The Edinburgh Book
of Twentieth-Century
Scottish Poetry

Edited by
Maurice Lindsay and Lesley Duncan

Edinburgh University Press

Selection, Introduction, editorial
arrangement and editorial materials
© Maurice Lindsay and Lesley Duncan, 2005
Poems © the individual poets

Edinburgh University Press Ltd
22 George Square, Edinburgh

Typeset in Sabon by
Norman Tilley Graphics, Northampton
and printed and bound in Great Britain
by Antony Rowe Ltd, Chippenham, Wilts

A CIP record for this book is available
from the British Library

ISBN 0 7486 2015 X (hardback)

The right of the contributors
to be identified as authors of this work
has been asserted in accordance with
the Copyright, Designs and Patents Act 1988.

The Editors and Publisher gratefully acknowledge
the grant made by the Barcapel Foundation Limited
through the Scottish Civic Trust.

The Publisher acknowledges subsidy
from the Scottish Arts Council

Scottish
Arts Council

Contents

Acknowledgements

The editors thank the staff of the Scottish Poetry Library, in particular Lizzie MacGregor, for all the help offered to them in the course of their researches; Dr Derick Thomson for his guidance on the Gaelic component of the book; and David Duncan for his computer expertise in the production of the manuscript.

Publisher's Acknowledgements
Grateful acknowledgement is made to the following sources for permission to reproduce material previously published elsewhere. Every effort has been made to trace the copyright holders, but if any have been inadvertently overlooked, the publisher will be pleased to make the necessary arrangements at the first opportunity.

Helen Adam, 'Song for a Sea Tower' and 'I Love My Love' from *Selected Poems & Ballads* (New York: Helikon Press, 1975). Reprinted by permission of Helikon Press. Margot Robert Adamson, 'Edinburgh' from *A Northern Holiday Poems* (London: Cobden-Sanderson, 1928). James Aitchison, 'The Inheritance' from *Brain Scans* (Dalkeith: Scottish Cultural Press, 1998); 'Dipper Territory' from *Dark Horse Magazine* and 'Landscape with Lapwings' from *Spheres* (London: Chatto & Windus, 1975). Reprinted by permission of the author. Marion Angus, 'The Fiddler' from *The Tinker's Road and Other Verses* (London & Glasgow: Gowans & Gray Ltd, 1924); 'Anemones', 'The Doors of Sleep', 'Alas! Poor Queen' and 'Mary's Song' from *Selected Poems of Marion Angus* (Edinburgh: Serif Books, 1950). J. K. Annand, 'Arctic Convoy' and 'Fur Coats' from *Selected Poems 1925–1990* (Edinburgh: Mercat Press, 1992); 'Mountain Pule' from *Bairn Rhymes* (Edinburgh: Mercat Press, 1998). Reprinted by permission of The Scottish National Dictionary Association. Meg Bateman, 'Lightness' and 'O Bonnie Man, Lovely Man' from *Aotromachd agus Dain Eile: Lightness and Other Poems* (Edinburgh: Polygon, 1997). Reprinted by permission of Birlinn and the author. D. M. Black, 'The Educators' from *The Educators* (London: Barrie and Rockcliff / The Cresset Press, 1969); 'The Water-Lily' from *The Happy Crow* (Edinburgh: M. Macdonald, 1974). Reprinted by permission of the author. Sheena Blackhall, 'Doric's

No Dodo ...' and 'The Spik o' the Lan' from *The Spik o' the Lan* (Aberdeen: Rainbow Publishing, 1986); 'Walk On' from *A Toosht o Whigmaleeries* (Aberdeen: Hammerfield Publishing, 1991). Reprinted by permission of the author. Captain Hamish Blair, 'The Bloody Orkneys' from *The Orkney Blast* (Orkney Islands: *The Orcadian*, date unknown). Reprinted by permission of *The Orcadian*. Alan Bold, 'Shore' from *This Fine Day* (Dunfermline: Borderline Press, 1979); '*from* Edinburgh Castle' from *Gambit* (Edinburgh: Edinburgh University Review, Summer, 1965), ed. Alan Bold. © Alan Bold. Reprinted by permission of Alice Bold. Deric Bolton, 'Schiehallion' and 'What Might Have Been' from *August Morning on Tweed* (Edinburgh: Galliard, 1991). Kate Y. A. Bone, 'Corners' and 'Catlike' from *Thistle By-Blaws* (West Linton: The Castlelaw Press, 1971). Reprinted by permission of Reinold Gayre. James Bridie (O. H. Mavor), 'The West End Perk' from *G.U.M.* Reprinted by permission of Ronald Mavor. George Mackay Brown, 'Ikey: His Will in Winter Written' and 'The Mother' from *The Herald* (Glasgow: *The Herald*, 20th December, 1996); 'The Lodging', 'Hamnavoe' and 'The Old Women' from *Loaves and Fishes* (London: Hogarth Press, 1959). Reprinted by permission of John Murray Publishers, *The Herald* and Archie Brown. Hamish Brown, 'A Salting of Snow', 'Dogs' and 'Counting Sheep' from *Time Gentleman* (Aberdeen: Aberdeen University Press, 1983). Reprinted by permission of the author. Margaret Gillies Brown, 'Village Woman' and 'Calgary Bay' from *Of Rowan and Pearl* (Argyll: Argyll Publishing, 2000). Reprinted by permission of Argyll Publishing. George Bruce, 'Love in Age' from *Collected Poems* (Edinburgh: Edinburgh University Press, 1970); 'A Gateway to the Sea' from *Landscape and Figures* (Kirkcaldy: Akros Publications, 1967); 'Inheritance' and 'Kinnaird Head' from *Sea talk* (Glasgow: William MacLellan, 1944); 'Departure and Departure and . . .' and 'Soup and Sherry' from *Pursuit* (Dalkeith: Scottish Cultural Press, 1999). Reprinted by permission of David Bruce, Marjorie Inglis and Lucina Prestige. Tom Bryan, 'Planting potatoes during Chernobyl' from *Wolfwind* (Edinburgh: Chapman, 1996). Reprinted by permission of the author. John Buchan, '*from* Alastair Buchan (1917)' and 'Fisher Jamie' from *Poems Scots and English* (Edinburgh and London: TC & EC Jack Ltd, 1917). Reprinted by permission of A. P. Watt Ltd on behalf of the Lord Tweedsmuir and Jean, Lady Tweedsmuir. Tom Buchan, 'The Everlasting Astronauts' and 'Scotland the Wee' from *Dolphins at Cochin* (London: Barrie & Rockliff / The Cresset Press, 1969). Elizabeth Burns, 'Jesus Speaks to the Church at Eastertime' and 'Ophelia' from *Ophelia and Other Poems* (Edinburgh: Polygon, 1991). Reprinted by permission of Birlinn. John Burnside, 'Anstruther' from *A Normal Skin* (London: Jonathan Cape, 1997). Reprinted by permission of The Random House Group Ltd. 'Out of Exile', 'Tundra's Edge' and 'Lost' from *The Hoop* (Manchester: Carcanet Press, 1988). Reprinted by permission of Carcanet Press Ltd. Ron Butlin, 'Advertisement for a Scottish

Servant' and 'The Bath' from *Histories of Desire* (Newcastle Upon Tyne: Bloodaxe, 1995). Reprinted by permission of the author. John M. Caie, 'The Puddock' from *The Kindly North: Verse in Scots and English* (Aberdeen: D. Wylie & Son, 1934). Janet Caird, 'John Donne, You Were Wrong' and 'Emigrants' from *John Donne, You Were Wrong* (Edinburgh: Ramsay Head Press, 1988). Reprinted by permission of Elisabeth Davenport and Janet Ronald. Sir Alec Cairncross, 'Covenanting Country' and 'Munich' from *Snatches* (Buckinghamshire: Colin Smythe Ltd, 1980). Reprinted by permission of Philip Cairncross. Angus Calder, 'Greeting, Not Greeting', 'Curling: Old Murrayfield Ice Rink' and 'October Opera for Kate' from *Waking in Waikato* (Callander: Diehard Publishers, 1997). Reprinted by permission of the author. Robert R. Calder, 'Love in the Abstract' from *Serapion* (Edinburgh: Chapman, 1996). Reprinted by permission of Chapman and the author. Gerry Cambridge, 'The Drunken Lyricist' from *The Shell House* (Dalkeith: Scottish Cultural Press, 1995); 'Shore Crab', 'Fallen Maple Leaves' and 'Foxgloves' from *"Nothing But Heather!": Scottish Nature in Poems, Photographs and Prose* (Edinburgh: Luath Press Ltd, 1999). Reprinted by permission of the author. Kate Clanchy, 'Mitigation', 'We Have Some Urgent Messages', 'Men From the Boys' and 'Timetable' from *Slattern* (London: Chatto & Windus, 1995). Reprinted by permission of Macmillan, London, UK and the author. W. D. Cocker, 'The Deluge' from *New Poems* (Glasgow: Brown, Son & Ferguson Ltd, 1949). Reprinted by permission of Brown, Son & Ferguson, Ltd, Glasgow. Stewart Conn, 'Stolen Light', 'Todd' and 'First Light' from *Stolen Light: Selected Poems* (Newcastle Upon Tyne: Bloodaxe, 1999). Reprinted by permission of the author. James Copeland, 'The Bayonet' and 'Ed' from *James Copeland's Shoogly Table Book of Verse* (Glasgow: Bramma, 1983). Robert Crawford, 'Sobieski-Stuarts' from *Spirit Machines* (London: Jonathan Cape, 1999); 'Scotch Broth' from *Masculinity* (London: Jonathan Cape, 1996). Reprinted by permission of The Random House Group Ltd. Helen B. Cruickshank, 'Comfort in Puirtith', 'The Wishin' Well', 'Sae Lang Has Sorrow' and 'Shy Geordie' from *Sea Buckthorn* (Dunfermline: H. T. Macpherson, 1954); 'Fate' from *The Ponnage Pool* (Edinburgh: M. Macdonald, 1968). Jenni Daiches, 'Horse in Glasgow', 'Jewish Cemetery, Frankfurt' and 'Geometry' from *Mediterranean* (Dalkeith: Scottish Cultural Press, 1995). Reprinted by permission of Scottish Cultural Press and the author. John Davidson, 'Epilogue – the Last Journey' and 'Snow' from *John Davidson: A Selection of his Poems* (London: Hutchinson, 1961). Christine De Luca, 'Dancing with Demons', 'Telling the Time' and 'Streams in the Desert' from *Wast wi da Valkyries* (Lerwick: The Shetland Library, 1997). Reprinted by permission of the author. Kirkpatrick Dobie, 'Aberfan' and 'King Claudius' from *Selected Poems* (Calstock: Peterloo Poets, 1992). © Peterloo Poets. Reprinted by permission of Peterloo Poets. Available post free from Peterloo Poets. Keith

Douglas, 'Vergissmeinnicht' and 'Simplify Me When I'm Dead' from *Selected Poems* (London: Faber and Faber Ltd, 1964). Reprinted by permission of Faber and Faber Ltd. Adam Drinan, '*from* The Men on the Rocks' and 'Florence: Sleeping in Fog' from *The Men of the Rocks* (London: Fortune Press, 1942); 'Measures' from *Modern Scottish Poetry: An Anthology of the Scottish Renaissance* (London: Faber and Faber Ltd, 1966). Carol Ann Duffy, 'Prayer', 'Close' and 'Valentine' from *Mean Time* (London: Anvil Press Poetry, 1993); 'War Photographer' from *Standing Female Nude* (London: Anvil Press Poetry, 1985); 'Warming Her Pearls' from *Selling Manhattan* (London: Anvil Press Poetry, 1987). Reprinted by permission of Anvil Press Poetry. Lesley Duncan, 'Festive Tolls' from *The Herald* (Glasgow: *The Herald*, 1989). 'The Visit', unpublished. Reprinted by permission of *The Herald* and the author. Douglas Dunn, 'Ships' and 'From the Night-Window' from *Terry Street* (Faber and Faber Ltd, 1969); 'France' from *Elegies* (Faber and Faber Ltd, 1985); 'Envoi' from *Selected Poems 1964–1983* (London: Faber and Faber Ltd, 1986). Reprinted by permission of Faber and Faber Ltd. Alison Fell, 'Pushing Forty' and 'Rannoch Moor' from *Kisses for Mayakovsky* (London: Virago, 1984); 'Pigeons' from *The Crystal Owl* (London: Methuen, 1987). Reprinted by permission of the author. Gillian Ferguson, 'Grey Kirk in the Mearns' from *Air for Sleeping Fish* (Newcastle Upon Tyne: Bloodaxe Books, 1997). Reprinted by permission of David Goodwin Associates and the author. Ian Hamilton Finlay, 'Bedtime', 'Gift', 'Finlay's House (in Rousay)' and 'O.H.M.S.' from *The Dancers Inherit the Party & Glasgow Beasts, on a Burd* (Edinburgh: Polygon, 1996). Reprinted by permission of Birlinn and the author. Lillias Scott Forbes, 'Turning a Fresh Eye' and 'The Half-Inch Tweeddale' from *Turning a Fresh Eye* (Kirkcaldy: Akros Publications, 1998). Reprinted by permission of Akros Publications and the author. Veronica Forrest-Thomson, 'Sonnet', 'In This House' and 'Not Pastoral Enough' from *Veronica Forrest-Thomson Collected Poems and Translations,* ed. Anthony Barnett (Lewes: Allardyce, Barnett, Publishers, 1990). © Jonathan Culler and The Estate of Veronica Forrest-Thomson 1967, 1974, 1976, 1990, 1999. © Allardyce, Barnett, Publishers 1990. Reprinted by permission of Allardyce, Barnett, Publishers. G. S. Fraser, 'Hometown Elegy' and 'Lean Street' from *Hometown Elegy* (London: Poetry London Editions, 1949); 'The Traveller Has Regrets' from *The Traveller Has Regrets* (Hanville Press, 1958). Reprinted by permission of Eileen Fraser. Robin Fulton, 'The End of an Age' and 'Forecast for a Quiet Night' from *Selected Poems 1963–78* (Edinburgh: Macdonald, 1980); 'A Note for Robert Henryson' from *Scots Poetry, Two* (Edinburgh: Edinburgh University Press, 1967). Reprinted by permission of the author. Robert Garioch, 'Elegy', 'I Was Fair Beat' and 'Nemo Canem Impune Lacessit' from *Complete Poetical Works* (Edinburgh: Macdonald, 1983). Reprinted by permission of the Saltire Society. Flora Garry, 'Rostov-on-Don (1942)' and 'The Professor's Wife' from *Collected Poems* (Edinburgh: Gordon Wright Publishing, 1995). Reprinted by permission of Steve Savage Publishers Ltd and The Estate of Flora Garry. Magi Gibson, 'Just Like Eve', 'Goldilocks' and 'Reading in Bed' from *Wild Women of a Certain Age* (Edinburgh: Chapman, 2000). Reprinted by permission of Chapman and the author. Valerie Gillies, 'We Meet Again', 'Summer Bull' and 'The Look-Alike' from *Bed of Stone* (Edinburgh: Canongate, 1994). Reprinted by permission of the author. Duncan Glen, 'Bell Barrow' from *Selected Poems 1965–1990* (Kirkcaldy: Akros Publications, 1991); 'My Faither' from *In Appearances* (Kirkcaldy: Akros Publications, 1971); 'Twa Warlds' from *Realities* (Kirkcaldy: Akros Publications, 1980). Reprinted by permission of Akros Publications and the author. W. S. Graham, 'Loch Thom' and 'Greenock at Night I Find You' from *Implements in their Places* (London: Faber and Faber Ltd, 1977); 'Letter VI' from *The Nightfishing* (London: Faber and Faber Ltd, 1955). © The W. S. Graham Estate. Reprinted by permission of Michael and Margaret Snow. Sir Alexander Gray, 'Scotland' and 'On a Cat, Ageing' from *Gossip* (Edinburgh: The Porpoise Press, 1928); 'The Fine Fechtin Mouse' from *Sir Halewyn, Examples in European Balladry & Folk Song* (London: Oliver & Boyd, 1949). Reprinted by permission of John Gray. Andrew Greig, 'Still', 'Interlude on Mutsagh Tower' and 'Ruth Says' from *The Order of the Day* (Newcastle Upon Tyne: Bloodaxe Books, 1990). Reprinted by permission of the author. George Campbell Hay, 'Still Gyte, Man', 'The Hind of Morning', 'Homer' and 'The Old Fisherman' from *Collected Poems and Songs of George Campbell Hay* (Edinburgh: Edinburgh University Press, 2000). Reprinted by permission of W. L. Lorimer Memorial Trust Fund and The Estate of George Campbell Hay. Hamish Henderson, 'The Flyting o' Life and Death' from *The Scottish Broadsheet* (May, 1963); 'The 51st Highland Division's Farewell to Sicily from *Ballads of World War II* (Glasgow: Lili Marlene Club of Glasgow, 1947); 'Elegies for the Dead in Cyrenaica: Prologue First Elegy' from *Elegies for the Dead in Cyrenaica* (London: John Lehmann, 1948). Reprinted by permission of Felicity Henderson. J. F. Hendry, 'The Constant North' from *The Bombed Happiness* (London: Routledge, 1942); 'The Ship' from *Marimarusa: Modern Scottish Poets 8* (Caithness Books, 1978). W. N. Herbert, 'The King and Queen of Dumfriesshire', 'Why the Elgin Marbles Must Be Returned to Elgin' and 'Looking Up from Aeroplanes' from *Cabaret McGonagall* (Newcastle Upon Tyne: Bloodaxe Books, 1996). Reprinted by permission of Bloodaxe Books. Alan Jackson, 'Hitch-Haiku', 'The Proddy Heebie Jeebies' and 'The Worstest Beast' from *The Grim Wayfarer* (London: Fulcrum Press, 1969); 'Confessio' from *Idiots Are Freelance* (Aberdeen: Rainbow Publishing, 1973). Reprinted by permission of Birlinn. Violet Jacob, 'The Water-Hen', 'Tam i' the Kirk' and 'The Neep-Fields by the Sea' from *The Scottish Poems of Violet Jacob* (London: Oliver & Boyd Ltd, 1944). Reprinted by permission of Malcolm Hutton. Kathleen

Jamie, 'Arraheids' and 'The Queen of Sheba' from *The Queen of Sheba* (Newcastle Upon Tyne: Bloodaxe Books, 1994); 'Mrs McKellar, Her Martyrdom' and 'Crossing the Loch' from *Jizzen* (London: Picador, 1999). Reprinted by permission of Macmillan Publishers Ltd. Jackie Kay, 'Teeth' from *Off Colour* (Newcastle Upon Tyne: Bloodaxe Books, 1998); 'Old Tongue' from *Scottish Poems Chosen by John Price* (London: Macmillan Children's Books, 2001). Reprinted by permission of PDF on behalf of Jackie Kay. I. W. King, 'If Ye Hivni . . .', an extract from *Fagbag* (Pallatine Press, Untitled Pamphlet). Reprinted by permission of Sally Evans and the author. Norman Kreitman, 'In Torrett, Minorca', 'Lizard' and 'Bonfire in April' from *Touching Rock* (Aberdeen: Aberdeen University Press, 1987); 'Glossy Mail' from *Against Leviathan* (Aberdeen: Aberdeen University Press, 1989). Reprinted by permission of the author. Frank Kuppner, '*from* An Old Guide-Book to Prague' from *What? Again? Selected Poems* (Manchester: Carcanet Press, 2000). Reprinted by permission of Carcanet Press Ltd. R. D. Laing, 'Sonnet 4' and 'Sonnet 16' from *Sonnets* (London: Michael Joseph, 1979). Helen Lamb, 'She Said/He Said' and 'Evidence' from *Strange Fish* (Dundee: Dundee Publishing, 1997). Reprinted by permission of the author. Tom Leonard, 'The Good Thief' and 'Feed Ma Lamz' from *Intimate Voices* (Buckfastleigh: Etruscan Books, 2003). Reprinted by permission of the author. Maurice Lindsay, 'At Hans Christian Andersen's Birthplace, Odense, Denmark' from *Collected Poems 1940–1990* (Edinburgh: Mercat Press, 1991); 'Hurlygush' from *Hurlygush* (Edinburgh: Serif Books, 1983); ''Tis Sixty Years Since', unpublished. Reprinted by permission of the author. Liz Lochhead, 'Noises in the Dark', 'My Rival's House', 'Poem for My Sister' and 'The Empty Song' from *Dreaming Frankenstein and Collected Poems* (Edinburgh: Polygon, 1984). Reprinted by permission of Birlinn. Roddy Lumsden, 'Yeah Yeah Yeah', 'Vanishing' and 'Prayer to Be with Mercurial Women' from *Yeah Yeah Yeah* (Newcastle Upon Tyne: Bloodaxe Books, 1997). Reprinted by permission of Bloodaxe Books. George MacBeth, 'Shotts' from *The Patient* (London: Hutchison, 1992); 'The Ward' from *The Colour of Blood: Poems by George MacBeth* (London, Melbourne, Toronto: Macmillan, 1967); 'Alsatian' from *Collected Poems, 1958–1970* (London: Macmillan, 1971). Reprinted by permission of Sheil Land Associates Ltd on behalf of The Estate of George MacBeth. Brian McCabe, 'Seagull' and 'Kite' from *Body Parts* (Edinburgh: Canongate, 1998). First published in Great Britain by Canongate Books Ltd, 14 High Street, Edinburgh, EH1 1TE. Reprinted by permission of Canongate Books Ltd. Norman MacCaig, 'No Choice', 'Toad', 'Praise of a Collie', 'Heron', 'Byre' and 'Double Life' from *Collected Poems* (London: Chatto & Windus, 1985). Reprinted by permission of The Random House Group Ltd. Hugh MacDiarmid, 'Empty Vessel' from *Penny Wheep* (Edinburgh: Blackwood, 1926); 'The Bonnie Broukit Bairn', 'The Eemis-Stane' and 'O Jesu Parvule' from *Sangschaw* (Edinburgh:

Blackwood, 1925); 'Milk-wort and Bog-Cotton' from *Scots Unbound and Other Poems* (Stirling: Enaes Mackay, 1932); 'O Wha's been here Afore Me, Lass?' from *A Drunk Man Looks at the Thistle* (Edinburgh: Blackwood, 1926); 'Lo! A child Is Born' from *Second Hymn to Lenin* (Edinburgh: Blackwood, 1935); 'Two Memories' and '*from* The Glass of Pure Water' from *Modern Scottiosh Poetry: An Anthology of the Scottish Renaissance* (London: Faber and Faber Ltd, 1966). Reprinted by permission of Carcarnet Press Ltd. Ellie McDonald, 'Widdershins' and 'Uncle' from *The Gagan Fruit* (Edinburgh: Chapman, 1992). Reprinted by permission of Chapman Publications and the author. Pittendrigh Macgillivray, 'Mercy o' Gode' from *Modern Scottish Poetry: An Anthology of the Scottish Renaissance* (London: Faber and Faber Ltd, 1966). Matt McGinn, 'Corrie Doon' and 'The Big Orange Whale' from *McGinn of the Calton* (Glasgow: Glasgow District Libraries, 1987). Alastair Mackie, 'Schoolquine', 'Pieta' and 'Primary Teachers' from *Ingaitherins: Selected Poems* (Aberdeen: Aberdeen University Press, 1987). Reprinted by permission of Bet Mackie. Albert D. Mackie, 'Molecatcher' and 'Newsboy' from *Modern Scottish Poetry* (Manchester: Carcanet Press, 1976). Reprinted by permission of John Mackie. Rayne Mackinnon, 'After the Snow' from *The Hitch-Hiker and Other Poems* (Walton-on-Thames: Outposts, 1976); 'Bruckner' and 'The Cuillin' from *The Blasting of Billy P* (Edinburgh: Netherbow Arts Centre, 1986); 'Scotland' from *Northern Elegies* (Edinburgh: Netherbow Arts Centre, 1986). Hamish MacLaren, 'Island Rose' from *Modern Scottish Poetry: An Anthology of the Scottish Renaissance* (London: Faber and Faber Ltd, 1966). Alasdair Maclean, 'Rams' and 'Question and Answer' from *Scottish Poetry 5* (Edinburgh: Edinburgh University Press); 'After Culloden' from *A Book of Scottish Verse* (London: Robert Hale, 2001). Reprinted by permission of David Higham. Sorley MacLean, 'Calvary', 'My Een Are Nae on Calvary', 'Dogs and Wolves', 'Shores', 'Hallaig' and 'Tumultuous Plenty in the Heavens' from *From Wood to Ridge* (Manchester: Carcanet Press, 1999). Reprinted by permission of Carcanet Press Ltd. Robert McLellan, 'Sang' from *Modern Scottish Poetry: An Anthology of the Scottish Renaissance* (London: Faber and Faber Ltd, 1966). Anne MacLeod, 'Shakespeare No More' and 'Persephone's Daughter' from *Standing by Thistles* (Dalkeith: Scottish Cultural Press, 1997). Reprinted by permission of the author. Hugh McMillan, 'Leaving Scotland by Train' from *Tramontana* (Glasgow: Dog and Bone, 1990); 'The X-Files: Bonnybridge, October '95' from *Aphrodite's Anorak* (Calstock: Peterloo Poets, 1995). Reprinted by permission of Peterloo Poets and the author. Adam McNaughtan, 'Oor Hamlet' and 'Jeelie Piece Song'. Reprinted by permission of MCPS and the author. Aonghas MacNeacail, 'A Proper Schooling' and 'Tonight You Being from Me' from *Oideachadh Ceart* (Edinburgh: Polygon, 1997). Reprinted by permission of the author. Hugh Macpherson, 'Looking for 78's in the '40s' from *Line Review. No*

108 (March 1989). Reprinted by permission of John MacPherson. Gerald Mangan, 'Glasgow 1956', 'Ailsa Craig' and 'Kirkintilloch Revisited' from *Waiting for the Storm* (Newcastle Upon Tyne: Bloodaxe Books, 1990). Reprinted by permission of the author. Angus Martin, 'Passchendaele' and 'Who Among Common Men of Their Time' from *The Song of the Quern* (Dalkieth: Scottish Cultural Press, 1998). Reprinted by permission of the author. Gordon Meade, 'The Scrimshaw Sailor' and 'The Great Spotted Woodpecker' from *The Scrimshaw Sailor* (Edinburgh: Chapman, 1996); 'In Eyemouth Harbour' from *Singing Seals* (Edinburgh: Chapman, 1991). Reprinted by permission of the author. Elma Mitchell, 'The Crucifixion Will Not Take Place', 'The Death of Adam' and 'Thoughts After Ruskin' from *People Etcetera* (Calstock: Peterloo Poets, 1987). © Harry Chambers. Reprinted by permission of Peterloo Poets. Naomi Mitchison, 'To a Fisherman with the Present of a Knife' and 'The Farm Woman: 1942' and 'The Scottish Renaissance in Glasgow: 1935' from *The Cleansing of the Knife* (Edinburgh: Canongate, 1978); 'Nettlebed Road' from *The Herald* (Glasgow: *The Herald*, 1997). Reprinted by permission of *The Herald* and Lois Godfrey. William Montgomerie, 'Flodden' from *Lines Review, No 79* (Edinburgh: M. Macdonald, 1981); 'Epitaph' from *Poetry Collection, Second Edition* (Glasgow: William McLellan, 1945). Reprinted by permission of Dian Elvin. Edwin Morgan, 'King Billy', 'Glasgow Green', 'Strawberries' and 'The First Men on Mercury' from *Collected Poems* (Manchester: Carcanet Press, 1996). Reprinted by permission of Carcanet Press Ltd. Ken Morrice, 'To a Shy Girl at a Party', 'Crossing the Alps' and 'Voyager' from *Talking of Michelangelo* (Dalkeith: Scottish Cultural Press, 1996). Reprinted by permission of Norah Morrice. Edwin Muir, 'Scotland 1941', 'Mary Stuart', 'Scotland's Winter', 'Song', 'Merlin' and 'One Foot in Eden' from *Collected Poems* (London: Faber and Faber Ltd, 1960). © 1960 Willa Muir. Reprinted by permission of Oxford University Press, Inc and Faber and Faber Ltd. Stephen Mulrine, 'The Coming of the Wee Malkies' from *Stephen Mulrine: Poems, Parkland Poets No 10.* (Kirkcaldy: Akros Publications, 1971). Neil Munro, 'Hey Jock, Are Ye Glad Ye Listed?', 'The Heather' and 'In Prison' from *The Poetry of Neil Munro* (Edinburgh: William Blackwood & Sons Ltd, 1931). Reprinted by permission of Lesley Bratton. Charles Murray, 'Gin I Was God', 'Charon's Song' and 'The Whistle' from *Hamewith – The Complete Poems of Charles Murray* (Aberdeen: Aberdeen University Press, 1979). Reprinted by permission of The Charles Murray Memorial Fund. Donald S. Murray, 'An Incomplete History of Rock Music in the Hebrides' from *West Coast Magazine*. Reprinted by permission of the author. William Neill, 'A Celtic History' from *Four Points of a Saltire* (Edinburgh: Reprographia, 1970); 'Lark' from *Wild Places: Poems in Three Leids* (Edinburgh: Luath Press, 1985); 'Are You There, Mr Punch?' from *Blossom, Berry, Fall & Selected Work* (Galloway: Fleet Intec, 1986). Reprinted by permission of the author.

Siusaidh NicNeill, 'Steel Yourself' and 'For Eric Blair' from *All My Braided Colours* (Dalkeith: Scottish Cultural Press, 1996). Reprinted by permission of the author. Dennis O'Donnell, 'The Young Men of Blackburn', 'The Crab' and 'Even Solomon' from *Two Clocks Ticking* (Edinburgh: Curly Snake Press Cencrastus, 1998). Reprinted by permission of the author. Donny O'Rourke, 'Wine and Wooing' and 'A Letter from My Father' from *The Waistband and Other Poems* (Edinburgh: Polygon, 1997). Reprinted by permission of the author. Janet Paisley, 'The Intellectual' and 'Feminist' from *Ye Cannae Win* (Edinburgh: Chapman, 2000); 'The Turning' from *Reading the Bones* (Edinburgh: Canongate, 1999). Reprinted by permission of Chapman and the author. Don Paterson, 'The Trans-Siberian Express' from *Nil Nil* (London: Faber and Faber Ltd, 1993); 'The Eyes' from *The Eyes* (London: Faber and Faber Ltd, 1999). Reprinted by permission of Faber and Faber Ltd. Walter Perrie, 'Exiles Leaving Lochboisdale, 1919' and 'Ascending Strathbraan' from *Exilics* poem-sequence. Reprinted by permission of the author. Tom Pow, 'A Favourite Stretch of Disused Railway' and 'The Years' from *Rough Seas* (Edinburgh: Canongate, 1987). Reprinted by permission of the author. Richard Price, 'Horseshoe Crab in Fragrante Delicto' from *Perfume and Petrol Fumes* (Callander: Diehard Publishers, 1999); 'On, Off, Over' from *Marks and Sparks* (Kirkcaldy: Akros Publications, 1995). Reprinted by permission of the author. John Purser, 'The Organist Confesses to His Mirror' from *A Share of the Wind* (Isle of Skye: Aquila, 1980); 'Love Poem' from *The Counting Stick* (Isle of Skye: Aquila, 1976). Reprinted by permission of the author. David Purves, 'Crabbit Angels' and 'Cleikit' from *Herts Bluid* (Edinburgh: Chapman, 1995). Reprinted by permission of the author. Kathleen Raine, 'To My Mountain' from *Stone and Flower* (London: Poetry London, 1943); 'Maire Macrae's Song' from *The Oval Portrait and Other Poems* (London: Enitharmon Press / Hamish Hamilton, 1977); 'Highland Graveyard' from *The Hollow Hill* (London: Hamilton, 1965). Reprinted by permission of Golgonooza Press. Tessa Ransford, 'First Thaw' from *Medusa Dozen and Other Poems* (Edinburgh: Ramsay Head Press, 1994); 'A Stable Relationship' from *When it Works it Feels Like Play* (Edinburgh: Ramsay Head Press, 1998); 'Viewpoint' from *Scottish Selection* (Kirkcaldy: Akros Publications, 1998). Reprinted by permission of Akros Publications and the author. Alastair Reid, 'Propinquity', 'Scotland', 'Weathering' and 'The Manse' from *Weathering* (Edinburgh: Canongate, 1978). Reprinted by permission of the author. Robert Rendall, 'The Horse-Mill' and 'Angle of Vision' from *An Island Shore: the Life and Work of Robert Rendall* (Orkney: Orkney Press, 1990). Alan Riach, 'Antenor' and 'Sankey Hymns' from *Clearances* (Dalkeith: Scottish Cultural Press and Christchurch, New Zealand: Hazard Press, 2001). Reprinted by permission of the author. James Robertson, 'Melt (Twa)' from *Fae The Flouers O Evil: Baudelaire in Scots'* (Fife: Kettillonia, 2001); 'Royalty' and 'George Buchanan in Old

Age' from *Stirling Sonnets* (Fife: Kettillonia, 2001). Reprinted by permission of Kettillonia and the author. Robin Robertson, 'Affair of Kites' and 'Flags of Autumn *from* Camera Obscura' from *A Painted Field* (London: Picador, 1997). Reprinted by permission of Macmillan, London, UK and the author. David Rorie, 'The Pawkie Duke' from *The Auld Doctor* (London: Constable & Co, 1920). Reprinted by permission of James Michie and The David Rorie Society. Dilys Rose, 'Queen Bee' and 'Figurehead' from *Madame Doubtfire's Dilemma* (Edinburgh: Chapman, 1989). Reprinted by permission of the author. R. Crombie Saunders, 'The Empty Glen' from *Modern Scottish Poetry: An Anthology of the Scottish Renaissance* (London: Faber and Faber Ltd, 1966). Alexander Scott, 'Scotched' from *Double Agent: Poems in English and Scots* (Kirkcaldy: Akros Publications, 1972); 'Continent o Venus', 'Calvinist Sang' and 'The Sodgers' from *The Latest in Elegies* (Glasgow: Caledonian Press, 1949). Reprinted by permission of Catherine Scott. Tom Scott, 'Auld Sanct-Aundrians – Brand the Builder' from *The Collected Shorter Poems of Tom Scott* (Edinburgh: Chapman / Agenda, 1993). Reprinted by permission of Chapman Publications and Heather Scott. Charles Senior, 'Fulmars' from *The Herald* (Glasgow: *The Herald*, 7th January 1967). Reprinted by permission of *The Herald*. Robert Service, 'The Shooting of Dan McGrew' from *Songs of a Sourdough* (Toronto: William Briggs, 1907). Reprinted by permission of Iris Davies-Service, Anne Longépé and William Krasilovsky. Burns Singer, 'Poem', 'The Local Ogres Are Against Me Here ...' and 'A Poem About Death' from *Collected Poems* (Manchester: Carcanet Press, 2001). Reprinted by permission of Carcanet Press Ltd. Iain Crichton Smith, 'Poem of Lewis' from *The Long River* (Edinburgh: M. Macdonald, 1955); 'John Knox' and 'Old Woman' from *Thistles and Roses* (London: Eyre and Spottiswoode, 1961); 'Returning Exile' from *The Exiles* (Manchester: Carcanet Press / Dublin: Raven Art Press, 1984); 'Two Girls Singing' from *The Law and the Grace* (London: Eyre and Spottiswoode, 1965). Reprinted by permission of Carcanet Press Ltd. Sydney Goodsir Smith, 'Elegy V *from* Under the Eildon Tree' from *Under the Eildon Tree: A Poem in XXIV Elegies* (Edinburgh: Serif Books, 1954); 'Ye Mongers Aye Need Masks for Cheeatrie' and 'Largo' from *The Deevil's Waltz* (Glasgow: W. M. MacLellan, 1946); 'Philomel' from *So Late Into the Nigth* (London: Peter Russell, 1952) . Reprinted by permission of Angus Peetz and Katherine M. Pal. Charles Hamilton Sorley, 'When You See Millions of the Mouthless Dead' from *The Poems and Selected Letters of Charles Hamilton Sorley* (Dundee: Blackness Press, 1978). William Soutar, 'The Philosophic Taed'; 'The Gowk' and 'The Tryst' from *Poems in Scots* (Edinburgh: The Moray Press, 1935); 'Who Are These Children?' and 'The Permanence of the Young Men' from *The Expectant Silence* (London: Andrew Dakers Ltd, 1944); 'Winter Beauty' from *Poems in Scots and English by William Soutar* (Edinburgh: Oliver & Boyd, 1961). Reprinted by permission of The

National Library of Scotland. Muriel Spark, 'We Were not Expecting the Prince Today' and 'The Yellow Book' from *All the Poems of Muriel Spark* (Manchester: Carcanet, 2004). Reprinted by permission of David Higham. Lewis Spence, 'Portrait of Mary Stuart, Holyrood' and 'Capernaum' from *Plumes of Time* (London: George Allen & Unwin, 1926). Kenneth Steven, 'The Calvinist' and 'The Long Silence' from *The Missing Days* (Dalkeith: Scottish Cultural Press, 1995); 'Lamb' and 'Edge' from *Iona* (Fife: Saint Andrews Press, 2000). Reprinted by permission of the author. William J. (Bill) Tait, 'On with the Dance! Let Freud be Unconfined!', 'The Contracting Universe' and 'Adjustin Mysel tae the Situation' from *Collected Poems: A Day Between Weathers* (Edinburgh: Paul Harris Publishing, 1980). Reprinted by permission of Brian Tait. Derick Thomson, 'Scarecrow', 'Lewis', 'St Kildan Congregation', 'The Second Island' from *Creachadh na Clarsaich* (Glasgow: Gairm, 1982). Reprinted by permission of the author. Valerie Thornton, 'Birds of Passage' first published in *Cencrastus No 25* (Spring, 1987). Reprinted by permission of the author. Ruthven Todd, 'Personal History' from *Horizon, vol. 2, no. 9* (September 1940); 'About Scotland, & c.' from *Life and Letters vol. 18, no. 12* (Summer, 1938). Reprinted by permission of Christopher Todd. Sydney Tremayne, 'The Falls of Falloch' from *Time and the Wind* (London: Collins, 1948); 'North of Berwick' and 'Mixed Weather' from *The Turning Sky* (London: Rupert Hart-Davis, 1969). Gael Turnbull, 'For Whose Delight' from *For Whose Delight* (Glasgow: Mariscat, 1995); 'And I Think it Yours' from *From the Language of the Heart* (Glasgow: Mariscat, 1983). Reprinted by permission of Mariscat Press and Dr Jill Turnbull. Anne Turner, 'Medusa' from *Contemporary Scottish Verse, 1959–1969* (London: Calder & Boyars, 1970). W. Price Turner, 'Full Supporting Programme' from *The Moral Rocking Horse* (London: Barrie and Jenkins, 1970); 'Homely Accommodation, Suit Gent' from *Fables for Love* (Calstock: Peterloo Poets, 1985). Raymond Vettese, 'Scottish Mythology', 'Photograph' and 'Scottish Names' from *The Richt Noise* (Edinburgh: Macdonald, 1988). Reprinted by permission of The Saltire Society and the author. Val Warner, 'Clearing Out' from *Under the Penthouse* (Manchester: Carcanet Press, 1973). Reprinted by permission of Carcanet Press Ltd. Roderick Watson, 'Is This Man, Martin Bormann? from *True History on the Walls* (Edinburgh: Macdonald, 1976). Reprinted by permission of the author. Kenneth White, 'Brandan's Last Voyage', 'Song of the Coffin Close' and 'McTaggart' from *Open World, the Collected Poems 1960–2000* (Edinburgh: Polygon, 2003). Reprinted by permission of the author. Colin Will, 'Satori in Fauldhouse' from *Seven Senses* (Callander: Diehard Publishers, 2000). Reprinted by permission of Diehard Publishers and the author. Jim C. Wilson, 'Pruning' from *The Herald* (Glasgow: *The Herald*, March 2000); 'Death in Venice' from *New Writing Scotland, Volume 15* (ASLS, 1997). Reprinted by permission of *The Herald* and the author.

Andrew Young, 'The Fear', 'Field-Glasses', 'The Falls of Glomach', 'Suilven' and 'Culbin Sands' from *Selected Poems* (Manchester: Carcanet Press, 1998). Reprinted by permission of Carcanet Press Ltd. Douglas Young, 'The Ballant o' the Laird's Bath', 'For a Wife in Jizzen' and 'Last Lauch' from *A Braird O' Thristles* (Glasgow: William MacLellan, 1947); 'For the Old Highlands' from *Auntran Blads* (Glasgow: William MacLellan, 1943). Reprinted by permission of Clara Young.

Introduction

The true, if not the only, end of poetry is delight, declared John Dryden. This anthology has been designed on Dryden's precept, rather than on purely academic principles, which may exclude the surprising and the offbeat. So readers will find here not only the definitive voices of twentieth-century Scottish poetry from MacDiarmid on, but unexpected contributors, ranging from Robert Service of Yukon fame to the psychiatrist R. D. Laing and those witty chroniclers of contemporary city life, Adam McNaughtan and Matt McGinn. By inclination the editors prefer the immediate and unpretentious to the grandiloquent. They also share a respect for craftsmanship and deft use of language, even if the old disciplines of rhyme and rhythm no longer hold automatic sway.

For non-Scottish readers, a little background information about the Scottish poetry scene may be of assistance.

At the end of the nineteenth century, Scottish poetry was barely emerging from the 'Kailyard' (or cabbage patch), with its sentimentality and over-concern with petty localised issues. Pittendrigh Macgillivray, though primarily a sculptor, was among the first to realise that the Scots language, increasingly fragmenting into local dialects, needed some sort of revitalisation if it were to survive effectively in literary use. Like Lewis Spence, Macgillivray looked backwards, towards the sixteenth century, in spelling and world-revival. It was left to Christopher Murray Grieve, in his poetic persona of Hugh MacDiarmid, to achieve a real revivification, devising what was variously called 'Plastic Scots' and 'Lallans', but resulting in *Sangschaw*, *Penny Wheep*, and *A Drunk Man Looks at the Thistle*; works of genius all three. Nevertheless, Macgillivray's verse was published early in the twentieth century so he is due the initial credit.

Two other writers helped to liberate the subject matter of Scottish poetry. One was the unhappy John Davidson, who in 1909 walked into the sea and drowned himself in the mistaken belief that he had cancer. His early poems, published in the late nineteenth century, include such frequently anthologised pieces as 'The Runable Stag' and 'Thirty Bob a Week' (which profoundly influenced both T. S. Eliot and Hugh MacDiarmid); but our selection comes from his later work, written in the first decade of the twentieth century, in which he propounds Humanism and a Nietzschean belief in the death of God. James (B. V.) Thomson, his older contemporary, had already burst the bonds of poetic conventionality with 'The City of Dreadful Night'. The constraints of the kailyard were thus well and truly shattered.

Those excellent North-East writers, Violet Jacob and Marion Angus, along with Charles Murray, represented a further effective use of Scots as it was still spoken, as did the work of Sir Alexander Gray from the same airt.

Then comes the MacDiarmid linguistic explosion, resulting in the appearance of the greatest Scottish poet of the century, particularly in his incomparable early Scots lyrics.

What Eric Linklater called 'the second wind' Scottish Renaissance (the label allegedly given to the MacDiarmid movement by a French professor, Denis Saurat, though possibly by MacDiarmid himself, using Saurat's name) then produced Sydney Goodsir Smith, Douglas Young, Robert Garioch and others, a group with which co-editor Maurice Lindsay was for a time associated.

With the possible exception of Edwin Morgan and Edwin Muir, no 'great' poet appeared in twentieth-century Scotland other than MacDiarmid – and, Gaelic scholars would claim, Sorley MacLean. However, there has been a plethora of admirable and enjoyable ones.

Sorley MacLean and three of the other most notable contemporary figures – Norman MacCaig, George Mackay Brown and Iain Crichton Smith – died in quick succession in the 1990s. Interestingly, three of the four came from the Northern or Western Isles (Mackay Brown from Orkney, though with a Highland mother, MacLean and Crichton Smith from Raasay and Lewis respectively). MacCaig had strong Highland connections. There are many possible theories about this imaginative outpouring from the country's peripheries. Is the Celtic connection at the heart of it or did the elemental nature of land and seascape form the creative sensibilities of the emerging poets? Thesis-writers will no doubt ponder, and pontificate on, such matters.

Meanwhile, even deprived of this major quartet, poetry flourished in Scotland as the new millennium loomed. In spite of the neglect of the classics of 'English' literature in schools, new poetry circulated via a variety of book publishers north and south of the Border, through such other mediums as the daily poem column of *The Herald* newspaper and the broadsheet *Poetry Scotland*, and through the revival of poetry pamphlets. Poetry was also written and discussed in the convivial setting of writers' groups.

Out of a diversity of talents and themes, at least two trends emerged. First the old agonising over the actual nature of the language used by Scottish poets has ceased. Poets – whether employing standard English, classical Scots, Lallans, regional dialects, city patois, or any permutation or combination of these – are linguistically relaxed. No place now for the fierce debates of the Muir–MacDiarmid era. Complexity of language is seen as an enrichment rather than a drawback. The increasing new confidence of Scots in their own cultural heritage (of which language is a central component) has no doubt influenced, and will in turn be further influenced by, the re-establishment of a Scottish Parliament.

A second major development in contemporary Scottish writing is the burgeoning of women writers. The successors of Helen Adam, Marion Angus and Violet Jacob are a feisty lot. The best known are probably Glasgow-based Liz Lochhead and Glasgow-born Carol Ann Duffy, but there are many others writing with candour and wit about all aspects of the human experience – including female sexuality.

A representative selection of Gaelic poetry is included in the anthology, both in its original version and in English translation.

In compiling this wide-ranging anthology, the editors have been impressed, above all, by the sheer range and energy of the poetry produced by their twentieth-century compatriots and by the many insights the poetry offers into a tumultuous era of war and peace and social change. They hope readers will share their enthusiasm.

Maurice Lindsay and Lesley Duncan

The Edinburgh Book of Twentieth-Century Scottish Poetry

Song for a Sea Tower
Helen Adam

There lived four sisters in a tower by the sea,
Between the blue waters and the lily lea.

One sister was a wolf, one a gentle sheep,
One a swan, and one a fish, from the fabled deep.

Four sisters loved a man, beautiful was he.
He swam in blue waters beside the lily lea.

The sheep gave him fleecy wool to warm his lonely bed.
The swan gave him feathers to crown his curly head.

The fish gave him gaudy rings from wrecks of vanity.
The wolf ran all alone around the lily lea.

The wolf ran all alone where the lilies proudly rise.
She gave the man nothing but a glance from her eyes.

A glance from her savage eyes beside the summer sea.
He left the wave and followed her along the lily lea.

Three enchanted sisters in a tower by the tide.
Where their hearts awakened, there they must abide.

Three spell-bound sisters, a sheep, a fish, a swan.
Floods beat against their tower. Time goes on and on.

'If we wait with patience, no matter what the pain,
From the green waters the God will come again.'

Three ancient sisters, faithfully they wait
For the young and loving man that the wolf ate.

I Love My Love

In the dark of the moon the hair rules – Robert Duncan

Helen Adam

There was a man who married a maid. She laughed as he led her
   home.
The living fleece of her long bright hair she combed with a golden
   comb.
He led her home through his barley fields, where the saffron
   poppies grew.
She combed, and whispered, 'I love my love.' Her voice like a
   plaintive coo.
Ha! Ha!
Her voice like a plaintive coo.

He lived alone with his chosen bride. At first their life was sweet.
Sweet was the touch of her playful hair binding his hands and feet.
When first she murmured adoring words, her words did not appall.
'I love my love with a capital A. To my love I give my All.
Ah! Ha!
To my love I give my All.'

She circled him with the secret web she wove as her strong hair
   grew.
Like a golden spider she wove and sang, 'My love is tender and
   true.'
She combed her hair with a golden comb, and shackled him to a
   tree.
She shackled him fast to the Tree of Life. 'My love I'll never set
   free.
No. No.
My love I'll never set free.'

Whenever he broke her golden bonds he was held with bonds of
   gold.
Oh! Cannot a man escape from love, from love's hot smothering
   hold?'
He roared with fury. He broke her bonds. He ran in the light of the
   sun.

Her soft hair rippled and trapped his feet as fast as his feet could
 run.
Ha! Ha!
As fast as his feet could run.

He dug a grave and he dug it wide. He strangled her in her sleep.
He strangled his love with a strand of hair, and then he buried he
 deep.
He buried deep when the sun was hid by a purple thunder-cloud.
Her helpless hair spread over the corpse in a pale resplendent
 shroud.
Ha! Ha!
A pale resplendent shroud.

Morning and night of thunder rain, and then it came to pass
That the hair sprang up though the earth of the grave, and it grew
 like golden grass.
It grew and glittered along her grave, alive in the light of the sun.
Every hair had a plaintive voice, the voice of his lovely one.

'I love my love with a Capital T. My love is tender and true.
I'll love my love in the barley fields when the thunder-cloud is blue.
My body crumbles beneath the ground, but the hairs of my head
 will grow.
I'll love my love with the hairs on my head. I'll never never let go.
Ha! Ha!
I'll never, never let go.'

The hair sang soft, and the hair sang high, singing of loves that
 drown,
Till he took his scythe by the light of the moon, and he scythed that
 singing hair down.
Every hair laughed a lilting laugh, and shrilled when his scythe
 swept through,
'I love my love with a Capital T. My love is tender and true.
Ha! Ha!
Tender, tender and true.'

All through the night he wept and prayed, but before the first bird
 woke,

Around the house in the barley fields blew the hair like billowing
  smoke.
Her hair blew over the barley fields where the slothful poppies
  gape.
All day long they cooed, 'My love can never escape.
No. No.
My Love can never escape.'

'Be still, be still, you devilish hair. Glide back to the grave and
  sleep.
Glide back to the grave and wrap her bones down where I buried
  her deep.
I am the man who escaped from love, though love was my fate and
  doom.
Can no man ever escape from love who breaks from a woman's
  womb?'

Over his house, when the sun stood high, her hair was a dazzling
  storm,
Rolling, lashing, o'er walls and roof, heavy, and soft, and warm.
It thumped on the roof. It hissed and glowed over every
  windowpane.
The smell of the hair was in the house. It smelled like a lion's mane.
Ha! Ha!
It smelled like a lion's mane!

Three times round the bed of their love, and his heart lurched with
  despair.
In through the keyhole, elvish bright, came creeping a single hair.
Softly, softly, it touched his lips, on his eyelids traced a sign.
'I love my love with a Capital Z. I mark him Zero and mine.
Ha! Ha!
I mark him Zero and mine.'

The hair rushed in. He struggled and tore, but whenever he tore a
  tress,
'I love my love with a Capital Z,' sang the hair of the sorceress.
It swarmed upon him. It swaddled him fast. It muffled his every
  groan.
Like a golden monster it seized his flesh, and then it sought the
  bone.

Ha! Ha!
And then it sought the bone.

It smothered his flesh and sought the bones: Until his bones were
  bare.
There was no sound but the joyful hiss of the sweet insatiable hair.
'I love my love,' it laughed as it ran, back to the grave its home.
Then the living fleece of her long, bright hair, she combed with a
  golden comb.

Edinburgh

Margot Robert Adamson

If they should ask what makes the stuff of us
We should call up such idle things and gone!
The theatre we knew on Grindley Street,
The midnight bell vibrating in the Tron.

A church tower's clock along the Lothian Road,
Whose face lit up would turn a lemon moon,
Seen o'er the pallid bleakness of the street
In the chill dusks that harry northern June,

A Sunday morning over Samson's Ribs,
The smoky grass that grows on Arthur's Seat;
Turned-yellow willow leaves in Dalkeith Road,
Dropt lanceheads on the pavement at our feet;

Glimpses got sometimes of the Forfar hills
With the white snows upon them, or, maybe,
Green waters washing round the piers of Leith
With all the straws and flotsam of the sea.

A certain railway bridge whence one can look
On a network of bright lines and feel the stress,
Tossing its plumes of milky snow, where goes
Loud in full pace the thundering North Express

Behind its great green engine; or in Spring
Black-heaved the Castle Rock and there where blows
By Gordon's window wild the wallflower still,
The gold that keeps the footprints of Montrose.

The Pentlands over yellow stubble fields
Seen out beyond Craigmillar, and the flight
Of seagulls wheeling round the dark-shared plough,
Strewing the landscape with a rush of white.

Such idle things! Gold birches by hill lochs,
The gales that beat the Lothian shores in strife,
The day you found the great blue alkanette,
And all the farmlands by the shores of Fife.

The Inheritance

James Aitchison

The war, the hospitals – he was away
so long he was a stranger when he died;
I knew his face better from holiday
snapshots than from the life; and when I tried
to weep there were few tears. Later, I thought
I owed him part of my life for the years
he lost and for his early death. I ought
to have known that my father re-appears
in me no matter what I think: I feel
about books, craftsmanship, woodlands at dusk
just as he once did, his coded will
decoded as I sit here at my desk
translating impulses that might fulfil
my father's purpose and complete his task.

Dipper Territory

James Aitchison

A subliminal pre-sighting? Before I can say
'This could be dipper territory,'
I see the whirring ball of russet, white
and grey go flicker-skimming across the stream.
It settles on a boulder, folds its wings,
and nods itself, twitches and bobs itself
into the bibbed roundness of a dipper.

When it walks under the water
the dipper defies its natural buoyancy,
defies the force of the downrush, the weight of cold.
It walks beneath the watersongs
of plunge and gulp, laughter-splash, guttural chattering
and a crystalline song like chiming icicles.
When the bird rises again, its feathers are dry.

Dippers live by rivers' origins.
Their presence proves the cleanliness of air
and earth and water in these fissured uplands.
They seldom venture downstream.
I could live without dippers. They can live
only if I keep some part of my mind
clean enough to be their habitat.

Landscape with Lapwings

James Aitchison

Another April and another day
with all the seasons in it, with lapwings
falling out of sunlight into rain,
stalling on a squall and then tumbling
over the collapsing wall of air
to float in zones of weightlessness again.

And on a day like this in such a place –
a few square miles of moorland in a round
of rounded hills, rain clouds and scattered trees,
with water flowing clearly over stone –
in such a place I feel the weights slip off
the way a lapwing would if it were me.

The place might form a frame of reference
for calculating weightlessness, and all
the weathers that are in one April day,
for drawing what conclusions can be drawn
from lapwings tumbling in and out of light
with such a total lack of gravity.

Alas! Poor Queen

Marion Angus

She was skilled in music and the dance
And the old arts of love
At the court of the poisoned rose
And the perfumed glove,
And gave her beautiful hand
To the pale Dauphin
A triple crown to win –
And she loved little dogs
And parrots
And red-legged partridges
And the golden fishes of the Duc de Guise
And a pigeon with a blue ruff
She had from Monsieur d'Elboeuf.

Master John Knox was no friend to her;
She spoke him soft and kind,
Her honeyed words were Satan's lure
The unwary soul to bind.
'Good sir, doth a lissome shape
And a comely face
Offend your God His Grace

Whose Wisdom maketh these
Golden fishes of the Duc de Guise?'

She rode through Liddesdale with a song;
'Ye streams sae wondrous strang,
Oh, mak' me a wrack as I come back
But spare me as I gang.'
While a hill-bird cried and cried
Like a spirit lost
By the grey storm-wind tost.

Consider the way she had to go,
Think of the hungry snare,
The net she herself had woven,
Aware or unaware,
Of the dancing feet grown still,
The blinded eyes –
Queens should be cold and wise,

And she loved little things,
Parrots
And red-legged partridges
And the golden fishes of the Duc de Guise
And the pigeon with blue ruff
She had from Monsieur d'Elboeuf.

The Fiddler

Marion Angus

A fine player was he . . .
'Twas the heather at my knee,
The Lang Hill o' Fare
An' a reid rose-tree,
A bonnie dryin' green,
Wind fae aff the braes,
Liftin' and shiftin'
The clear-bleached claes.

Syne he played again . . .
'Twas dreep, dreep o' rain,
A bairn at the breist
An' a warm hearth-stane,
Fire o' the peat,
Scones o' barley-meal
An the whirr, whirr, whirr,
O' a spinnin'-wheel.

Bit aye, wae's me!
The hindmaist tune he made . . .
'Twas juist a dune wife
Greetin' in her plaid,
Winds o' a' the years,
Naked wa's atween,
And heather creep, creepin'
Ower the bonnie dryin' green.

Anemones

Marion Angus

Anemones, they say, are out
By sheltered woodland streams,
With budding branches all about
Where Spring-time sunshine gleams;

Such are the haunts they love, but I
With swift remembrance see
Anemones beneath a sky
Of cold austerity –

Pale flowers too faint for winds so chill
And with too fair a name –
That day I lingered on a hill
For one who never came.

Mary's Song

Marion Angus

I wad ha'e gi'en him my lips tae kiss,
Had I been his, had I been his;
Barley bried and elder wine,
Had I been his as he is mine.

The wanderin' bee it seeks the rose;
Tae the lochan's bosom the burnie goes;
The grey bird cries at evenin's fa',
'My luve, my fair one, come awa'.'

My beloved sall ha'e this he'rt tae break,
Reid, reid wine and the barley cake,
A he'rt tae break, and a mou' tae kiss,
Tho' he be nae mine, as I am his.

The Doors of Sleep

Marion Angus

Jenny come ower the hill,
Ye hae broke yer troth lang syne
An' ta'en yer hand frae mine,
But nichts are warm and still.

White as a flo'er in May
Gang glimmerin' by my bed –
White flo'er sae sune tae fade
At early dawnin' day.

Come by the doors o' sleep,
Whaur ne'er a word sall fa'
O' the ring ye gi'ed awa,
The tryst ye failed tae keep;
When nichts are clear and still,
Jenny – come ower the hill.

Arctic Convoy

J. K. Annand

Intil the pitmirk nicht we northwart sail
Facin the bleffarts and the gurly seas
That ser' out muckle skaith to mortal men.
Whummlin about like a waukrife feverit bairn
The gude ship snowks the waters o a wave.
Swithers, syne pokes her neb intil the air,
Hings for a wee thing, dinnlin, on the crest,
And clatters in the trouch wi sic a dunt
As gey near rives the platin frae her ribs
And flypes the tripes o unsuspectin man.

Northwart, aye northwart, in the pitmirk nicht.
A nirlin wind comes blawin frae the ice,
Plays dirdum throu the rails and shrouds and riggin,
Ruggin at bodies clawin at the life-lines.
There's sic a rowth o air that neb and lungs
Juist canna cope wi sic a dirlin onding.

Caulder the air becomes, and snell the wind.
The waters, splairgin as she dunts her boo,
Blads in a blatter o hailstanes on the brig
And geals on guns and turrets, masts and spars,
Cleedin the iron and steel wi coat o ice.

Northwart, aye northwart, in the pitmirk nicht.
The nirlin wind has gane, a lownness comes;
The lang slaw swall still minds us o the gale.
Restin aff-watch, a-sweein in our hammocks,
We watch our sleepin messmates' fozy braith
Transmogrify to ice upon the skin
That growes aye thicker on the ship-side plates.

Nae mair we hear the lipper o the water,
Only the dunsh o ice-floes scruntin by;
Floes that in the noon-day gloamin licht
Are lily leafs upon my lochan dubh.
But nae bricht lily-flouer delytes the ee,

Nae divin bird diverts amang the leafs,
Nae sea-bird to convoy us on our gait.
In ilka deid-lown airt smools Davy Jones,
Ice-tangle marline spikes o fingers gleg
To claught the bodies o unwary sailors
And hike them doun to stap intil his kist.
Whiles 'Arctic reek' taks on the orra shapes
O ghaistly ships-o-war athort our gait,
Garrin us rin ram-stam to action stations
Then see them melt awa intil the air.

Owre lang this trauchle lasts throu seas o daith,
Wi ne'er a sign o welcome at the port,
Nae 'Libertymen fall in!' to cheer our herts,
But sullen sentries at the jetty-heid,
And leesome-landsome waitin at our birth.

At length we turn about and sail for hame,
Back throu rouch seas, throu ice and snaw and sleet,
Hirdin the draigelt remnant o our flock
Bieldin them weel frae skaith o enemie.
But southwart noo we airt intil the licht
Leavin the perils o the Arctic nicht.

Fur Coats

J. K. Annand

Said the whitrick to the stoat,
'I see ye've on your winter coat.
I dinna see the sense ava!
Ye're shairly no expectin snaw?'

To the whitrick said the stoat,
'At least it's mair nor you hae got.
I'm gled I dinna hae to wear
The same auld coat throughout the year.'

Said the whitrick to the stoat,
'I wadna make owre muckle o't.
While nene will covet my auld coat
Your ermine fur wi tip o black
Will aiblins cleed a Provost's back.'

Mountain Pule

J. K. Annand

I saw ferlies in thon mountain pule.
Its deeps I couldna faddom, but I kent
Ilk drap o water in its shadowy mass
Begoud as crystal on a slender stem
Heich on the mountainside, syne wi its peers
Whummelt owre craigs, mellin wi licht and air,
Afore it settled in thon lownsome place.

Sae wi your mind. The deeps o thocht that dern
Intil't I'll never faddom, but whiles there kythes
Ayont your smile the dew that kittles up
And nourishes my spreit as thon deep pule
Sustained amang the stanes a gowden flouer.

Aotromachd

Meg Bateman

B' e d' aotromachd a rinn mo thàladh,
aotromachd do chainnte 's do ghàire,
aotromachd do lethchinn nam làmhan,
d' aotromachd lurach ùr mhàlda;
agus 's e aotromachd do phòige
a tha a' cur trasg air mo bheòil-sa,
is 's e aotromachd do ghlaic mum chuairt-sa
a leigeas seachad leis an t-sruth mi.

Lightness

It was your lightness that drew me,
the lightness of your talk and your laughter,
the lightness of your cheek in my hands,
your sweet gentle modest lightness;
and it is the lightness of your kiss
that is starving my mouth,
and the lightness of your embrace
that will let me go adrift.

Fhir luraich 's fhir àlainn

Meg Bateman

Fhir luraich 's fhir àlainn,
thug thu dàn gu mo bhilean,

Tobar uisge ghil chraobhaich
a' taomadh thar nan creagan,

Feur caoin agus raineach
a' glasadh mo shliosan;

Tha do leabaidh sa chanach,
gairm ghuilbneach air iteig.

Tha ceòban cùbhraidh na Màighe
a' teàrnadh mu mo thimcheall,

'S e a' toirt suilt agus gutha
dham fhuinn fada dìomhain,

Fhir luraich 's fhir àlainn,
thug thu dàn gu mo bhilean.

O Bonnie Man, Lovely Man

O bonnie man, lovely man,
You've brought a song to my lips,

A spring of clear gushing water
spilling over the rocks,

Soft grasses and bracken
covering my slopes with green;

Your bed is in cotton-grass
With curlews calling in flight,

Maytime's sweet drizzle
is settling about me,

Giving mirth and voice
to my soils long barren,

O bonnie man, lovely man,
You've brought a song to my lips.

The Educators

D. M. Black

In their
limousines the
teachers come: by
hundreds. O the
square is

blackened with dark suits, with grave
scholastic faces. They
wait to be summoned.
These are the
educators, the

father-figures. O you could
warm with love for the firm lips, the
responsible foreheads. Their
ties are strongly set, between their collars. They
pass with dignity the exasperation of waiting.

A
bells rings. They turn. On the
wide steps my
dwarf is standing, both hands raised. He
cackles with laughter. Welcome, he cries, welcome,
to our elaborate Palace. It is indeed. He
is stumbling in cartwheels over the steps. The
teachers turn to each other their grave faces.

With
a single grab they have him up by the shoulders. They
dismantle him. Limbs, O
limbs and delicate organs, limbs and
guts, eyes, the tongue, the
lobes of the brain, glands; several tonsils,
eyes, limbs, the tongue,
a kidney, pants, livers, more
kidneys, limbs, the tongue
pass from hand to hand, in their serious hands. He is
utterly gone. Wide
crumbling steps.

They
return to their cars. They
drive off smoothly, without disorder;
watching the road.

The Water-Lily

D. M. Black

When the lily establishes herself in the
cleanish water – the cleanest she can find – she
does not only unfurl and sweep abroad her
floating pads (to delight the frogs) and the flowers with
which she speaks to the kingfishers, no, but also
(let the goldfish confirm) she sends her taproot
to the black mud. Who knows what plastic bottles,
what foul slime it will cope with! As she fingers
to and fro for a purchase, (gains the nourishment
only earth can provide), it may also happen that,
piercing through to some heavy oilyish bubble she
makes climb up to the light a sickly splendour.
When the sages who daylong smoke their pipes on the
nearby benches observe it they say nothing;
the breeze fractures it into a million ripples.

Doric's No Dodo . . .

for Cuthbert Graham

Sheena Blackhall

Fowk spik aboot Scots –
Ay, wir ain Doric leid –
As if 'twis a dodo
Wha'd drappit doon deid!
As mad tae conserve an preserve the auld wirds,
As a gleg taxidermist, wi putrifeed birds,
They wrangle ower spellin, gash gulls wi their gab,
Ower a muckle weet haddie streekt oot on a slab.

I've news fur them –
Scots disna bide in a buik!
It's alive, an it's kickin,
Gin they wid bit look.
Tak a keek frae the waas

O their ivory tower,
Tak a traivel ben Buchan,
Inbye, an' oot-ower,
They'd ken it wis livin,
A weel-haunelt shelt,
Fowk spik it wi niver
A thocht foo it's spelt!
A buik for a tongue?
It's a boon fur the few!
We ken it b'hairt –
We've a tongue, in wir mou!

The Spik o' the Lan

Sheena Blackhall

The clash o' the kintra claik
Rins aff ma lug, as rain
Teems ower the glaissy gape
O' the windae pane.

The chap o' the preacher's wird,
Be it wise as Solomon,
It fooners on iron yird
Brakks, upon barren grun.

Bit the lowe o' a beast new born,
The grieve at his wirk,
The blyter o' brierin corn,
The bicker o' birk
The haly hush o' the hill:
Things kent, an at haun
I'd harken tae that wi' a will.
The Spik o' the lan!

Walk On

Sheena Blackhall

No eagle stays a wind in cosmic motion,
No mountain stops a roving wisp of straw,
No fisherman draws in the wishless ocean,
No daybreak falls beneath the fox's paw.

No hatter binds a sunbeam to a brook,
No nail impales a shadow fast.
Progress – the turning pages of a book
No hand restrains . . . the new inters the past.

Snow stills the land to sleep, spring stirs to grow
A season's holding – season's letting go.
March ticks life upward, ever moving on,
A wakening roebuck leaping into dawn.

Daunting, indeed, the troubled traveller's load
Where memory impedes tomorrow's road.
An empty dwelling has a world to gain
Where grief's the tenant . . . bitterness and pain.

Be as the bending snowdrop in the dew,
The storms of love and enmity pass through.
For thorns that seek to tear us on the way
Sink deepest when embraced. Our frailty
Fashions us fetters of our very own,
Slowing each step with yesterdays of stone.

Only the now is real. The past is gone.
Firm, set your heel upon the path. Walk on!

The Bloody Orkneys
Captain Hamish Blair

This bloody town's a bloody cuss –
No bloody trains, no bloody bus,
And no one cares for bloody us –
In bloody Orkney.

The bloody roads are bloody bad,
The bloody folks are bloody mad,
They'd make the brightest bloody sad,
In bloody Orkney.

All bloody clouds, and bloody rains,
No bloody kerbs, no bloody drains,
The Council's got no bloody brains,
In bloody Orkney.

Everything's so bloody dear,
A bloody bob, for bloody beer,
And is it good? – no bloody fear,
In bloody Orkney.

The bloody 'flicks' are bloody old,
The bloody seats are bloody cold,
You can't get in for bloody gold
In bloody Orkney.

The bloody dances make you smile,
The bloody band is bloody vile,
It only cramps your bloody style,
In bloody Orkney.

No bloody sport, no bloody games,
No bloody fun, the bloody dames
Won't even give their bloody names
In bloody Orkney.

Best bloody place is bloody bed,
With bloody ice on bloody head,
You might as well be bloody dead,
In bloody Orkney.

Shore

Alan Bold

Sheets of water are washed out on the shore as
The sea bubbles, seems to boil, then sends
Gouts of spray steaming in towards the land.
End-on the waves brighten to reveal
Fantastic swaying columns of suspended seaweed
Whose loose luxuriant curls of brown and red
Are smashed against a tepid sandstone bed.
There is a ferocious crash, and then a pause
Before the sea provides its own applause.

from *Edinburgh Castle*

Alan Bold

As if a few odd bombs were bouncing round
The globe, the third world war engulfed us all.
That day many people walked the streets as they had
For ten or twenty years, or perhaps more.
The buses kept on moving and the roads
Though hardly perfect – had just done so far.
Out on some remote island in the East
The thing had gone too far; the brink was brinked
And then the guts of cities spewed their load.
We could only wait. Other places,
So we heard, were ripped apart, and flames
Were seen for miles. All the pipes, the tubes
That carry power underneath a town
Were gone. All was just one tangled mesh
Of wire, rock, rubble, and some human bones.
This is what we heard, but our means
Of communication were faltering.

Fingers scraped in cities far away
From underneath a tomb of rotten earth
(Where plants no longer photosynthesise).

The flesh that melted from the bones, like wax
Melting from an iron armature,
Gave us reason to be lucky *here*.
We had been missed out in the capitals
The two sides thought of as strategic points
And so – we had the world to ourselves!

Schiehallion

Deric Bolton

Stop the car beside the litter bin,
Crunch the ice-cream cone, the box,
Of chocolate crisps, the sandwich bag,
A pepper tin for gulls, gently coax
The radio to sing a song of Italy,
Before this mountain god, wound up
In shrouds of nylon twist, or terylene
Or dacron, propathene, but now the sound
Steps percolate the air, they coalesce
Around the mountain edge and rip
The heathers, clarifying wave and slap
Of breeze across the ridge and cairns;
O, hemisphere of mountain, regular and smooth,
Used subtly to determine once the length
And mass of Earth, but now before
My eyes, still city-filmed, you change,
Washed by this migrant music weave,
These canned and tinned and bottled violins.
You rip the pages, turn back days
And months and years, cause clouds to slide
And tumble, cantering slowly back along
These braes to Tay and Angus and Strathmore; I see
Clearly upon the summit now your boots
O, One, stepping towards that mine in Normandy
And you, O, Two, your footprints here, another century
But here indelibly upon this air, thumbing
A lift to Delhi, Kabul and the Hindu Kush.
And I was here, too, I was Number Three,
O, canned and tinned and bottled melody.

What Might Have Been
Deric Bolton

Between what was
And might have been,
There was no wall
Until you intervened
With thoughts of sorrow
And regret
But as the trains ran green
Through evenings, still with chalk,
Leaf-filled with June,
O, why then did you hesitate, begin
To doubt how much that is
Equates with what your eyes
Had seen
Or intellect could tell
There might have been?

Corners
Kate Y. A. Bone

I am a constant corner sitter, I
Like the right-angled privacy of nooks
Where trusted friends immortalise themselves
In books beside me on my corner shelves.
A book, a cigarette, a drink, a cat,
What corner could be better than all that?

I am a further corner sitter, I
Like the delight of sitting in the sun.
Here there are blackbirds, pausing in their search,
A mist of greenness climbs upon the larch.
A flower, a bird, the humming of a bee,
These make a sheltered sanctuary for me.

I am a constant corner sitter, I
Like the right-angled privacy of nooks.

Catlike

Kate Y. A. Bone

What fun to be able to purr
Loudly like her;
To respond to the stroking of fur
With this burr.

And then to be able to spit –
No wet, no hit –
But breathily to emit
Venom and wit.

Like her to be able to sleep,
Not just in a heap,
But elegantly keep
Secrets so deep.

To awake at the sound of a voice
Saying 'Rejoice'.
To have such a wonderful choice
Of amorous boys.

To dote with pride as a mother,
Almost to smother
Sister and brother
In an overfond fluther.

In the end to forget
The whole suckling set
With no sort of fret
At once having met.

And loudly to purr
At the stroking of fur.
What fun to be her.

The West End Perk

James Bridie (O. H. Mavor)

It's long pest midnight, there's no one in the street,
The consteble is sleeping at the corner of his beat.

The cold white erc-lemps fizz like gingerade,
And I'm below your window with this cherming serenade.

Open your window, the night is beastly derk,
The phentoms are dencing in the West-End Perk,
Open your window, your lover brave to see,
I'm here all alone, and there's no one here but me!

Over the Cowkeddens a gentle stillness spreads,
All good little Redskins are tucked up in their beds.
A deep and holy stillness broods the Gorbals o'er,
And softly blow the zephyrs down on Goven's peaceful shore.

(As if with a cold in the head.)
Still do bovebed frob your lofty widdow-sill?
Well, I bust be bovig off, I fear I've got a chill,
Do tibe for eddy bore pethetic sighs or such,
So suffice it to assure you I adbire you very buch.

Opedd your widdow, the dight is beastly derk,
The phedtobs are dedsig id the West-End Perk.
Opedd your widdow, your lover brave to see,
I'b here all alode, ad there's do wudd here . . . atishee!

Ikey: His Will in Winter Written

George Mackay Brown

I, Ikey Faa, being of whole and sound mind, (nobody thinks it but
   me),
do hereby bequeath and leave my possessions
to the following persons, heartily praying that
those beneficiaries make full use

of the same, to their own hearty good and the
good of all the world beside.

Item: the birds of the isle, hawk and swan,
eider and blackbird and dotterel, to the
child JOHN SWEYNSON that gave me and the birds a
bite to eat in last winter's snow, and I in the
high winds of March gave the said John a
kite I had made out of sticks and paper for to fly among the
said birds.

Item: the fish in the tides and rips and
races about this isle, to JOCK SINCLAIR fisherman in the
said isle: that he having to return the
fattest fish to the laird's plate and kitchen, in
exchange for a farthing or a halfpenny:
since also the fingers of the laird have not baited hooks, nor his
    lady's fingers
to my knowledge stunk with fish-guts,
and there is no true truce and tryst-time
as between hall and haul:
which season and compact are well
kent to the fishermen. I have had this and that cod-head
from John's goodwife.

Item: the flowers of the sun, from the first
snowdrop to the last blown rose petal,
to GERDA FLAWS, for I have not
seen such delight in flowers in any
house-bound creature, no, not in butterfly and
bee; and I pray the said Gerda to
ensure and guarantee all traffic as between
bee and butterfly, sun and raindrop and
the feast in the open bud. I wish for her
a long happy butter-time and
bannock-time and bairn-time, happy among flowers.

Item: I leave the land of this isle from the
lowest rooted tangle in the ebb to the
hawk over the hill to MANSIE GRAY and all others who
changed it, in a thousand years and more,

from a bog to a green-and-gold patchwork;
and yet it wears Mansie Gray
out, the land, it grinds him down and it
grays him, bows and breaks him, to keep the big
laird's house with nine empty echoing rooms and
another in the city of Edinburgh; and forbye
to stock the said dwellings
with beef and bread and wine, silk and fiddles and etchings and
    harps.
I have eaten croft-crusts with thankfulness from Mansie Gray's
    table.

Item: The burns and the winds to millers.

Item: Rain and sun and corn to the makers of ale.

Item: to the factor, a breath and a heartbeat and
a breath, calculations, one at a time: as far as the last breath:
such as are never noted among the ciphers and in the ledger in his
    office.

I, Ikey Faa, write this with a stick on snow and
mud in the quarry, three days before Yule,
having a hoast on me that does not
mend, and a fiercer burning in the
blood than I have known.

I have rejoiced greatly in the
elements that are soon to shake me out and away, all but earth –
    'twixt
Yule and Hogmanay, as near as I can
guess – and I leave what is mine and all men's and God's to them
    that
will enjoy and use it best.

As *Witness* – a sparrow (his splash in the ditch)
a mouse (his scurry and snow mark)

                              *

(Will I manage to struggle to the ale-house
before closing time? If I do, will the thin-lipped
prevaricator that keeps the place give me the loan of a
last whisky?)

Hamnavoe

George Mackay Brown

My father passed with his penny letters
Through closes opening and shutting like legends
      When barbarous with gulls
      Hamnavoe's morning broke

On the salt and tar steps. Herring boats,
Puffing red sails, the tillers
      Of cold horizons, leaned
      Down the gull-gaunt tide

And threw dark nets on sudden silver harvests.
A stallion at the sweet fountain
      Dredged water, and touched
      Fire from steel-kissed cobbles.

Hard on noon four bearded merchants
Past the pipe-spitting pier-head strolled,
      Holy with greed, chanting
      Their slow grave jargon.

A tinker keened like a tartan gull
At cuithe-hung doors. A crofter lass
      Trudged through the lavish dung
      In a dream of cornstalks and milk.

Blessings and soup plates circled. Euclidian light
Ruled the town in segments blue and gray.
      The school bell yawned and lisped
      Down ignorant closes.

In 'The Arctic Whaler' three blue elbows fell,
Regular as waves, from beards spumy with porter,
      Till the amber day ebbed out
      To its black dregs.

The boats drove furrows homeward, like ploughmen
In blizzards of gulls. Gaelic fisher girls

Flashed knife and dirge
Over drifts of herring,

And boys with penny wands lured gleams
From the tangled veins of the flood. Houses went blind
      Up one steep close, for a
      Grief by the shrouded nets.

The kirk, in a gale of psalms, went heaving through
A tumult of roofs, freighted for heaven. And lovers
      Unblessed by steeples, lay under
      The buttered bannock of the moon.

He quenched his lantern, leaving the last door.
Because of his gay poverty that kept
      My seapink innocence
      From the worm and black wind;

And because, under equality's sun,
All things wear now to a common soiling,
      In the fire of images
      Gladly I put my hand
      To save that day for him.

The Lodging

George Mackay Brown

The stones of the desert town
Flush; and, a star-filled wave,
Night steeples down.

From a pub door here and there
A random ribald song
Leaks on the air.

The Roman in a strange land
Broods, wearily leaning
His lance in the sand.

The innkeeper over the fire
Counting his haul, hears not
The cry from the byre;

But rummaging in the till
Grumbles at the drunken shepherds
Dancing on the hill;

And wonders, pale and grudging,
If the queer pair below
Will pay their lodging.

The Mother

George Mackay Brown

On Monday she stood at the wooden wash-tub,
Suds to the elbow,
A slave among the storm-gray shirts and sheets.

Tuesday, she pegged the washing high –
The garden a galleon in a gale!
Then lamplight, the iron, the crisp sun-smelling folds.

The rooms thrummed with Gaelic rhythms,
A low monotone, on a Wednesday
(And every day), ancient Celtic work-spells.

She was never free like the lipsticked shop-girls
On Thursday afternoon; all her tasks
Were like bluebells in a jar on the window-sill.

On Friday she rose above textures of oat and barley
Into the paradise of cakes.
I licked cream from the wooden spoon.

Saturday night, I followed her basket and purse.
The grocer, silver-spectacled, was king
Of the apples, cheeses, syrup, sweetie-jars, cloves.

We sat, seven, in the high pew on Sunday.
After the psalms, her paper poke
Made sweet thunders all through the sermon.

The Old Women

George Mackay Brown

Go sad or sweet or riotous with beer
Past the old women gossiping by the hour,
They'll fix on you from every close and pier
An acid look to make your veins run sour.

'No help,' they say, 'his grandfather that's dead
Was troubled with the same dry-throated curse,
And many a night he made the ditch his bed.
This blood comes welling from the same cracked source.'

On every kind of merriment they frown.
But I have known a gray-eyed sober boy
Sail to the lobsters in a storm, and drown.
Over his body dripping on the stones
Those same old hags would weave into their moans
An undersong of terrible holy joy.

A Salting of Snow

Hamish Brown

The farmer said,
'Just a salting of snow' –
an odd way of putting it
for salt and snow we usually see
in the mess of busy streets.

But it was apt,
with the fawn haunches of the Howgills

spread with the salt-snow
and nicely grilling in a winter sun
set at a low number.

We raised the dust of it
as we tramped the white fells
the short day through.
Just a salting of snow,
but enough to flavour
the day so the ordinary
turned into a feast.

Dogs
Hamish Brown

We humans talk
Of treating other
Humans as dogs;
But my dumb beast
Treats me as a dog,
Thank God.

Counting Sheep
Hamish Brown

Sleep is postponed
when words sheep over
the gates of the mind.
It is too late, past dawn,
to gather wool from thorns
and barbed-wire fences.
The beasts have to be grabbed,
dipped and disinfected,
sheared in an hour
while fighting awake
hung-over from day.

Who would be a shepherd
with flocks of words loose
on the fells of the mind
in March moonlight?
I would wash my mind
of the stinking fold,
but I cannot sleep
till I count my sheep.

Village Woman

for Mrs Hodge

Margaret Gillies Brown

It's her durability that astounds.
She lives in the echo of hills,
Near run of the pearled river
In a folk-weave village
Skelped by the wind.

She is –
Child bearer,
Housekeeper,
Hen husbander,
Potato picker –
Born to bend into strong breezes.

Now at seventy –
Grandmother,
Great grandmother,
She feels loss if the storm lessens . . .

Looks for more gale
To fight against.

Calgary Bay

Margaret Gillies Brown

It was probably raining
When they left Mull
And there must have been weeping.
Standing on the beach,
Semi-circling the bay in palest gold,
I can feel tears in the wet wind.
Some left to make a new Calgary
Thousands of miles across an ocean,
Deep in the heart of land waves,
Frozen in winter.
They could see in the distance
Mountains higher and rockier
But not these green baize hills,
And their homes were not
These lonely cottages
With solemn eyes on the sea.

It's quiet here now.
My mind drifts backwards
A century or more
To those people making way for sheep.
I watch the emigrants leave:
In little boats they make for the big ship
With white sails.
Some get caught in the rip tide
Which almost pulls them back.
The anchor lifts,
There's weeping on shore and ship.

Today there's only the staccato bleating
On the hillside,
The lonely children of early tourists
Running on salty feet,
Wrestling with the wind,
Making castles they hope won't break
In a welter of sea . . .

And where the crescent thins to nothingness
A sandpiper calls from the black boulders.

A Gateway to the Sea (1)

At the East Port, St Andrews

George Bruce

Pause stranger at the porch: nothing beyond
This framing arch of stone, but scattered rocks
And sea and these on the low beach
Original to the cataclysm and the dark.

Once one man bent to the stone, another
Dropped the measuring line, a third and fourth
Together lifted and positioned the dressed stone
Making wall and arch; yet others
Settled the iron doors on squawking hinge
To shut without the querulous seas and men.
Order and virtue and love (they say)
Dwelt in the town – but that was long ago.
Then the stranger at the gate, the merchants,
Missioners, the blind beggar with the dog,
The miscellaneous vendors (duly inspected)
Were welcome within the wall that held from sight
The water's brawl. All that was long ago.
Now the iron doors are down to dust,
But the stumps of hinge remain. The arch
Opens to the element – the stones dented
And stained to green and purple and rust.

Pigeons settle on the top. Stranger,
On this winter afternoon pause at the porch,
For the dark land beyond stretches
To the unapproachable element; bright
As night falls and with the allurement of peace,
Concealing under the bland feature, possession.
Not all the agitations of the world
Articulate the ultimate question as do those waters
Confining the memorable and the forgotten;
Relics, records, furtive occasions – Caesar's politics
And he who was drunk last night:
Rings, diamants, snuff boxes, warships,
Also the less worthy garments of worthy men.
Prefer then this handled stone, now ruined

While the sea mists wind about the arch.
The afternoon dwindles, night concludes,
The stone is damp unyielding to the touch,
But crumbling in the strain and stress
Of the years: the years winding about the arch,
Settling in the holes and crevices, moulding
The dressed stone. Once one man bent to it,
Another dropped the measuring line, a third
And fourth positioned to make the wall and arch
Theirs. Pause stranger at this small town's edge –
The European sun knew those streets
O Jesu parvule; Christus Victus, Christus Victor,
The bells singing from their towers, the waters
Whispering to the waters, the air tolling
To the air – the faith, the faith, the faith.

All this was long ago. The lights
Are out, the town is sunk in sleep.
The boats are rocking at the pier,
The vague winds beat about the streets –
Choir and altar and chancel are gone.
Under the touch the guardian stone remains
Holding memory, reproving desire, securing hope
In the stop of water, in the lull of night
Before dawn kindles a new day.

Love in Age

George Bruce

Now that we have had our day, you
having carried, borne children,
been responsible through the wearing years,
in this moment and the next
and still the next as our love
spreads to tomorrow's horizon,
we talk a little before silence.

Let the young make up their love songs,
about which subject they are securely ignorant.
Let them look into eyes that mirror
themselves. Let them groan and ululate
their desire into a microphone. Let them
shout their proclamations over the tannoy
– a whisper is enough for us.

Inheritance

George Bruce

This which I write now
Was written years ago
Before my birth
In the features of my father.

It was stamped
In the rock formations
West of my hometown.
Not I write,

But, perhaps, William Bruce,
Cooper.
Perhaps here his hand
Well articled in his trade.

Then though my words
Hit out
An ebullition from
City or flower,

There not my faith,
These the paint
Smeared upon
The inarticulate,

The salt crusted sea-boot,
The red-eyed mackerel,
The plate shining with herring,
And many men,

Seamen and craftsmen and curers,
And behind them
The protest of hundreds of years,
The sea obstinate against the land.

Kinnaird Head

George Bruce

I go North to cold, to home, to Kinnaird,
Fit monument for our time.

This is the outermost edge of Buchan.
Inland the sea birds range,
The tree's leaf has salt upon it,
The tree turns to the low stone wall.
And here a promontory rises towards Norway,
Irregular to the top of thin grey grass
Where the spindrift in storm lays its beads.
The water plugs in the cliff sides,
The gull cries from the clouds
This is the consummation of the plain.

O impregnable and very ancient rock,
Rejecting the violence of water,
Ignoring its accumulations and strategy,
You yield to history nothing.

Departure and Departure and . . .

George Bruce

Someone is waving a white handkerchief
from the train as it pulls out with a white
plume from the station and rumbles its way
to somewhere that does not matter. But
it will pass the white sands and the broad sea
that I have watched under the sun and moon
in the stop of time in my childhood as I am
now there again and waiting for the white
handkerchief. I shall not see her again
but the waters rise and fall and the horizon
is firm. You who have not seen that line
hold the brimming sea to the round earth
cannot know this pain and sweetness of departure.

Soup and Sherry

George Bruce

It was 3.30 in the afternoon, mid-November
and I was calling on Bill Gillies.
(Sir William Gillies, R.S.A., R.A. etcetera.)
'Come in,' he says, 'We'll have soup.
You won't be drinking and driving
so we'll have sherry.' Didn't like
the idea of the combination, but
the lentil soup was hottering
on the stove so there was nothing for it
but swallow it with the sherry.
There was a painting on the easel
of Temple, the village where we were.
It didn't look like the rainy street
off which I'd just come. In it
the moon was up and silvering
the length of it, pavement, tarmac road,
squat houses, and touching up

two black trees, winter trees,
but each twig starting from its branch
as if Spring were in it. I looked out
the window. Nothing like the painting.
No glimmering windows along the street.
He was stirring the soup. He didn't look up.
'I catched a painting last night.'
I could see him casting on the Esks,
North Esk, South Esk, Leithen Water, Falla.
How many paintings got away? 'Soup's ready.'
How many poems slip back into my dark sea?

Planting Potatoes during Chernobyl

Tom Bryan

The seed went in
two days before the Chernobyl Cloud
shiva-danced over the strath.
We joked about tubers
glowing in the dark.

It rained for six weeks.

The leaves grew to lovely sheen.
Tiny flowers lured bees and butterflies;
roots swelled; Edsel Blues – skins of livid heather.
Kerr's Pinks: soft carnation hue, marble-fleshed.
All perfect, as new potatoes.
Leave them for maincrop?
Eat and run?
Dig before the roots turn to slush
and cells run riot?

Let them grow.
Death and potatoes go a long way back
in my family.
Old Irish men in North America
would not risk potatoes again.

They planted maize
because the sun could cure what soil could not.

In that newer world,
death was above ground,
in the clear light of day.

from *Alastair Buchan (1917)*

A. E. B.
Born 12th June, 1894
Died of wounds received at Arras, 9th April, 1917

John Buchan

A mile or two from Arras town
The yellow moorland stretches far,
And from its crest the roads go down
Like arrows to the front of war.

All day the laden convoys pass,
The sunburnt troops are swinging by,
And far above the trampled grass
The droning planes climb up the sky.

In April when I passed that way
An April joy was in the breeze;
The hollows of the woods were gay
With slender-stalked anemones.

The horn of Spring was faintly blown,
Bidding a ransomed world awake,
Nor could the throbbing batteries drown
The nesting linnets in the brake.

And as I stood beside the grave,
Where 'mid your kindly Scots you lie,
I could not think that one so brave,
So glad of heart, so kind of eye,

Had found the deep and dreamless rest,
Which men may crave who bear the scars
Of weary decades on their breast,
And yearn for slumber after wars.

You scarce had shed your boyhood's years,
In every vein the blood ran young,
Your soul uncramped by ageing fears,
Your tales untold, your songs unsung.

As if my sorrow to beguile,
I heard the ballad's bold refrain:
'I'll lay me downe and bleed a-while,
And then I'll rise and fight again.'

Fisher Jamie

John Buchan

Puir Jamie's killed. A better lad
Ye wouldna find to busk a flee
Or burn a pule or wield a gad
Frae Berwick to the Clints o' Dee.

And noo he's in a happier land. –
It's Gospel truith and Gospel law
That Heaven's yett maun open stand
To folk that for their country fa'.

But Jamie will be ill to mate;
He lo'ed nae music, kenned nae tunes
Except the sang o' Tweed in spate,
Or Talla loupin' ower its linns.

I sair misdoot that Jamie's heid
A croun o' gowd will never please;
He liked a kep o' dacent tweed
Whaur he could stick his casts o' flees.

If Heaven is a' that man can dream
And a' that honest herts can wish,
It maun provide some muirland stream,
For Jamie dreamed o' nocht but fish.

And weel I wot he'll up and speir
In his bit blate and canty way,
Wi' kind Apostles standin' near
Whae in their time were fishers tae.

He'll offer back his gowden croun
And in its place a rod he'll seek,
And bashfu'-like his herp lay doun
And speir a leister and a cleek.

For Jims had aye a poachin' whim;
He'll sune grow tired, wi' lawfu' flee
Made frae the wings o' cherubim,
O' castin' ower the Crystal Sea . . .

I picter him at gloamin' tide
Steekin' the backdoor o' his hame
And hastin' to the waterside
To play again the auld auld game;

And syne wi' saumon on his back,
Catch't clean against the Heavenly law,
And Heavenly byliffs on his track,
Gaun linkin' doun some Heavenly shaw.

The Everlasting Astronauts

Tom Buchan

These dead astronauts cannot decay –
they bounce on quilted walls of their tin grave
and very gently collide with polythene balloons
full of used mouthwash, excrements and foodscraps.

They were chosen not for their imagination
but for their compatibility with machines –
glancing out at the vast America of the universe
they cried, 'Gee boys, it's great up here!'

Now, tumbling and yawing, their playpen hurries
into the continuum and at last they are real explorers
voyaging endlessly among unrecorded splendours
with Columbus, Peary, Magellan and Drake.

Scotland the Wee
Tom Buchan

Scotland the wee, crèche of the soul,
of thee I sing

land of the millionaire draper, whisky vomit
and the Hillman Imp

staked out with church halls, gaelic sangs
and the pan loaf

eventide home for teachers and christians,
nirvana of the keelie imagination

Stenhousemuir, Glenrothes, Auchterarder, Renton
– one way street to the coup of the mind.

Jesus Speaks to the Church at Eastertime
Elizabeth Burns

I have plans for you
you snoozer
you drowsy sluggish church

I resurrect myself
am off that cross
knowing what torture is:

your hand's palm (place where
sparrow, flax-flower
wheat-chaff were cupped)

has nails hit through it
cartilage crumbles like biscuit
body gapes, blood crusts

I get limbs out
of those bloodied ribbons
musky gravecloths

step out past boulder and soldiers
into wet grass
Morning in a garden

Breakfast on a beach
Fingers falter at scabbed skin
touch, touch

I shake you like a mother at dawn
trying to wake a child
who flops like a rag doll

You doze and will not look
at daylight
your dreams are easier

I resurrect
You eat chocolate eggs
sugary and melting

You mix me in with spring:
hatched birds, daffodils
all gaudy yellow things

never thinking of the southern hemisphere
where it is not spring
never looking at the church at the tip of Africa

It does not need posies, ribbons, baby rabbits
It has tasted crucifixion
real as nails or tear-gas

Its gold and green
are not colours of primroses
but of freedom, potent

But here you lie in bed, snug and indulged
You do not see there is a day outside
And people living in it

Oh wilted church, what rags of hymns you sing
what mumbled scraps of prayers you speak
on the narrow track to your imagined heaven

Oh gaunt church, gaunt people
so silent and not dancing
not screaming

Ophelia

Still harping on daughters

Elizabeth Burns

Always the daughter
her movements round the castle
charted by her father

She has a wide-armed gangly innocence
she is motherless and milky
an innocent in the court
Her flesh is thin as manuscript
her eyes are animal and scared
Ribbons hang from her hair
her skirts are hitched up awkwardly
cling to her gawky legs
make her gauche among armour

Always the daughter

But Hamlet – he –
she licks the ink of his letters
fingers the string of pearls he gave her
that swing between her breasts
– he – but he is ungraspable

He will not talk to her as adult:
he confides in Horatio
walks off, untouchable, to man's talk
He basks in the words of Horatio:
the days are not long enough to listen to his wisdom
He wants it to be just the two of them together

plotting Denmark's future:
no women to distract them

He laughs now at the old love letters
he once wrote her, tosses them in the fire
He wants her gone
His words clang in her head:
Get thee to a nunnery

She is trapped in this tilted castle
and this man who has drawn such promises from her
who has given her gifts of pearls
spits in her eye and slaps her face:
his handmark makes a red flag
across her pale cheek

He will not listen, he will not
listen when she says she loves him,
love big as these pounding waves
that salt the windows
Every word she wrote and spoke was true
but Hamlet will not hear her

Each day she tiptoes on a slippery bank –
one step and she would over-edge from sanity
feeling rocks grown slithery with moss
slide from her grasp as whirlpool water looms

This is not the beautiful floating death by water
She will not have her skirts drawn out around her
billowed along by the current
her hair floating like some golden weed
and a cloak of wildflowers scattered round her

This death by water
will be sticky with mud
Her wet clothes will drag her down
and the stones in her pockets
sink her quickly

She reaches out to Hamlet
through filmy salt-splattered windows –
he drifts through her fingers
she cannot make herself heard –

Madness flows between them like a river
They say that his is faked
They say that hers is real

She gives herself over to flowers
and songs and bitter-scented herbs
rubbed and rubbed through her fingers

It is very hazy and blossomy here, and loud –
she cannot make herself heard
between the rantings of the courtiers

She is walled by this castle, she is liege
Her father's eyes are on her
The ramparts clutch at her –

she looks to shores of Elsinore
and sees the men set sail
for England, and for France

But she will float away

bedraggled down the stream –
water will take her

She has her pockets weighted
and her hair garlanded

She went down singing
so they say

Ophelia
Ophelia
Ophelia –

Tundra's Edge

John Burnside

Here is the wolf. The wind, the sound of rain,
the kitchen light that falls across the lawn –
these things are his. This house is his domain.

Here is the wolf. He slips in with the dawn
to raid your mirrors. Shadows will persist
for days, to mark the distance he has gone

in search of you. Yet still you will insist
the wolf died out in these parts long ago:
everyone knows the wolf does not exist.

You catch no scent. And where the mirrors glow
those are not eyes, but random sparks of light.
You never dream of running with the snow.

Yet here is Wolf. He rustles in the night.
Only the wind, but you switch on the light.

Lost

John Burnside

The fog walks down the hill and finds our yard:
curious, like a tourist, filling up
corners, measuring spaces, rescuing
mystery from the commonplace. We take
no little pride in our slight membership
of this all-knowing whiteness; echoes fall
two yards away and plunge into the deep
beside us, like the voices in a well,
and home was unremarkable until
it disappeared into the hinterland
behind our practised blindness, where we keep
private forests, mountains, shifting sands
on lucid, instinct maps of holy ground
we render to the fog when we are found.

Out of Exile

John Burnside

When we are driving through the border towns
we talk of houses, empty after years
of tea and conversation;
of afternoons marooned against a clock
and silences elected out of fear,
of lives endured for what we disbelieved.

We recognise the shop fronts and the names,
the rushing trees and streets into the dark;
we recognise a pattern in the sky:
blackness flapping like a broken tent,
shadow foxes running in the stars.
But what we recognise is what we bring.

Driving, early, through the border towns,
the dark stone houses clanging at our wheels,

and we invent things as they might have been:
a light switched on, some night, against the cold,
and children at the door, with bags and coats,
telling stories, laughing, coming home.

Anstruther

John Burnside

Watching the haar move in
I think of the times we came out here, as children,

and disappeared like ghosts
into the fog:

ghosts for ourselves, at least; we were still
involved with substance

and swallows flickering along the rim
of light and sand

avoided us, no matter how we tried
to be invisible.

The far shore, that I used to think
was somewhere strange,

the lighthouse that once seemed large
and fishing boats beneath the harbour wall

are forming anew
within this fold of mist,

more real than ever, harder and more precise,
and nothing ghostly in the way

the cold welds to my skin
and lets me know

how quick I am, how quick I have to be
to go on walking, blindly, into silence.

Advertisement for a Scottish Servant
Ron Butlin

Would you like a very Scottish servant all your own
who'll do for, spiritually speaking, you alone?
A lad o' pairts: a prophet, historian and more,
a therapist/composer who understands the score?
Guaranteed – your past and future contrapuntally combined
into a pre-determined present so defined
you'll never need to think or feel again!

Your gardener for life, his motto: prune first then restrain
the slightest sign of growth. He'll cut you down to size
(for your own good) then train your roots to do
their darkest: dig deep, grasp, immobilise;
if needs be, split your soul in two.
He'll anticipate your every beck and call –
he *kent your faither*, after all!

As a Scottish-school economist he takes great pains
where pain was never due. No credit-giving Keynes,
he soon has Adam Smith's close-fistedness outclassed
insisting every childhood trauma last
your lifetime. All you'll need to know is what he'll tell you,
even when you're sleeping he'll compel you
treat his dreams as if they were your own.

Say 'Yes' – he's yours! Your very own: flesh, blood and bone
passed on as Scottish fathers pass him on
to Scottish sons (with references supplied
unto the seventh generation). A tendency to patricide
but nothing serious – just words – so never heed him.
This very Scottish servant –
who needs him?

The Bath

Ron Butlin

Standing in the middle of a field: claw-footed,
white-lipped, porcelain-plungered, fully stretched
for the reading of detective novels in;
ocean-going, and of Jurassic proportions
all but extinct in this designer-world.

Less than two miles from the river Annan. There was mud
to walk through, thistles, nettles and cows to avoid;
barbed wire to climb over. A cloudless sky:
the sun had a perfect view of me the day
I first climbed in, trying it for size.

The Puddock

John M. Caie

A puddock sat by the lochan's brim,
An' he thocht there was never a puddock like him.
He sat on his hurdies, he waggled his legs,
An' cockit his heid as he glowered throu' the seggs.
The bigsy wee cratur' was feelin' that prood
He gapit his mou' an' he croakit oot lood:
'Gin ye'd a' like tae see a richt puddock,' quo' he,
'Ye'll never, I'll sweer, get a better nor me.
I've fem'lies an' wives an' a weel-plenished hame,
Wi' drink for my thrapple an' meat for my wame.
The lasses aye thocht me a fine strappin' chiel,
An' I ken I'm a rale bonny singer as weel.
I'm nae gaun tae blaw, but th' truth I maun tell –
I believe I'm the verra MacPuddock himsel'.' . . .

A heron was hungry an' needin' tae sup,
Sae he nabbit th' puddock and gollup't him up;
Syne runkled his feathers: 'A peer thing,' quo' he,
'But – puddocks is nae fat they eesed tae be.'

John Donne, You Were Wrong . . .

No man is an island – John Donne

Janet Caird

John Donne, you were wrong.
We are all islands and the sea
breaks on the shore in foam
rolls back to the deep and leaves
flotsam and jetsam haphazard on the pebbles.

Lighthouses, beacons,
criss-cross the dark –
warnings, greetings, s.o.s.,
that die with daylight.

Small skiffs beached on the shingle
below beetling cliffs
must soon drift on
under the tyranny of the tide.

Signals,
brief landfalls,
the intervening sea –
each man is an island.

Emigrants

Janet Caird

We see them in old films
thronging the rails of huge liners
and their excitement, trepidation, grief
when the ship moves and the gap widens.
From the wharf friends wave and wave and reach
for the paper streamers soaring from the ship
last frail contacts
soon to split and drift on the indifferent waves.

Do the stay-at-homes forget
they too will climb the gangway and be emigrants
while others watch the ship
lessen and lessen into the horizon
and over the curve of the world?

Greeting, Not Greeting

for Peta Sandars

Angus Calder

To wake to the reassurance of grey stone streets
under a clouded, adequate Edinburgh sky,
finding one has the right change in one's pocket
for once: and for once there seems no cause to cry . . .
It is unnecessary to fly on a rocket.
Here is a day which one greets, not greeting.

Curling: Old Murrayfield Ice Rink

Angus Calder

Ice-capers! Time cannot stale
our pot-bellied skittishness. Watch us
frisking like penguins who've guzzled
too many tunas
off Tristan da Cunha. But who
dares lampoon us? Directed
by skeely skips, we address
elementals with modest finesse.
Not 'bowls on the rocks' this, but stones
over ice: final realities.

Ice in captivity, certainly,
stones smoothed to human shining,
but heavy
real stones. See them sinuate
target-wards suavely.

Truly this joust has more import
than slim-shanked cavortings across there
by teeny-bopping, insouciant
easy
skaters.

Sweat, greybeards!
Concentrate. Sweep
hard, harder –
we might
    yet
        win.

October Opera for Kate
Angus Calder

Götterdämmerung on the radio –
the crazed Valkyrie
hurls herself into the flames
as the Gods' home crumbles.
A dwarf greets over gold.
Fishy maidens triumph.

We were both of us right
to mistrust Wagner
I think, as I plod
through this slow autumn.
(How long green lingers
on the trees this year.)

Mozart's the man – 'They're all like that',
'Pardon, Countess, pardon' – transitional
quick emotions survived, not
self-immolation
after hero-sized betrayals –
but cynical, not so?

Somewhere in between
there's the ground no opera occupies,
where music's the laughter
of a child on a seashore,
where a well-cooked meal
sustains as arias don't.

Brunnhilde burns as stews shouldn't.
A hurt child can afford no pardon.

Love in the Abstract

Robert R. Calder

Can even the soundest or loftiest notion
know anything of the contingent human being
who, their mind in a fixed state, is its possession?

Does this dulling of my late perplexity,
some time now since she was with me,
say the her I thought me with just could not be?

Is that stranger now with her with another stranger,
and was there ever more than two bare dice
bounced in a bag, and thrown, to us two together?

'We . . . ll, yes *and* no' is maybe not nonsense if now
I now do know her and the pang left is better not dismissed,
and know I didn't have her and so didn't lose her,

nor she lose me: *undiscovered from undiscovered*
parted a while back. Yet another pang comes: emotion's
so abstract . . . I wish we could have met each other!

(variation on an Arab poem)

Covenanting Country
Sir Alec Cairncross

In this wide moorland fringed with dirty haze
Voices fall quivering on the windless air;
The lazy seagulls trace a circling maze,
And pompous crows glean what the reapers spare.
Here the hot sky is empty of all rancour;
The quiet rivers wash away pretence.
Is this deep-rooted land a natural anchor
To peaceful living and secure good sense?
This is the home of ancient persecution,
Ungovernable wills, the spirit of denial,
Fanaticism. Men went to execution
'As to a marriage', mocking at their trial.
And we, who purpose with a calmer mind –
Can we be as implacable, less blind?

1937

Munich
Sir Alec Cairncross

A wilful, credulous, obstinate, old man
Decked in the honour of dishonoured friends
Parades betrayal as a novel plan
For everlasting peace, and makes amends
For Britain's misdeeds with Bohemian land:
Venting atonement on disarmed allies,
And finding justice, by some sleight of hand,
In yielding to injustice. Men of lies
Have had their way. Henceforward we are bound
As junior partners on the side of error.
We must watch helpless from unhallowed ground
Who might have won delivery from the Terror.
Uncrucified, you bring us others' sorrow
And shame that former Gods were wont to borrow!

1938

The Drunken Lyricist

Gerry Cambridge

We met that grey dull evening on the east shore.
Roaring round the bend he came, flat out
at fifteen miles an hour, and stopped. We had to shout
till he turned off his engine. *It's going to pour*
it looks like: me. *Oa, I'm haardly cancerned*
thee night wi weather, man! he said, flat cap askew.
Gap-toothed smile. Torched cheeks. Eyes' Atlantic blue.
Hiv you seen any? Weemun? Whisky burned
its golden road in him, and he would search.
's that wun, man? – the shore's dark speck.
Not waiting a reply, through the bright wreck
of that grey evening, he roared off, with a lurch.
His tractor almost reared on its back tyres.
Fifteen miles an hour flat out, parched by amber fires.

Shore Crab

Gerry Cambridge

Haw, Jimmy, dinnae mess wi me.
Fancy yer chances, eh? Eh? We'll see.
Naw, they dinnae caw
me Shug the Claw
fer naethin. Mon, square go then. Srang,
ye feart? Ahve taen a haill gang
o the likes o ye at wance.
Dinnae reckon yer chance
noo, eh? When ye get tae hell
ah'll be waitin there fer ye. Caw
me a scroonger, eh? Aye, awa
an rin ti yer maw
ya wimp! Mind o Shug the Claw.

Fallen Maple Leaves

Gerry Cambridge

Like jigsaw pieces to an unfound puzzle,
drawn up from where we lie now we were each
a bud that swayed on the blue and white,
then made all summer a submarine shade
with our rustling high society. Now we
are colours of blood and butter and bronze,
wind-shaken down from our lofty tree,
and not to be shamed by our last flamboyance
before we re-enter mud's democracy.

Foxgloves

Gerry Cambridge

Come now, bees, you want to, don't you?
Why else am I here in my purplish-red,
stately and tall at the dark wood's edge?
With the leopard spots on my petal's lips
I will draw you in, with the silk
of my every gloving bell
enclose you well
in your deep desire for the sticky drops
in my shaking steeple.
Yes, thrum and vibrate in my bells
my buzzing loves, I'll dust your hair
with the glorious gold that's a half of life
in return for your clumsy lust! Yes,
visit my softness again and again,
do not be put off by wind and rain –
let me slenderly spring in my satin dress
for your kin for a thousand summers,
my bells all trembling in the air's caress.

Mitigation
Kate Clanchy

We think you know the secret places,
the ones you called, perhaps, *Big Sands*,
The Den, or *Grassy Hill*. They loom up large
behind your eyes. Those hands that stroke
your signet ring, were once, like ours, blunt-
fingered, small, and clutched at grass or clenched
a stone and loved the tender, ticking throat

of panicked bird or retching child.
You watched the films, played Dracula.
That doll was yours whose head came off.
You stored her up behind the fort, the patch
of dirt around her mouth. There's something
buried in the park, a shallow grave, a rotting
thrush. You know the place. And know

the swooping railway tracks and why
we stole a child, like sweeties, from the shops.
You twitch and feel the small wet thrill.
You balked, you bottled, ran, that's all.
We heard you from the Policeman's van.
We heard your hands, the short, sharp slaps
of grown-ups clamouring to get back.

We Have Some Urgent Messages
Kate Clanchy

Above all, in droves, they simply leave,
one dry evening, wordless, whistling.
Nightly, the radio calls them home,
known as Jeannie, last seen . . .

No answer comes. They have stepped
from the noise to the edge of their lives,
the margin where the light seeps
under the thick curved glass that holds us in.

Men From the Boys

Kate Clanchy

Imagine this man as a lonely boy:
at the biscuit-smelling, sour milk stage,
shirt misbuttoned, strangled tie,
pockets stocked with fists and secrets.

The inky boy in the front row desk,
who writes his name, address, adds
England, Earth, the Universe, concocts
a six month scheme for their general good;

get dressed in robes to bury voles,
makes the cat a home that goes unused
or tries to help the birds with nests;
gives over spring to crushing flies

to keep a fledgling half alive; and spends
dank winter afternoons spinning
treacle over spoons or making tapes
of private jokes with laughter

added later. This boy writes runes
in milk on library books, and *Out*,
Forbidden on his door. You know
that if you grab him now

you'll hold a bag of kicking bones.
He wants no comfort, mother, home.
He'll work the whole thing out alone.

Timetable
Kate Clanchy

We all remember school, of course:
the lino warming, shoe bag smell, expanse
of polished floor. It's where we learned
to wait: hot cheeked in class, dreaming,
bored, for cheesy milk, for noisy now.
We learned to count, to rule off days,
and pattern time in coloured squares:
purple English, dark green Maths.

We hear the bells, sometimes,
for years, the squeal and crack
of chalk on black. We walk, don't run,
in awkward pairs, hoping for the open door,
a foreign teacher, fire drill. And love
is long aertex summers, tennis sweat,
and somewhere, someone singing flat.
The art room, empty, full of light.

The Deluge
W. D. Cocker

The Lord took a staw at mankind,
A righteous an' natural scunner;
They were neither to haud nor to bind,
They were frichtit nae mair wi' his thun'er.

They had broken ilk edic' an' law,
They had pitten his saints to the sword,
They had worshipped fause idols o' stane;
'I will thole it nae mair,' saith the Lord.

'I am weary wi' flytin' at folk;
I will dicht them clean oot frae my sicht;
But Noah, douce man, I will spare,
For he ettles, puir chiel, to dae richt.'

So he cried unto Noah ae day,
When naebody else was aboot,
Sayin': 'Harken, my servant, to Me
An' these, my commands, cairry oot:

'A great, muckle boat ye maun build,
An ark that can float heich an' dry,
Wi' room in't for a' yer ain folk
An' a hantle o' cattle forby.

'Then tak' ye the fowls o' the air,
Even unto the big bubbly-jocks;
An' tak' ye the beasts o' the field:
Whittrocks, an' foumarts, an' brocks.

'Wale ye twa guid anes o' each,
See that nae cratur rebels;
Dinna ye fash aboot fish:
They can look efter theirsels.

'Herd them a' safely aboard,
An' ance the Blue Peter's unfurled,
I'll send doun a forty-day flood
And de'il tak' the rest o' the world.'

Sae Noah wrocht hard at the job,
An' searched to the earth's farthest borders,
An' gathered the beasts an' the birds,
An' tellt them to staun' by for orders.

An' his sons, Ham an' Japheth an' Shem,
Were thrang a' this time at the wark;
They had fell'd a wheen trees in the wood
An' biggit a great, muckle ark.

This wasna dune juist on the quate,
An' neebours would whiles gether roun';
Then Noah would drap them a hint
Like: 'The weather is gaun to break doun.'

But the neebours wi' evil were blin'
An' little jaloused what was wrang,
Sayin': 'That'll be guid for the neeps,'
Or: 'The weather's been drouthy ower lang.'

Then Noah wi' a' his ain folk,
An' the beasts an' the birds got aboard;
An' they steekit the door o' the ark,
An' the lippened theirsels to the Lord.

Then doun cam' a lashin' o' rain,
Like the wattest wat day in Lochaber;
The hailstanes like plunkers cam' stot,
An' the fields turned to glaur, an' syne glabber.

An' the burns a' cam' doun in a spate,
An' the rivers ran clean ower the haughs,
An' the brigs were a' soopit awa',
An what had been dubs becam' lochs.

Then the folk were sair pitten aboot,
An' they cried, as the weather got waur:
'Oh! Lord, we ken fine we ha'e sinn'd
But a joke can be cairried ower faur!'

Then they chapp'd at the ark's muckle door,
To speer gin douce Noah had room;
But Noah ne'er heedit their cries,
He said: 'This'll learn ye to soom.'

An' the river roar'd loudly an' deep;
An' the miller was droon't in the mill;
An' the watter spread ower a' the land,
An' the shepherd was droon't on the hill.

But Noah, an' a' his ain folk,
Kep' safe frae the fate o' ill men,
Till the ark, when the flood had gi'en ower,
Cam' dunt on the tap o' a ben.

An' the watters row'd back to the seas,
An' the seas settled doun and were calm.
An' Noah replenished the earth –
But they're sayin' he took a guid dram!

Stolen Light

Stewart Conn

A shiver crosses Loch Stenness
as of thousands of daddy-long-legs
skittering on the surface.
In total stillness
thunderclouds close in.

Lead-shot from a blunderbuss
the first flurries come.
The elements have their say;
the depths riven
as by some monster.

The impulse to run
hell-for-leather
lest this a prelude
to one of the Great Stones
clumping to the water.

A friend is writing
a book on poetry
and inspiration.
Brave man – imagine him
in flippers and wet-suit

poised on the edge:
a charging of nerve-ends
too rapid to track,
or underwater treasure
you hold your breath and dive for?

Todd

Stewart Conn

My father's white uncle became
Arthritic and testamental in
Lyrical stages. He held cardinal sin
Was misuse of horses, then any game

Won on the sabbath. A Clydesdale
To him was not bells and sugar or declension
From paddock, but primal extension
Of rock and soil. Thundered nail

Turned to sacred bolt. And each night
In the stable he would slaver and slave
At cracked hooves, or else save
Bowls of porridge for just the right

Beast. I remember I lied
To him once, about oats: then I felt
The brand of his loving tongue, the belt
Of his own horsey breath. But he died,

When the mechanised tractor came to pass.
Now I think of him neighing to some saint
In a simple heaven or, beyond complaint,
Leaning across a fence and munching grass.

First Light

Stewart Conn

Near Nunnerie, where Daer and Potrail meet,
highstepping it through early morning mist:
a troupe of llamas; one brown, four white,
their head-erect posture midway between
goat and camel, last thing we dreamt we'd see.

Approaching the bank, they stop in unison
and stand motionless, maybe in contemplation
of their near perfect reflections, or simply
for a good nostrilful of us, then move on;
all but the largest, who gazes quizzically

as if asking, 'Do you suspect we exist
only as some mutation of the spirit
of the place? Have it as you please.'
Then dismissing philosophical fripperies
he turns and splashes through a hoop of light.

The Bayonet

James Copeland

Grim and gaunt the sergeant-major,
Gimlet gaze on raw recruits,
Calling them to proper order,
Eyeing them from cap to boots.

Please attend my latest subject,
Quietly he began – and then
Whipped the scabbard from the object:
This is called The Bayonet, men!

At his roar the soldiers quivered,
Listen now and listen well!
And the bravest of them shivered,
Such the tale he had to tell.

This is not the blade for shaving!
This is not for toasting bread!
Bare it to the foe you're braving,
Lunge and twist and leave him dead.

Face the foe or he will slay you!
Give him not the slightest chance!
Let no thoughts of mercy stay you!
Scream with rage as you advance!

Yours the life and his the dying!
In your thoughts no higher plan!
Not for you bereavement's sighing!
War is war and man is man!

Place your boot against the slaughtered,
Pull the blade from out his breast,
He was brave but he was bettered,
Leave him now and face the rest.

This is my council be attending,
He is dead who stands afraid!
Still be there the battle ending,
Wipe your sweat and clean your blade.

Now the sergeant-major quietened,
Eyeing each and smiling then,
Saying, to their courage heightened:
Thus – the bayonet, gentlemen.

Ed

James Copeland

Ed,
Like the dead,
Lay in his bed,
Deep was his dread
Of the workaday battle.

Woke
With a sigh,
A whimpering cry,
A pain-laden – Why?
To the letterbox rattle.

Knew
What it meant,
What had been sent,
The rates and the rent
And the – Dear Sir Unless.

Ed,
Like the dead,
Out of his head,
Where to get bread,
That was nobody's guess.

No
Bloody joke,
Bloody well broke,
Must have a smoke,
Last fag in the packet.

Ed,
Like the dead,
Sat up in his bed,
The fag glowing red
And a smouldering jacket.

Head
Drooping lower,
Started to snore,
Then with a roar,
Great flames leaping higher.

Ed,
Like the dead,
Smoking in bed,
Of whom it was said,
Was a big ball of fire.

Sobieski-Stuarts

Robert Crawford

On scuffed chaise-longues in Europe's drawing-rooms
Sobieski-Stuarts audition for thrones.

Their Gaelic is not the Gaelic of Borrodale
But the Gaelic of Baden-Baden.

Draped in ancient, oddly pristine
Manic-depressive tartans,

Soi-distant with calipered wrists,
Statuesque for early cameras,

Soon they pirouette to receive
Double malts and weary autograph hunters,

Couples rubicundly stripping the willow
After the band has gone home.

Trains connect for the Hook of Holland,
Luxembourg, St Germain.

Underneath heavy evening cloud
The sun sets, a jabot of light.

Scotch Broth

Robert Crawford

A soup so thick you could shake its hand
And stroll with it before dinner.

The face rising to its surface,
A rayfish waiting to be stroked,

Is the pustular, eat-me face of a crofter,
Turnipocephalic, white-haired.

Accepting all comers, it's still our nation's
Flagsoup, sip-soup; sip, sip, sip

At this other scotch made with mutton
That intoxicates only

With peas and potatoes, chewy uists of meat.
All races breathe over our bowl,

Inhaling Inverness and Rutherglen,
Waiting for a big, teuchtery face

To compose itself from carrots and barley
Rising up towards the spoon.

Comfort in Puirtith

Helen B. Cruickshank

The man that mates wi' Poverty,
An' clasps her tae his banes,
Will faither lean an' lively thochts,
A host o' eident weans –
But wow! they'll warstle tae the fore
Wi' hunger-sharpit brains!

But he that lies wi' creeshy W'alth
Will breed a pudden thrang,
Owre cosh tae ken their foziness,
Owre bien tae mak' a sang –
A routh o' donnert feckless fules
Wha dinna coont a dang!

The Wishin' Well

Helen B. Cruickshank

A lass cam' sabbin'
Tae my brink,
Tae dip her hand
An' wishin,' drink.
'O, water, water,
Gi'e tae me
This wish I wish,
Or else I dee!'

Back cam' the lass
Years efter-hand,
An' peered again
At my dancin' sand.
'I mind,' she said
'O' drinkin' here,
But – Losh keep me,
What *did* I speir?'

Sae Lang Has Sorrow

Helen B. Cruickshank

Sae lang has Sorrow tenanted
The hoose o' Life wi' me,
An saut-like seasoned ilka meal
Wi' sharpened ecstasie,
That gin she cam' tae say Fareweel,
An' Joy hersel' cam' ben,
I doobt I wadna welcome her,
The bonny smilin' quean.

And at the lanely hinderend
Gin I sud tak' the road
Tae regions yont the yett o' Daith,
A sorrowless abode,

I doobt I wadna feel at hame
Sans sorrow an' sans sin,
But fleein' frae the wersh-like place
I'd tirl *anither* pin.

Fate

From an old fable

Helen B. Cruickshank

Fate fell upon a man,
Beat him
Well nigh to death.
And as she paused for breath
'Why thus assault me?'
The poor fellow said.

Dealing the wretch
A yet more grievous blow
Upon the head,
'Now that you ask me
Why, damme if I know
Myself' Fate said.

Shy Geordie

Helen B. Cruickshank

Up the Noran Water,
In by Inglismaddy,
Annie's got a bairnie
That hasna got a daddy.
Some say it's Tammas's
And some say it's Chay's;
An' naebody expec'it it,
Wi' Annie's quiet ways.

Up the Noran Water,
The bonnie little mannie
Is dandlit an' cuddlit close
By Inglismaddy's Annie.
Wha the bairnie's faither is
The lassie never says;
But some think it's Tammas's,
And some think it's Chay's.

Up the Noran Water,
The country folk are kind;
An' wha the bairnie's daddy is
They dinna muckle mind.
But oh! the bairn at Annie's breist,
The love in Annie's e'e!
They mak' me wish wi' a' my micht
The lucky lad was me!

Horse in Glasgow

Jenni Daiches

A horse comes out of the dark,
graith a-glitter in the light
and rain, haunches heavy
and steady, hoofs striking
the street like full buckets.

Beside the huge dipping
head walks a man, fingers
linked in wet leather,
silent as an old friend.

And we two turn to watch
their remote and measured way,
in Glasgow, and almost touch.
The space between holds wordless
praise for the great beast
for a moment possessing the city.

People churn and spill
against the perfect pulse
ringing into the dark.

Jewish Cemetery, Frankfurt

Jenni Daiches

Deep autumnal green has soaked the earth.
Through the barred gate it invites like velvet,
beckons an intrusion under the awkward
arms of the broad old trees, boldly red,
fraily yellow as a night's alluring moon.
The wall is also old, its rough centuries warm
to the hand. The people passing would think it odd
if a woman rested her head against it and wept.
The trees are helpless within the spiralled leaves.
Beyond are the stones, huddled, dark, leaning
to the right, the left, forward, shawled in the light
of a lenient afternoon. Their faces void,
their grey garments folded close. I listen.
I believe there's a thread of an ancient song. The city
takes a breath. The trams, the river traffic, the market
stalls, dissolve. I smell the fire and the blood,
the acrid smoke of fear. Where once a temple
stood some simple words confine catastrophe.
If only I had love enough for all.

Geometry

for M.B.

Jenni Daiches

We talked till late
of circles and straight
lines, of gendered time,
of women living in the round
and the onwardness of men.

And then,
today I made a circle, walked
from Seven Sisters Road
to Upper Street and found
bistros and brasseries
but the shop gone
that cut the butter
into quarter pounds.

The Hare and Hounds
still there, thank God, where
he and I ate lunch
that very first of days.
Then to the Angel
to complete the circle
I'd begun
when I was unforgettably young.

Meanwhile the men
race on, leaving the earth
rather than bend,
as if life were straight,
as if to follow a curve
were to deviate.

Epilogue – the Last Journey

John Davidson

I felt the world a-spinning on its nave,
I felt it sheering blindly round the sun;
I felt the time had come to find a grave:
I knew it in my heart my days were done.
I took my staff in hand; I took the road,
And wandered out to seek my last abode.
Hearts of gold and hearts of lead
Sing it yet in sun and rain,
'Heel and toe from dawn to dusk,
Round the world and home again.'

O long before the bere was steeped for malt,
And long before the grape was crushed for wine,
The glory of the march without a halt,
The triumph of a stride like yours and mine
Was known to folk like us, who walked about,
To be the sprightliest cordial out and out!
Folk like us, with hearts that beat,
Sang it too in sun and rain –
'Heel and toe from dawn to dusk,
Round the world and home again.'

My feet are heavy now, but on I go,
My head erect beneath the tragic years.
The way is steep, but I would have it so;
And dusty, but I lay the dust with tears,
Though none can see me weep: alone I climb
The rugged path that leads me out of time –
Out of time and out of all,
Singing yet in sun and rain,
'Heel and toe from dawn to dusk,
Round the world and home again.'

Farewell the hope that mocked, farewell despair
That went before me still and made the pace.
The earth is full of graves, and mine was there
Before my life began, my resting-place;
And I shall find it out and with the dead
Lie down for ever, all my sayings said –
Deeds all done and songs all sung,
While others chant in sun and rain,
'Heel to toe from dawn to dusk,
Round the world and home again.'

Snow

John Davidson

I

'Who affirms that crystals are alive?'
I affirm it, let who will deny: –
Crystals are engendered, wax and thrive,
Wane and wither; I have seen them die.

Trust me, masters, crystals have their day,
Eager to attain the perfect norm,
Lit with purpose, potent to display
Facet, angle, colour, beauty, form.

II

Water-crystals need for flower and root
Sixty clear degrees, no less, no more;
Snow, so fickle, still in this acute
Angle thinks, and learns no other lore:

Such its life, and such its pleasure is,
Such its art and traffic, such its gain,
Evermore in new conjunctions this
Admirable angle to maintain.

Crystalcraft in every flower and flake
Snow exhibits, of the welkin free:
Crystalline are crystals for the sake,
All and singular, of crystalry.

Yet does every crystal of the snow
Individualize, a seedling sown
Broadcast, but instinct with power to grow
Beautiful in beauty of its own.

Every flake with all its prongs and dints
Burns ecstatic as a new-lit star:
Men are not more diverse, finger-prints
· More dissimilar than snow-flakes are.

Worlds of men and snow endure, increase,
Woven of power and passion to defy
Time and travail: only races cease,
Individual men and crystals die.

III

Jewelled shapes of snow whose feathery showers,
Fallen or falling wither at a breath,
All afraid are they, and loth as flowers
Beasts and men to tread the way to death.

Once I saw upon an object-glass,
Martyred underneath a microscope,
One elaborate snow-flake slowly pass,
Dying hard, beyond the reach of hope.

Still from shape to shape the crystal changed,
Writhing in its agony; and still,
Less and less elaborate, arranged
Potently the angle of its will.

Tortured to a simple final form,
Angles six and six divergent beams,
Lo, in death it touched the perfect norm
Verifying all its crystal dreams!

IV

Such the noble tragedy of one
Martyred snow-flake. Who can tell the fate
Heinous and uncouth of showers undone,
Fallen in cities! – showers that expiate

Errant lives from polar worlds adrift
Where the great millennial snows abide;
Castaways from mountain-chains that lift
Snowy summits in perennial pride;

Nomad snows, or snows in evil day
Born to urban ruin, to be tossed,
Trampled, shovelled, ploughed and swept away
Down the seething sewers: all the frost

Flowers of heaven melted up with lees,
Offal, recrement, but every flake
Showing to the last in fixed degrees
Perfect crystals for the crystal's sake.

V

Usefulness of snow is but a chance
Here in temperate climes with winter sent,
Sheltering earth's prolonged hibernal trance:
All utility is accident.

Sixty clear degrees the joyful snow,
Practising economy of means,
Fashions endless beauty in, and so
Glorifies the universe with scenes

Arctic and antarctic: stainless shrouds,
Ermine woven in silvery frost, attire
Peaks in every land among the clouds
Crowned with snows to catch the morning's fire.

Dancing with Demons

Christine De Luca

I have seen angels:
they wear uniform
and tend the senile
in locked wards.

Their messages are simple.
'Here's your cocoa, George;
no, try the other hand.
I'll hold it for you.'

No light attends their ministerings
as they console
the mad and mindless,
search out the dignity

that's dribbling, stumbling,
shouting.

'No, Betty, keep your tights on.
It's not quite bedtime yet, love,
won't be long.'

They smooth the edges
bear the unbearable,
stare into the face
of their own frailness,
contain the furies
till they ease
in death's slip stream.

I have seen angels:
they partner fear,
dance with our demons,
tend the senile
in locked wards.

Streams in the Desert
Christine De Luca

You cannot recognise me now
but welcome me, companion for a time.
I walk the wilderness with you,
search like the wandering Israelites.
Will there be answers in this secret place
of thunder, of murmurings?

The wilderness within you has been stripped.
Only the grain is left. And yet, depite erosion,
much remains to cross the chasms;
a touch, a smile. Your muddled words
are full of thoughtfulness.

I sing for you, and wonderfully
you join in, add harmony.

Then shall the tongue of the dumb sing:
for in the wilderness shall waters break out,
streams in the desert.

I feel as Moses must have felt
striking the rock.

(from Psalm 81, v7; Exodus 17; Isaiah 35, v6)

Telling the Time
Christine De Luca

From the windowsill, the stillest
of grey squirrels eyes me, anticipates
a second helping. It is her season
of making ready, of waiting.

Our caterpillar in the sweetie jar
has woven a cocoon. It is brown
with round ends, precision engineering.
He measures metamorphosis in months.

In a basin, orphaned tadpoles lie quiet,
unmoved by night or day, hung
between jellied egg and gulping frog-ness.
They wait weeks for legs and lungs.

Our grey cat brushes past, spelling
tea-time round my legs.
His stomach is his clock, accurate
as the quartz of his eye. He is fed

whenever he comes, spoiled creature.
But for me, I stalk time, hunt it
through the sun's clear demarcations;
pounce on the season, the moment.

Aberfan

Kirkpatrick Dobie

In mining Wales at Aberfan
across the fields the mountain ran
and choked the little children where
they stood in rows at morning prayer.

Before the parents knew their dead
they knew what some pronouncer said
and how he felt and how he looked
and fathers saw themselves rebuked
that such a broken busy man
should bear the grief of Aberfan.
But others were as quick as he
to show how sorry they could be,
for sorrow must compete no less
than any other business.
Grave, gracious, condescending, quick,
candid, confiding, every trick!
They ran where each sensation led,
did it like Marlborough – 'for bread'.
The knowing boys who only know
life as a story, death a show.

And shows and shams and Abbadon
were all they had at Aberfan,
and money poured in like a flood
to make a deeper sea of mud.

Christ! was there nobody to shame them?
Reproach and drive them out and blame them?
With everything that there belongs –
a tongue to scourge! A whip with thongs!
Nothing! The Church saw nothing wrong.
They only wanted to belong.
Their only horror was the fate
of seeming to be out of date.
Not love, but what they called compassion
they followed, for it was the fashion.

But better far for Aberfan
had all the loving hearts withdrawn
and held their tongues and dried their eyes
and stayed at home divinely wise,
leaving the village to the fact,
the brute unmitigated act,
awe-ful, obscure, but wholly kin
to that bleak world they wandered in.
The silence of the empty street,
the grimy grass beneath their feet,
the moving moon in a dark sky
had been their kinder company.

But tragic, tragic Aberfan,
where all around the show-men ran
and showed the people how they bled
and left them deader than their dead.

King Claudius

Kirkpatrick Dobie

Being so bad, how did he get to be king?
Being so wicked, how was he voted in?
Begin
with that.
That is the question.

Hamlet at thirty must have been well known.
So, what was wrong
other than he was seen to be unstable
compared to one so eminently able,
mad, or if less than mad,
then the more bad;
on any estimate far worse than Claudius,
far more disastrous?

Consider, when you talk of murder
(to go no further)

Rosencranz, Guildenstern, sent to Hell –
for what? Because 'betwixt the fell
incensed points of mighty opposites'.
(Poor nits)
Gertrude, Ophelia, and Polonius!
It's Jack the Ripper as compared to Claudius.

Granted the latter's crime was fratricide –
though who are we to talk? – Besides,
he could have been a youth of promise too
whose expectation withered as it grew
under a strutting stuff-shirt till
he more than had his fill
of that feigned 'front of Jove' displayed to Heaven
as if anticipating television.
'Hyperion's curls!' (How vulgar could you get?
How tarted-up effeminate?)
Recall those 'sledded Polacks on the ice'.
Why so precise?
Where else would sledded Polacks be?

Easy to see
how Claudius, catching Gertrude's eye
in some such spate of blank blank verse verbosity,
saw love and murder meet.
And from that vision never could retreat.

What's certain is
that being so *un*majestical,
so little of a bore upon a pedestal,
not mad,
nor altogether bad,
King Claudius claims his due;
and recollect, of all that posturing crew,
he, only he, at close of day
retires to pray,
and for the first time speaking for himself
and his soul's health,
obliges you to feel
something of his appeal.

One thinks of Churchill on Lloyd George's death,
touching with moderated breath
that tortuous ascent
and then, abruptly and without exegesis –
'He *coveted* the place!
Perhaps the place was his.'

Vergissmeinnicht
Keith Douglas

Three weeks gone and the combatants gone
returning over the nightmare ground
we found the place again, and found
the soldier sprawling in the sun.

The frowning barrel of his gun
overshadowing. As we came on
that day, he hit my tank with one
like the entry of a demon.

Look. Here in the gunpit soil
the dishonoured picture of his girl
who has put: *Steffi. Vergissmeinnicht*
in a copybook gothic script.

We see him almost with content,
abased, and seeming to have paid
and mocked at by his own equipment
that's hard and good when he's decayed.

But she would weep to see today
how on his skin the swart flies move;
the dust upon the paper eye
and the burst stomach like a cave.

For here the lover and the killer are mingled
who had one body and one heart.
And death who had the soldier singled
has done the lover mortal hurt.

Simplify Me When I'm Dead
Keith Douglas

Remember me when I am dead
and simplify me when I'm dead.

As the processes of earth
strip off the colour and the skin
take the brown hair and blue eye

and leave me simpler than at birth,
when hairless I came howling in
as the moon came in the cold sky.

Of my skeleton perhaps
so stripped, a learned man will say
'He was of such a type and intelligence,' no more.

Thus when in a year collapse
particular memories, you may
deduce, from the long pain I bore

the opinions I held, who was my foe
and what I left, even my appearance
but incidents will be no guide.

Time's wrong-way telescope will show
a minute man ten years hence
and by distance simplified.

Through that lens see if I seem
substance or nothing: of the world
deserving mention or charitable oblivion

not by momentary spleen
or love into decision hurled,
leisurely arrive at an opinion.

Remember me when I am dead
and simplify me when I'm dead.

from *The Men on the Rocks*
Adam Drinan

Our pastures are bitten and bare
our wool is blown to the winds
our mouths are stopped and dumb
our oatfields weak and thin.
Nobody fishes the loch
nobody stalks the deer.
Let us go down to the sea.
The friendly sea likes to be visited.

Our fathers sleep in the cemetery
their boats, cracked, by their side.
The sea turns round in his sleep
pleasurecraft nod on the tide.
Sea ducks slumber on waves
sea eagles have flown away.
Let us put out to sea.
The fat sea likes to be visited.

Fat sea, what's on your shelf?
all the grey night we wrestled.
To muscle, to skill, to petrol,
Hook oo rin yo! . . . one herring!
and of that only the head.
Dogfishes had the rest,
a parting gift from the sea.
The merry waves like to be visited.

Merry sea, what have you sent us?
A rusty English trawler?
The crew put into the hotel
the engineer overhauls her.
Gulls snatch offal to leeward.
We on the jetty await
gifts of the cod we can't afford.
The free sea likes to be visited.

Free were our father's boats
whose guts were strown on the shore.

Steam ships were bought by the rich
cheap from the last war.
They tear our nets to pieces
and the sea gives them our fishes.
Even he favours the rich.
The false sea likes to be visited.

Florence: Sleeping in Fog
Adam Drinan

Our olives safe from mildew
slumber toward sweet oil.
Cats and cars in stall
and our children snug.
In a basket a convex dog.

But round the house it clams,
the halitosis of old water,
round and over the home,
a moulding, a suppurating,
subsisting return of flood.

Measures
Adam Drinan

Three measures of breadth I take
that the heart, the hand, and the foot make:
the candid inches between the eyes of confidence,
the width of a gull's back in the hand that shot it,
and stretch of a water that cannot be walked upon.

And three measures of slenderness I put to these,
in which the eye, the ear, and the mind meet:
the slimness of a boy's ankle while he is alive to dance,
the whisper that draws a hill across a strath,
and that which separates self-respect from self-regard.

Prayer
Carol Ann Duffy

Some days, although we cannot pray, a prayer
utters itself. So, a woman will lift
her head from the sieve of her hands and stare
at the minims sung by a tree, a sudden gift.

Some nights, although we are faithless, the truth
enters our hearts, that small familiar pain;
then a man will stand stock-still, hearing his youth
in the distant Latin chanting of a train.

Pray for us now. Grade I piano scales
console the lodger looking out across
a Midlands town. Then dusk, and someone calls
a child's name as though they named their loss.

Darkness outside. Inside, the radio's prayer –
Rockall. Malin. Dogger. Finisterre.

War Photographer
Carol Ann Duffy

In his darkroom he is finally alone
with spools of suffering set out in ordered rows.
The only light is red and softly glows,
as though this were a church and he
a priest preparing to intone a Mass.
Belfast. Beirut. Phnom Penh. All flesh is grass.

He has a job to do. Solutions slop in trays
beneath his hands which did not tremble then
though seem to now. Rural England. Home again
to ordinary pain which simple weather can dispel,
to fields which don't explode beneath the feet
of running children in a nightmare heat.

Something is happening. A stranger's features
faintly start to twist before his eyes,
a half-formed ghost. He remembers the cries
of this man's wife, how he sought approval
without words to do what someone must
and how the blood stained into foreign dust.

A hundred agonies in black-and-white
from which his editor will pick out five or six
for Sunday's supplement. The reader's eyeballs prick
with tears between the bath and pre-lunch beers.
From the aeroplane he stares impassively at where
he earns his living and they do not care.

Close

Carol Ann Duffy

Lock the door. In the dark journey of our night,
two childhoods stand in the corner of the bedroom
watching the way we take each other to bits
to stare at our heart. I hear a story
told in sleep in a lost accent. You know the words.

Undress. A suitcase crammed with secrets
bursts in the wardrobe at the foot of the bed.
Dress again. Undress. You have me like a drawing,
erased, coloured in, untitled, signed by your tongue.
The name of a country written in red on my palm,

unreadable. I tell myself where I live now,
but you move in close till I shake, homeless,
further than that. A coin falls from the bedside table,
spinning its heads and tails. How the hell
can I win. How can I lose. Tell me again.

Love won't give in. It makes a hired room tremble
with the pity of bells, a cigarette smoke itself
next to a full glass of wine, time ache

into space, space, wants no more talk. Now
it has me where I want me, now you, you do.

Put out the light. Years stand outside on the street
looking up to an open window, black as our mouth
which utters its tuneless song. The ghosts of ourselves,
behind and before us, throng in a mirror, blind,
laughing and weeping. They know who we are.

Valentine

Carol Ann Duffy

Not a red rose or a satin heart.

I give you an onion.
It is a moon wrapped in brown paper.
It promises light
like the careful undressing of love.

Here.
It will blind you with tears
like a lover.
It will make your reflection
a wobbling photo of grief.

I am trying to be truthful.

Not a cute card or a kissogram.

I give you an onion.
Its fierce kiss will stay on your lips,
possessive and faithful
as we are,
for as long as we are.

Take it.
Its platinum loops shrink to a wedding-ring,
if you like.

Lethal.
Its scent will cling to your fingers,
cling to your knife.

Warming Her Pearls
for Judith Radstone

Carol Ann Duffy

Next to my own skin, her pearls. My mistress
bids me wear them, warm them, until evening
when I'll brush her hair. At six, I place them
round her cool, white throat. All day I think of her,

resting in the Yellow Room, contemplating silk
or taffeta, which gown tonight? She fans herself
whilst I work willingly, my slow heat entering
each pearl. Slack on my neck, her rope.

She's beautiful. I dream about her
in my attic bed; picture her dancing
with tall men, puzzled by my faint, persistent scent
beneath her French perfume, her milky stones.

I dust her shoulders with a rabbit's foot,
watch the soft blush seep through her skin
like an indolent sigh. In her looking-glass
my red lips part as though I want to speak.

Full moon. Her carriage brings her home. I see
her every movement in my head. . . . Undressing,
taking off her jewels, her slim hand reaching
for the case, slipping naked into bed, the way

she always does. . . . And I lie here awake,
knowing the pearls are cooling even now
in the room where my mistress sleeps. All night
I feel their absence and I burn.

Festive Tolls

*Written on the execution of the deposed President Ceauşescu
of Romania on Christmas Day 1989*

Lesley Duncan

Christmas, bloody Christmas, we would say,
Unmoved by seasonal piety.
The festive toll of bell and till,
Alike, induced fastidious chill,
The vapid carols on TV
Offending almost equally
With piped goodwill in superstore.
Christ for commerce? What a bore.

But then this year it came to pass
In far-off Timosuar', alas,
Christmas *was* bloody:
Innocents martyred at a tyrant's shrine,
As Herod did in Palestine,
And then the tyrant crucified,
The natal Christ thus twice denied.

The Visit

Lesley Duncan

Mary, more than quite contrary, bars the door.
What do you want? the hostile brat of
Eighty years demands, her clockwork legs awhir,
The Windsor handbag bristling on her arm.
Feigning good humour, I edge into the lounge,
Note the plastic flowers, the faint, sweet smell
Of faeces overlaid with freshener.

The gang are crowded round the goggle-box
Feast-ending or just gazing
At the blank screen of their intellects.
A daughter bends to kiss her mummy,

A creature bandaged in white shawls,
With skin Egyptian dry.

Oh, others' living dead
Are somehow easier to view.

On, then, to rehearse my own mortality.
She lies in bed, undentured mouth agape.
Agape indeed, for we will share this fate.
Long past the consolations of religion
(No presbyterian rites to smooth the passage
To senility or death) or hope of reuniting
With her late-acquired, late husband,
She whimpers for her parents,
Octogenarians dead these forty years,

The parents who exacted service
From their unmarried daughter,
Her comely days consigned to duty
While siblings took flight
And all her care for granted.

And did not her father (my grandparent)
Mock his brown-eyed girl for legs
Like table's and a 'hooker-doon'
(That nose that marks us kin),
In excess of Scotch candour
Or else to scotch her vanity
In case a suitor beckoned?

Oh damn that generation
Who could not think their young of any worth
Because they thought so little of themselves.
And yet they too were once a lad and lass,
She tall and straight in satin,
He dapper with his ice-blue gaze,
And maybe, too, the burden
Of their own old oppressed them.

My aunt dreams on,
The leaves of distant memory

Adrift at random through her brain
As if exposed by irate blackbirds.
(And too late now to ask her
If she ever called them *merles*,
The way her thrushes sang as *mavises*.)
My brain is drifting too
To thoughts of lust and shopping lists.
I must get out of here,

For others' living dead
Are somehow easier to bear.

Ships

Douglas Dunn

When a ship passes at night on the Clyde,
Swans in the reeds, picking oil from their feathers,
Look up at the lights, the noise of new waves,
Against hill-climbing houses, malefic cranes.

A fine rain attaches itself to the ship like skin.
Lascars play poker, the Scottish mate looks
At the last lights, one that is Ayrshire,
Others on lonely rocks, or clubfooted peninsulas.

They leave restless boys without work in the river towns.
In their houses are fading pictures of fathers ringed
Among ships' complements in wartime, model destroyers,
Souvenirs from uncles deep in distant engine rooms.

Then the boys go out, down streets that look on water.
They say, 'I could have gone with them,'
A thousand times to themselves in the glass cafés,
Over their American soft drinks, into their empty hands.

From the Night-Window

Douglas Dunn

The night rattles with nightmares.
Children cry in the close-packed houses,
A man rots in his snoring.
On quiet feet, policemen test doors.
Footsteps become people under streetlamps.
Drunks return from parties,
Sounding of empty bottles and old songs.
Young women come home
And disappear into white beds
At the edge of the night.
All windows open, this hot night,
And the sleepless, smoking in the dark,
Making small red lights at their mouths,
Count the years of their marriages.

France

Douglas Dunn

A dozen sparrows scuttled on the frost.
We watched them play. We stood at the window,
And, if you saw us, then you saw a ghost
In duplicate. I tied her nightgown's bow.
She watched and recognised the passers-by.
Had they looked up, they'd know that she was ill –
'Please, do not draw the curtains when I die' –
From all the flowers on the windowsill.

'It's such a shame,' she said. 'Too ill, too quick.'
'I would have liked us to have gone away.'
We closed our eyes together, dreaming France,
Its meadows, rivers, woods and *jouissance*.
I counted summers, our love's arithmetic.
'Some other day, my love. Some other day.'

Envoi
Douglas Dunn

Why did I bring you to this Hull,
This rancid and unbeautiful
Surprise of damp and Englishness?
Mad for an education, for poetry,
I studied at our window,
My mind dying in shy cadences.
What cost of life was there, in poverty,
In my outlaw depressions, in your coping
With lonely, studious bohemia!

Now I choose to remember
Bus-rides together into Holderness,
Exploring the hedgerowed heat
On country walks by fields of mustard.
That view was broad and circular
Where everywhere seemed everywhere!

A curse on me I did not write with joy.

Pushing Forty
Alison Fell

Just before winter
we see the trees show
their true colours:
the mad yellow of chestnuts
two maples like blood sisters
the orange beech
braver than lipstick

Pushing forty, we vow
that when the time comes
rather than wither
ladylike and white

we will henna our hair
like Colette, we too
will be gold and red
and go out
in a last wild blaze

Pigeons

Alison Fell

Pigeons
are tossing up
seeds
and bread.
Their pecking is snappish,
they want
what they want
and the rest
goes in whirligigs
like salt over their shoulders.

Today
when I said
I was writing about you –
for women will make meat and bread
of their long tearings –
you looked like that puffed
angry one
in its purple ruff;

yes,
that's
what you looked like.

Rannoch Moor

Alison Fell

Behind us, Glencoe of the Slaughter,
Achnacone, field of dogs,
Achtriachan, where the water-bull
lurks among thin fish tickled by weed,
and the Great Herdsman of Etive
over us like a black axe

To pace the moor, and mark it,
like a cat bruises the grass
for its bed,
or be claimed instead –
scars of burnt heather, dead
weariness, the sheep paths
misleading, and the bogs
pitted with white water

Slow steps mark the line
on the moor sour with struggle,
where darkness is brought to the brim,
and the bog-cotton bursts
like puffs of smoke
after a musket,
and the broken bleached roots
of the old forest
are white bones under
the petrol shimmer of methane

Slow march in the whine
of telegraph wires,
while the wind chops
at my breath,
and the peat mud sticks to my feet
like rafts

Grey Kirk in the Mearns
Gillian Ferguson

Perched, a stained skull
on an ancient skeleton
of wind-picked hill,

the grey kirk
clutches veils of sleet
about its scoured bone.

Glazed sockets
spill no colour
on melting snow.

Once fleshed
with bodies broken
on this brutal soil,

it was the head
of its cold religion.
Empty,

it still wears the frown
of dour old ministers
set in stone.

Bedtime
Ian Hamilton Finlay

So put your nightdress on
It is so white and long
And your sweet night-face
Put it on also please
It is the candle-flame
It is the flame above
Whose sweet shy shame
My love, I love, I love.

Gift

Ian Hamilton Finlay

How silly and how dear, how very dear
To send a dehydrated porcupine
By letter post, with love. It did appear
That it was such – a gift, but more a sign
Of love, from her I love, that girl of mine.

I did not think it too exceptional
(Acceptance being one part of being in love)
And yet I thought it strange, for you could call
It strange to send a dried-up porcupine
With love. My dear, I thought. O darling mine.

And stroked with love its quills so soft and fine
At which I saw it was not animal
But vegetable. Yes, it was vegetable –
The prickly part of some old hoary pine
She had detached and sent me, plus a line

There scribbled in her dear and silly scrawl:
'I hope it did not prick you, dearest mine,
I did not mean you to be hurt at all.'

Finlay's House (in Rousay)

Ian Hamilton Finlay

And this is Finlay's house –
A wild stone on the floor,
Lots and lots of books
And a chair where you can't sit for
– No, not the tar –
The hooks, the lost fish-hooks.

Dried fish festoon the wall
And that stone sticks the door.

Spiders spin in nooks.
The visitors tend to fall.
They trip first, then they fall –
They catch on the lost fish-hooks.

I ought to shift that stone
But it seems easier
To unscrew the door.
Am I an awful man?
I'm better housed than ducks
And like to lose fish-hooks.

O.H.M.S.

Ian Hamilton Finlay

To my creel and stack-net island
Of the little hills, low and dark,
Her Majesty's Government graciously sent
Me an Assistance clerk.

He frowned, 'May I come in?'
– To inspect me, he meant. 'Please do.
I shall sit on this old oil drum
And leave the chair for you.'

'Some questions require to be answered.'
'You must ask me whatever you wish.
– Those things strung on the knotted string
You are staring at, are fish.'

'Fish? – I thought they were socks.'
He wrote me all down in his book.
O little dark island, I brought him, and after
Did you give me a darker look?

Turning a Fresh Eye
Lillias Scott Forbes

A time there was I hated this old chair,
This cast-off chair that ventures to outlive me:
I would have seen it dead by now or auction bound,
Wheeled out under dun sackcloth of my days
Wrapped in frail shroud and ragged flags of youth.

But now as I am loath to break old bonds
By grant of my reprieve it still holds court
As if in wait for some imperious occupant,
Not as formerly, one of four stools for penitents
When we, borne on their liveried damask
Mouse-mute before our parents ate our meal.

My friends arrives, spies this old chair,
Fondles the fretwork spirals, burnished arabesques –
'Such craftsmanship lies here, such loving care!'
I turn a fresh eye on this outworn frame.

How I should long to take my seat again,
My family all complete, time's scurry ceased,
Enthroned, a child once more, to feel and to surprise
The touch of love that glows within the grain,
My father's glance round the familial feast.

The Half-Inch Tweeddale
Lillias Scott Forbes

Coltherdscleugh and Cauldcleuchheid
Sae lang's ye mind thae words
Loupin oot at ye fae the hauf-inch Tweeddale map
Ye've sma cause tae be warsellin wi sair heid
Ower the demise o the guid Scots tongue:
No tae speak o' Meg's Shank or Catcleuch Shin,
Phenzhopehaugh, Tushielaw, Faw Side

An for a richt dowie dollop o glaur
For getting yer gruntles intae . . .
Muckle Dod Fell.

Sonnet
Veronica Forrest-Thomson

My love, if I write a song for you
To that extent you are gone
For, as everyone says, and I know it's true:
We are all always alone.

Never so separate trying to be two
And the busy old fool is right.
To try and finger myself from you
Distinguishes day from night.

If I say 'I love you' we can't but laugh
Since irony knows what we'll say.
If I try to free myself by my craft
You vary as night from day.

So, accept the wish for the deed my dear.
Words were made to prevent us near.

In This House
Veronica Forrest-Thomson

All the photographs are faded.
All the clocks are slow.
Last year's words lie stale like smoke
on used up air; the piano keys
are touched only to be dusted.
Rooms and furnishings
have been so long familiar

that they are merely memories;
and now is happening elsewhere.

But, habit being a substitute for will,
though the mirrors are tired of our faces,
and spring comes later each year,
we go on lighting flowers like candles
at windows dissolved by rain.

Not Pastoral Enough

Homage to William Empson

Veronica Forrest-Thomson

It is the sense, it is the sense, controls,
Landing every poem like a fish.
Unhuman forms must not assert their roles.

Glittering scales require the deadly tolls
Of net and knife. Scales fall to relish.
It is the sense, it is the sense, controls.

Yet languages are apt to miss on souls
If reason only guts them. Applying the wish,
Unhuman forms must not assert their roles,

Ignores the fact that poems have two poles
That must be opposite. Hard then to finish
It is the sense, it is the sense, controls,

Without a sense of lining up for doles
From other kitchens that give us the garnish:
Unhuman forms must not assert their roles.

And this (forgive me) is like carrying coals
To Sheffield. Irrelevance betrays a formal anguish.
It is the sense, it is the sense, controls,
'Unhuman forms must not assert their roles.'

Home Town Elegy

for Aberdeen in Spring

G. S. Fraser

Glitter of mica at the windy corners,
Tar in the nostrils, under blue lamps budding
Like bubbles of glass and blue buds of a tree,
Night-shining shopfronts, or the sleek sun flooding
The broad abundant dying sprawl of the Dee:
For these and for their like my thoughts are mourners
That yet shall stand, though I come home no more,
Gas works, white ballroom, and the red brick baths
And salmon nets along a mile of shore,
Or beyond the municipal golf-course, the moorland paths
And the country lying quiet and full of farms.
This is the shape of a land that outlasts a strategy
And is not to be taken with rhetoric or arms.
Or my own room, with a dozen books on the bed
(Too late, still musing what I mused, I lie
And read too lovingly what I have read),
Brantôme, Spinoza, Yeats, the bawdy and wise,
Continuing their interminable debate,
With no conclusion, they conclude too late,
When their wisdom has fallen like a grey pall on my eyes.
Syne we maun part, there sall be nane remeid –
Unless my country is my pride, indeed,
Or I can make my town that homely fame
That Byron has, from boys in Carden Place,
Struggling home with books to midday dinner,
For whom he is not the romantic sinner,
The careless writer, the tormented face,
The hectoring bully or the noble fool,
But, just like Gordon or like Keith, a name:
A tall, proud statue at the Grammar School.

Lean Street

G. S. Fraser

Here, where the baby paddles in the gutter,
Here, in the slaty greyness and the gas,
Here, where the women wear dark shawls and mutter
A hasty word as other women pass.

Telling the secret, telling, clucking and tutting,
Sighing, or saying that it served her right,
The bitch! – the words and weather both are cutting
In Causewayend, on this November night.

At pavement's end and in the slaty weather
I stare with glazing eyes at meagre stone,
Rain and the gas are sputtering together
A dreary tune! O leave my heart alone,

O leave my heart alone, I tell my sorrows,
For I will soothe you in a softer bed
And I will numb your grief with fat tomorrows
Who break your milk teeth on this stony bread!

They do not hear. Thought stings me like an adder,
A doorway's sagging plumb-line squints at me,
The fat sky gurgles like a swollen bladder
With the foul rain that rains on poverty.

The Traveller Has Regrets

G. S. Fraser

The traveller has regrets
For the receding shore
That with its many nets
Has caught, not to restore,
The white lights in the bay,
The blue lights on the hill,

Though night with many stars
May travel with him still,
But night has nought to say,
Only a colour and shape
Changing like cloth shaking,
A dancer with a cape
Whose dance is heart-breaking,
Night with its many stars
Can warn travellers
There's only time to kill
And nothing much to say:
But the blue lights on the hill,
The white lights in the bay
Told us the meal was laid
And that the bed was made
And that we could not stay.

The Wee Cock Sparra

Hugh Frater and Duncan Macrae

A wee cock sparra sat on a tree,
A wee cock sparra sat on a tree,
A wee cock sparra sat on a tree
Chirpin awa as blithe as could be.

Alang came a boy wi' a bow and an arra,
Alang came a boy wi' a bow and an arra,
Alang came a boy wi' a bow and an arra
And he said: 'I'll get ye, ye wee cock sparra.'

The boy wi' the arra let fly at the sparra,
The boy wi' the arra let fly at the sparra,
The boy wi' the arra let fly at the sparra,
And he hit a man that was hurlin' a barra.

The man wi' the barra cam owre wi' the arra,
The man wi' the barra cam owre wi' the arra,
The man wi' the barra cam owre wi' the arra,
And said: 'Ye take me for a wee cock sparra?'

The man hit the boy, tho he wasne his farra,
The man hit the boy, tho he wasne his farra,
The man hit the boy, tho he wasne his farra
And the boy stood and glowered; he was hurt tae the marra.

And a' this time the wee cock sparra,
And a' this time the wee cock sparra,
And a' this time the wee cock sparra
Was chirpin awa on the shank o' the barra.

The End of an Age
Robin Fulton

The chestnut they said had stood for seventy years.
Its whiteness in May, redness in September,
thin scrolls of long fingery twigs,
were things expected of it.
The tree was an obvious landmark like a hill.

The little people hurrying about the place,
their heads packed with intricacies,
their feet not in the habit of standing still,
slightly envied the tree
for adding such tiny cubits to itself.

At last, for safety's sake it had to come
and, falling, for the first time became heavy.
A man with an axe sorting it all out
but making slow work
said, 'A tree's complicated when it's down.'

A Note for Robert Henryson
Robin Fulton

Winter can't have changed much for us,
the shape of windows perhaps but not the hard
flowers on them the weak sun can't soften.

Four walls have a lot to keep out
still and much the same to keep in,
a fire a book whisky and common sense.

From me to you is not many miles,
we could walk together now and on the snow
our hunchback shadows would be like twins.

Your outer weather then I understand
and almost your inner: late medieval
though to you not yet so far past
and still rich with clarity and fear.

Forecast for a Quiet Night
Robin Fulton

A secret cone will drop in Rothiemurcus,
causing not the slightest local disturbance.

A quiet wind will stroke Loch Araich-linn,
an indiscretion no-one can possibly notice.

By dawn imperceptible frosty wrinkles
will have puckered the edges of countless backwaters.

By dawn too a generation of mice
will have been snipped by a night-shift of owls
working separately and almost in silence.

And the mild local disturbance behind the eyes
of the invalid
will have been noted only by the next of kin.

Elegy

Robert Garioch

They are lang deid, folk that I used to ken,
their firm-set lips aa mowdert and agley,
sherp-tempert een rusty amang the cley:
they are baith deid, thae wycelike, bienlie men,

heidmaisters, that had been in pouer for ten
or twenty year afore fate's taiglit wey
brocht me, a young, weill-harnit, blate and fey
new-cleckit dominie, intill their den.

Ane tellt me it was time I learnt to write –
round-haund, he meant – and saw about my hair:
I mind of him, beld-heidit, wi a kyte.

Ane sneerit quarterly – I cuidna square
my savings-bank – and sniftert in his spite.
Weill, gin they arena deid, it's time they were.

I Was Fair Beat

Robert Garioch

I spent a nicht amang the cognoscenti,
a hie-brou clan, ilk wi a beard on him
like Mark Twain's miners, due to hae a trim,
their years on aiverage roun three-and-twenty.

Of poetry and music we had plenty,
owre muckle, but ye maun be in the swim:
Kurt Schwitter's Ur-sonata that gaes 'Grimm
glimm gnimm bimmbimm,' it fairly wad hae sent ye

daft, if ye'd been there; modern jazz wi juicy
snell wud-wind chords, three new anes, I heard say,
by thaim that kent, new, that is, sen Debussy.

Man, it was awfie. I wad raither hae
a serenata sung by randy pussy,
and what a time a reel of tape can play!

Nemo Canem Impune Lacessit
Robert Garioch

I kicked an Edinbro dug-luver's dug,
leastways, I tried: my timing wes owre late.
It stopped whit it wes daein on my gate
and skelpit aff to find some ither mug.

Whit a sensation! If a clockwark thug
suid croun ye wi a brolly owre yir pate,
the Embro folk wad leave ye to yir fate;
it's you, maist like, wad get a flee in yir lug.

But kick the Friend of Man! Or hae a try!
The Friend of Wummin, even, that's far waur
a felony, mair dangerous, forby.

Meddle wi puir dumb craiturs gin ye daur.
That maks ye a richt cruel bruitt, my! my!
And whit d'ye think yir braw front gate is for?

Rostov-on-Don (1942)
Flora Garry

The Mountains of the Caucasus
Invest that foreign sky.
Under the bridge-heads of that Don
Men, dead, go floating by.

Bell heather blooms on Bennachie
Red this bright summer day

And down by Inverurie town
Men work among the hay.

Why should I thole this alien woe,
For dule unkent repine?
The flower of war incarnadines
Another Don than mine.

The Professor's Wife

Flora Garry

I wis a student at King's.
Ma folk hid a craft in Glenardle.
'Learnin's the thing,' they wid say,
'To help ye up in the wardle.'

They vrocht fae daylicht to dark.
Fine div I min' on ma midder,
Up ower the queets amo dubs,
Furth in the weetiest widder.

Swypin the greep in the byre,
Forkin the crap on the laan,
Treetlin wi' water an aess an peats,
Aye a pail in her haan.

I wis a student at King's.
O the craft I nivver spoke.
Peer and prood wis I
An affrontit o ma folk.

An fyles on a stull Mey nicht
I wid tak a daaner roun
By Spital an College Bounds
To the lythe o the Aal Toon.

An I wid stan an glower
In at the windows wide

O the muckle hooses there
Far the professors bide.

At cannel-licht an flooers
Shinin silver an lace,
An, braw in a low-neckit goon,
The professor's wife at her place.

'Fine,' says I to masel,
'Fine to be up in the wardle,'
An thocht wi a groo, on the brookie pots
In the kitchen at Glenardle.

'Learnin's the thing,' says I,
'To help ye up in the wardle,'
I wed a professor come time
And gid hyne awaa fae Glenardle.

I bide in a muckle dark hoose
In a toon that's muckle an dark,
An it taks me maist o the day
To get fordalt wi ma wark.

Traachlin wi sitt an styoo,
Queuein for maet for oors,
A body his little time or hert
For cannel-licht and flooers.

Ma hans are scorie-hornt,
An fyles I fin masel
Skushlin ma feet, as ma midder did
Oot teemin the orra pail.

The aal folk's lyin quaet
In the kirkyard at Glenardle.
It's as weel; they'd be gey sair-made
At the state noo-a-days o the wardle.

'Learnin's the thing,' they wid say,
'To gie ye a hyste up in life.'
I wis eence a student at King's.
Noo I'm jist a professor's wife.

Just Like Eve
Magi Gibson

I could have brought you
whisky to warm you on winter nights,
poems full of words to fill your silences

I could have brought you
armfuls of flowers
to fill your rooms with summer,
scented petals to scatter where you dream

I could have brought
olives, shiny, black and green,
anchovies and Parmesan,
Chianti, deep blood-red

I could have brought
figs, dates, kumquats, lychees
tastes to make your senses sing
to set your soul adrift

Instead I brought
forbidden fruit
the one and only gift
you would not accept

Goldilocks
Magi Gibson

She wakes beside a man
with greying stubble on his chin.
She notes how the muscles on the arm
hauled heavily across her breasts
feel no longer young, no longer firm,
how on his neck the thin pale flesh
crinkles like boiled milk skin.

She calculates his age
as if he was a tree
she'd sliced through
and could count the rings.

Old enough to be her father –
that makes her smile, snuggle closer.

She shuts her eyes
but does not dream.
This bed is warm,
a sheltered lair
she has burrowed into.
It smells of him
of sweat, of stale cologne
of last night's beer
of big strong daddy bear.

In the scullery she rummages
for cereal, milk, a bowl
turns the radio low
lights a fag, finds a comb
runs its blunt teeth through her hair,
makes herself at home.

Reading in Bed
Magi Gibson

afterwards he sleeps
limbs spread on crumpled sheets
air dark with summer heat

a hieroglyph
of hair, skin, muscle, bone

her fingers read
for pleasure

We Meet Again
Valerie Gillies

For the first time in seven years
we meet.
Your son says to my daughter
'I hate girls: go away.'
She smiles her formidable smile.
Fates get their yarn in a twist.

They'll wait.
While he swings on his tarzan rope
or casts a new lure in the sea,
she'll hang back from her brothers
till she can make this fellow
look for the land he first came from.

Who will remember today
when they discover
their own surprising eden?
As, in the pretty far back,
once it was you and me.

Summer Bull
Valerie Gillies

A blusterer of a bull
stayed with us that summer.
He was full of surprising moves.
One morning he ran easily as the minotaur
up the dark alley by the byre.

Hearing his locomotive sound
I came to the kitchen doorway
to see my boy standing out
in the open yard watching the hard-head
circle and cut-circle round him.

The bull tossed hens through the air,
and clipped biddies flew for the first time.
He whirled them in eddies,
bore them up and over the boy
at a standstill, smiling.

Tiptoe, in profile, a Cretan vaulter
poised for the swift ton of violence
which left him untouched at the stormcentre.
Only my dead thought lay on the ground
the day my dearborn kept his nerve.

The Look-Alike

Valerie Gillies

I was asleep when the guest came.
Today he is a man sitting at our table
talking of open boats and million-pound trawlers.

I see the way he moves his hand and head.
It reminds me of you,
it has me loving him instantly.

He tells about the big herring, with scales,
taken in the drift net; but I am seeing you,
right to the cut of your hair.

How could he look like you
when this whole world cannot hold or satisfy me?
Send me the kind of smile I like.

I am setting out the cups
when the kitchen door shuts on my forehead
and I dream stars.

I see you, only you, with a clarity
that feels more passionate to me
than the laughter or the cry of any other man.

Bell Barrow

Duncan Glen

I can raise up the deid.
A Bell Barrow wi proper ditch
proper rampart
  a cairn
echteen fuit high
and a hunner and twenty aroond the base.
Ablow lie large dresst flaags wi capstane.
  And toom.
Juist a sma heap o earth
in that impossible chamber
  and soon
   flettened.

But fairmers are still walkin the sma hills
some hae New Town for neighboor
some hae sons in city streets wi open minds
some hae taen to golf

the Bell Barrow is
the tenth green

My Faither

Duncan Glen

Staunin noo aside his braw bress-haunled coffin
I mind him fine aside the black shinin range
In his grey strippit troosers, galluses and nae collar
For the flannel shirt. My faither.

I ken him fine thae twenty or mair years ago
Wi his great bauchles and flet auld kep;
And in his pooch the spottit reid neepkin
For usin wi snuff. My faither.

And ben in the lobby abune the braw shoon and spats
Aside the silk waistcoat and claw-haimmer jaicket
Wi its muckle oxter pooch, hung the lum hat.
They caw'd him Jock the Lum. My faither.

And noo staunin wi thae braw shinin haunles
See him and me baith laid oot in the best
Black suitin wi proper white aw weill chosen.
And dinna ken him. *My father*.

Twa Warlds

Duncan Glen

I sit in my moulded black chair
near to Matisse's 'Draped Nude' (1936).

Sometimes someane touches a canvas
and I staun up, which is usually enough.
I'm no a man o unnecessary words.

Sometimes I adjust the thermostat.
Sometimes I tak a daunder roond the gallery
and if it's empty staun by my favourite wark.

It's Henri Matisse's 'Draped Nude'
by the door.
Next to it is his 'The Inattentive Reader' (1919)
bequeathed by M. Shearman
through the Contemporary Art Society 1940.
No. 5141.

I'm especially fond o its frame
wi decoratit gilt in twa layers
gien a wee sunken ledge at the tap
atween its back and front.

There I keep my ball-point pen.

Loch Thom

W. S. Graham

1

Just for the sake of recovering
I walked backward from fifty-six
Quick years of age wanting to see,
And managed not to trip or stumble
To find Loch Thom and turned round
To see the stretch of my childhood
Before me. Here is the loch. The same
Long-beaked cry curls across
The heather-edges of the water held
Between the hills a boyhood's walk
Up from Greenock. It is the morning.

And I am here with my mammy's
Bramble jam scones in my pocket.
The Firth is miles and I have come
Back to find Loch Thom maybe
In this light does not recognise me.

This is a lonely freshwater loch.
No farms on the edge. Only
Heather grouse-moor stretching
Down to Greenock and One Hope
Street or stretching away across
Into the blue moors of Ayrshire.

2

And almost I am back again
Wading the heather down to the edge
To sit. The minnows go by in shoals
Like iron-filings in the shallows.

My mother is dead. My father is dead
And all the trout I used to know
Leaping from their sad rings are dead.

3

I drop my crumbs into the shallow
Weed for the minnows and pinheads.
You see that I will have to rise
And turn round and get back where
My running age will slow for a moment
To let me on. It is a colder
Stretch of water than I remember.

The curlew's cry travelling still
Kills me fairly. In front of me
The grouse flurry and settle. GOBACK
GOBACK GOBACK FAREWELL LOCH THOM.

Greenock at Night I Find You
W. S. Graham

1

As for you loud Greenock long ropeworking
Hide and seeking rivetting town of my child
Hood, I know we think of us often mostly
At night. Have you ever desired me back
Into the set-in bed at the top of the land
In One Hope Street? I am myself lying
Half-asleep hearing the rivetting yards
And smelling the bone-works with no home
Work done for Cartsburn School in the morning.

At night. And here I am descending and
The welding lights in the shipyards flower blue
Under my hopeless eyelids as I lie
Sleeping conditioned to hide from happy.

2

So what did I do? I walked from Hope Street
Down Lyndoch Street between the night's words

To Cartsburn Street and got to the Cartsburn Vaults
With half an hour to go. See, I am back.

3

See, I am back. My father turned and I saw
He had the stick he cut in Sheelhill Glen.
Brigit was there and Hugh and double-breasted
Sam and Malcolm Mooney and Alastair Graham.
They all were there in the Cartsburn Vaults shining
To meet me but I was only remembered.

Letter VI

W. S. Graham

A day the wind was hardly
Shaking the youngest frond
Of April I went on
The high moor we know.
I put my childhood out
Into a cocked hat
And you moving the myrtle
Walked slowly over.
A sweet clearness became.
The Clyde sleeved in its firth
Reached and dazzled me.
I moved and caught the sweet
Courtesy of your mouth.
My breath to your breath.
And as you lay fondly
In the crushed smell of the moor
The courageous and just sun
Opened its door.
And there we lay halfway
Your body and my body
On the high moor. Without
A word then we went
Our ways. I heard the moor

Curling its cries far
Across the still loch.

The great verbs of the sea
Come down on us in a roar.
What shall I answer for?

Scotland
Sir Alexander Gray

Here in the Uplands
The soil is ungrateful;
The fields, red with sorrel,
Are stony and bare.
A few trees, wind-twisted –
Or are they but bushes? –
Stand stubbornly guarding
A home here and there.

Scooped out like a saucer,
The land lies before me;
The waters, once scattered,
Flow orderedly now
Through fields where the ghosts
Of the marsh and the moorland
Still ride the old marches,
Despising the plough.

The marsh and the moorland
Are not to be banished;
The bracken and heather,
The glory of broom,
Usurp all the balks
And the fields' broken fringes,
And claim from the sower
Their portion of room.

This is my country,
The land that begat me.

These windy spaces
Are surely my own.
And those who here toil
In the sweat of their faces
Are flesh of my flesh,
And bone of my bone.

Hard is the day's task –
Scotland, stern Mother –
Wherewith at all times
Thy sons have been faced:
Labour by day,
And scant rest in the gloaming,
With Want an attendant,
Not lightly outpaced.

Yet do thy children
Honour and love thee.
Harsh is thy schooling,
Yet great is the gain:
True hearts and strong limbs,
The beauty of faces,
Kissed by the wind
And caressed by the rain.

On a Cat, Ageing

Sir Alexander Gray

He blinks upon the hearth-rug,
And yawns in deep content,
Accepting all the comforts
That Providence has sent.

Louder he purrs and louder,
In one glad hymn of praise
For all the night's adventures,
For quiet and restful days.

Life will go on for ever,
With all that cat can wish;
Warmth and the glad procession
Of fish and milk and fish.

Only – the thought disturbs him –
He's noticed once or twice,
The times are somehow breeding
A nimbler race of mice.

The Fine Fechtin Mouse

Sir Alexander Gray

'Fairest o' fair, O, hear my cry;
O, open and let your love inby;
Sae lang have I been here standin,
Ay, ay, ay standin,
That I'm frozen all-utterly.'

'Deed, and I winna open to ye,
Nor to ony gangrel, as weel ye may be;
But first, you maun tell me strauchtly,
Ay, ay, ay, strauchtly,
That there's nane that you lo'e but me.'

'Dear lass, I lo'e you; weel you ken
That you've aye been the only ane.
But sae lang have I been here standin,
Ay, ay, ay, standin,
That I'm frozen cauld to the bane.'

In the nicht in the nicht, in the middle o' the nicht,
A dunt at the winnock gae's baith a fricht.
And her mither, O ay, *she* heard it,
Ay, ay, ay, SHE heard it:
'Are you sure, Jean, that a' thing's a' richt?'

'O mither, it's only Baudrons, the cat:
He's efter a moose, and that's what he's at;
And dod, but he's grippit the beastie;
Ay, ay, ay, the beastie –
She's a fine fechtin moose for a' that.'

Still

Andrew Greig

Here is stillness, there is still more
while the light is fading. Hands slow
then settle, they could mediate
or just be resting while birds pour
late songs from TV aerials.
Now whatever is trying to find you,
finds you; tea-pot, vase, radio
begin to shine, the early stars tune in.

Where are you when the light is fading?
Pulling on the red nightdress,
half-listening to the radio?
You are somewhere doing
something shadowy to me –
thanks be for that obscurity.
I loved you once; now you've gone dim
I still love someone, that is bearable.

This is the dusk of loving;
the birds are empty and these
are little sorrows, pin-prick ones.
Bearable instances, sad pretty stars
now dribble out above the last
note of the concluding song.
Here comes the calm, the insurmountable
parting. The aerial shakes still.

Interlude on Mustagh Tower
Andrew Greig

In these high places we are melting out
of all that made us rigid; our ice-screws
hang loose on the fixed ropes to the Col.
Monday in the Himalaya, the clouds are down,
our objective is somewhere, but obscure –
let it soar without us for a day!
We lounge in thermals on the glacier,
brewing and shooting the breeze, that improbable
project of conversation among the living.
Laughter rings across the ice. Why not?
None of us will die today – yon's immortality
you can draw on in a cigarette,
harsh and sweet, the way we like it.
Steam rises from the billy, Sandy pours.
It is true high, worked for, that we pass
hand to hand between us with our brews.
Men on ice, going nowhere and laughing
at everything we cannot see but know
is there – among the cloud, on the Col,
a hand of some sort is tightening our screws.

Ruth Says
Andrew Greig

This is not passion, but with pleasure
I see you note how well I am
undressed in black. Clear sight shows
our age, lines curved around the mouth
like brackets, as though we smile
as an aside (as though desire were
a little joke we like to tell
from time to time).

We are not in love, we are not drowning
in needy dreams, so we may lay down
our weary arms, unconfused
by fate and feeling; I am composed
as we surrender, eyes wide open
even as they close.

Still Gyte, Man?

George Campbell Hay

'Still gyte, man? Stude I in yere claes
I'd thole nae beggar's nichts an' days,
chap-chappan, whidderan lik a moose,
at ae same cauld an' steekit hoose.'

'What stane has she tae draw yere een?
What gars ye, syne she aye has been
as toom an' hertless as a hoor,
gang sornan kindness at her dure?'

*'Though ye should talk a hunner year,
the windblown wave will seek the shore,
the muirlan watter seek the sea.
Then, wheesht man. Sae it is wi me.'*

The Hind of Morning

George Campbell Hay

She snorts and stamps upon the eastern hill,
the Hind of Morning, longing for the day,
the Hind of Morning, mad to leap away,
and flings her head up, scorning to be still.

On high her hooves strike up a streaming fire,
that wavers, slanting past the haloed peaks;

her quick feet spurn the summits, and she seeks
to trample night and burn it up entire.

The Hind of Morning leaps and will not stay,
she stretches West and West with flinging stride,
the Hind of Morning pacing in her pride,
The Hind of Morning is away, away.

Homer

George Campbell Hay

They say that you were blind, yet from the shore
you saw the long waves cresting out at sea:
before the climbing dawn from heaven's floor
you saw the dark night flee.

The torrents whirling in the springtime thaw,
the shady slopes of Ida many-pined,
the curving flash of falling swords you saw –
they lie: you were not blind.

The Old Fisherman

George Campbell Hay

Greet the bights that gave me shelter,
they will hide me no more with the horns of their forelands.
I peer in a haze, my back is stooping;
my dancing days for fishing are over.

The shoot that was straight in the wood withers,
the bracken shrinks red in the rain and shrivels,
the eyes that would gaze in the sun waver;
my dancing days for fishing are over.

The old boat must seek the shingle,
her wasting side hollow the gravel,

the hand that shakes must leave the tiller;
my dancing days for fishing are over.

The sea was good night and morning,
the winds were friends, the calm was kindly –
the snow seeks the burn, the brown fronds scatter;
my dancing days for fishing are over.

The Flyting o' Life and Daith
Hamish Henderson

Quo life, the warld is mine.
The floo'ers and trees, they're a' my ain.
I am the day, and the sunshine
Quo life, the warld is mine.

Quo daith, the warld is mine.
Your lugs are deef, your een are blin
Your floo'ers maun dwine in my bitter win'
Quo daith, the warld is mine.

Quo life, the warld is mine.
I hae saft win's, an' healin' rain,
Aipples I hae, an' breid an' wine
Quo life, the warld is mine.

Quo daith, the warld is mine.
Whit sterts in dreid, gangs doon in pain
Bairns wintin' breid are makin' mane
Quo daith, the world is mine.

Quo life, the warld is mine.
Your deidly wark, I ken it fine
There's maet on earth for ilka wean
Quo life, the warld is mine.

Quo daith, the warld is mine.
Your silly sheaves crine in my fire

My worm keeks in your barn and byre
Quo daith, the warld is mine.

Quo life, the warld is mine.
Dule on your een! Ae galliard hert
Can ban tae hell your blackest airt
Quo life, the warld is mine.

Quo daith, the warld is mine.
Your rantin' hert, in duddies braw,
He winna lowp my preeson wa'
Quo daith, the warld is mine.

Quo life, the warld is mine.
Though ye bigg preesons o' marble stane
Hert's luve ye cannae preeson in
Quo life, the warld is mine.

Quo daith, the warld is mine.
I hae dug a grave, I hae dug it deep,
For war an' the pest will gar ye sleep.
Quo daith, the warld is mine.

Quo life, the warld is mine.
An open grave is a furrow syne.
Ye'll no keep my seed frae fa'in in.
Quo life, the warld is mine.

The 51st Highland Division's Farewell to Sicily

Hamish Henderson

The pipie is dozie, the pipie is fey,
He winna come roon' for his vino the day.
The sky ow'r Messina is unco an' grey,
An' a' the bricht chaulmers are eerie.

Then fare weel ye banks o' Sicily,
Fare ye weel ye valley and shaw.
There's nae Jock will mourn the kyles o' ye,
Puir bliddy swaddies are wearie.

Fare weel, ye banks o' Sicily,
Fare ye weel, ye valley and shaw,
There's nae hame can smoor the wiles o' ye,
Puir bliddy swaddies are wearie.

Then doon the stair and line the waterside,
Wait your turn, the ferry's awa'.
Then doon the stair and line the waterside,
A' the bricht chaulmers are eerie.

The drummie is polisht, the drummie is braw
He cannae be seen for his webbin' ava.
He's beezed himsel' up for a photy an a'
Tae leave wi' his Lola, his dearie.

Sae fare weel, ye dives o' Sicily
(Fare ye weel, ye shieling an' ha'),
We'll a' mind shebeens and bothies
Whaur kind signorinas were cheerie.

Fare weel, ye banks o' Sicily
(Fare ye weel, ye shieling an' ha');
We'll a' mind shebeens and bothies
Whaur Jock made a date wi' his dearie.

Then tune the pipes and drub the tenor drum
(Leave your kit this side o' the wa').
Then tune the pipes and drub the tenor drum
A' the bricht chaulmers are eerie.

(Tune: Farewell to the Creeks)

Elegies for the Dead in Cyrenaica
Hamish Henderson

Alles geben Götter, die unendlichen,
Ihren Lieblingen ganz.
Alle Freunden, die unendlichen,
Alle Schmerzen, die unendlichen, ganz.
Goethe

Prologue
for John Spiers

Obliterating face and hands
The dumb-bell guns of violence
Show up our godhead for a sham.
Against the armour of the storm
I'll hold my human barrier,
Maintain my fragile irony.

I've walked this brazen clanging path
In flesh's brittle arrogance
To chance the simple hazard, death.
Regretting only this, my rash
Ambitious wish in verse to write
A true and valued testament.

Let my words knit what now we lack
The demon and the heritage
And fancy strapped to logic's rock.
A chastened wantonness, a bit
That sets on song a discipline,
A sensuous austerity.

First Elegy
End of a Campaign

There are many dead in the brutish desert,
        who lie uneasy
among the scrub in this landscape of half-wit

stunted ill-will. For the dead land is insatiate
and necrophilous. The sand is blowing about still.
Many who for various reasons, or because
                of mere unanswerable compulsion, came here
and fought among the clutching gravestones,
                shivered and sweated,
cried out, suffered thirst, were stoically silent, cursed
the spittering machine-guns, were homesick for Europe
and fast embedded in quicksand of Africa
                agonized and died.
And sleep now. Sleep here the sleep of the dust.

There were our own, there were the others.
Their deaths were like their lives, human and animal.
There were no gods and precious few heroes.
What they regretted when they died had nothing to do with
                race and leader, realm indivisible,
laboured Augustan speeches or vague imperial heritage.
(They saw through that guff before the axe fell.)
                Their longing turned to
the lost world glimpsed in the memory of letters:
an evening at the pictures in the friendly dark,
two knowing conspirators smiling and whispering secrets;
        or else
a family gathering in the homely kitchen
with Mum so proud of her boys in uniform:
                their thoughts trembled
between moments of estrangement, and ecstatic moments
of reconciliation: and their desire
crucified itself against the unutterable shadow of someone
whose photo was in their wallets.
Then death made his incision.

There were our own, there were the others.
Therefore, minding the great word of Glencoe's
son, that we should not disfigure ourselves
with villainy of hatred; and seeing that all
have gone down like curs into anonymous silence,
I will bear witness for I knew the others.
Seeing that littoral and interior are alike indifferent
and the birds are drawn again to our welcoming north
why should I not sing *them*, the dead, the innocent?

The Constant North
for Dee

J. F. Hendry

Encompass me, my lover,
With your eyes' wide calm.
Though noonday shadows are assembling doom,
The sun remains when I remember them;
And death, if it should come,
Must fall like quiet snow from such clear skies.

Minutes we snatched from the unkind winds
Are grown into daffodils by the sea's
Edge, mocking its green miseries;
Yet I seek you hourly still, over
A new Atlantis loneliness, blind
As a restless needle held by the constant north we always
      have in mind.

The Ship

J. F. Hendry

Here is a ship you made
Out of my breasts and sides
As I lay dead in the yards
Under the hammers.

Here is the hull you built
Out of a heart of salt,
Sky-rent, the prey of birds
Strung on the longshore.

Here is her rigging bound
Nerve, sinew, ice and wind
Blowing through the night
The starred dew of beads.

Here her ribs of silver
Once steerless in a culvert
Climb the laddered centuries
To hide a cloud in a frame.

The King and Queen of Dumfriesshire
W. N. Herbert

The King and Queen of Dumfriesshire sit
in their battery-dead Triumph, gazing ahead
at an iced-over windscreen like a gull rolled flat.
They are cast in bronze, with Henry Moore holes
shot in each other by incessant argument;
these are convenient for holding her tartan flask,
his rolled-up *Scotsman*. The hairy skeleton
of a Border terrier sits in the back window,
not nodding. On the back seat rests
their favourite argument, the one about
how he does not permit her to see the old friends
she no longer likes and he secretly misses;
the one which is really about punishing each other
for no longer wanting to make love.
The argument is in the form of a big white bowl
with a black band around it hand-painted with fruit.
It has a gold rim, and in it lies
a brown curl of water from the leaking roof.
Outside, the clouds continue
to bomb the glen with sheep, which bare
their slate teeth as they tumble,
unexpectedly sneering.
The King and Queen of Dumfriesshire sit
like the too-solid bullet-ridden ghosts
of Bonny and Clyde, not eating their
tinned salmon sandwiches, crustless, still
wrapped in tinfoil, still in the tupperware.
They survey their domain, not glancing at
each other, not removing from the glove compartment
any of the old words they have always used,
words like 'twae', like 'couthy', like 'Kirkcudbright',
which keep their only threat at bay: of separation.

Why the Elgin Marbles Must be Returned to Elgin

W. N. Herbert

Because they are large, round and bluey,
        and would look good on the top of Lady Hill.
Because their glassy depths would give local kids
        the impression that they are looking at
        the Earth from outer space.
Several Earths in fact, which encourages humility
        and a sense of relativity.
Because local building contractors would use
        JCBs to play giant games in Cooper Park
        and attract tourists to Morayshire:
        'Monster Marble Showdown Time!'
Because the prophecy omitted from the Scottish Play
        must be fulfilled:
        'When the marbles come back to Elgin
        the *mormaer* will rise again.'
(A *mormaer* being a Pictish sub-king.
Which Macbeth was, not a thane.
Nor a tyrant, for that matter.
More sort of an Arthur figure, you know,
        got drunk and married Liza Minelli, with
        Gielgud as Merlin the butler.)
Because they're just gathering dust
        sitting in the British Museum, never mind
        the danger that if someone leans against them
        they might roll and squash a tourist like a bug.
Because the Greeks, like the rest of Europe,
        don't know where Scotland is, and so
        won't be able to find them.
Because if they come looking we can just
        push the marbles into the Firth off Burghead
        and show them the dolphins instead.
Greeks like dolphins. Always have.
Because it will entertain the dolphins
        watching the Elgin marbles roll with the tides
        and perhaps attract whales.

Because whales can balance the marbles
    on the tops of their spouts,
    then ex-Soviet tourist navies can come
    and fire big guns at them
    like in a funfair.
Because the people of Morayshire were
    originally Greek anyway, as proven by
    Sir Thomas Urquhart in his *Pantochronochanon*.
And by the fact they like dolphins.
Because we are not just asking for them,
    we demand their return, and this
    may be the marble that sets the heather
    alight, so to speak.
Because if the Stone of Destiny is
    the MacGraeae's tooth, then
    the Elgin marbles are
    the weird sisters' glass eyes.
Because Scotland must see visions again,
    even if only through
    a marble of convenience.

Looking Up from Aeroplanes

W. N. Herbert

Do you too soon forget the brown
frownland far below,
between the slippery blotchings of
cloud-shadows, the
zip-fasteners of farm-lanes,
the telephone pad-hatchings of the towns
and look up?
           Into
that darkening of the blue
through the occasional vapour trail
like a larval tubule to
the grainy upper layers
grazed thin by stubbly cheeks,
the sore lips of peering
angels,

           each one packed together with
the others like a white fish,
touching each other and
the whole sky at every point raised
by their massive iris
whose pupil is the blinded sun.

Hitch-Haiku

Alan Jackson

nae hat
an the cauld rain fallin

dearie me

Confessio

Alan Jackson

'I put the peas in Galileo's telescope'

The Proddy Heebie Jeebies

Alan Jackson

the proddy heebie jeebies
are bitin' intae me
my voluntary rescue team
has foundered in the sea

the polis stand by helpless
they're feared tae dae a thing
in their constitution
rex is still the king

i lash about quite manful
it doesnae do nae good
a hernia a rupture
i cant digest my food

the boys is whizzing over
land and sea to help
nietzsche blake and a chinaman
they gie the prots a skelp

the proddies come back fightin
frae a base inside my skull
cunnin old buggers fishers o men
theyve drained life to the full

and there i'll have to leave you
this interim report
of rank disturbance of the peace
and take myself to court

The Worstest Beast

Alan Jackson

the worstest beast that swims in the sea
is man with his bathing trunks down to his knee

the worstest beast that goes through the air
is man with his comb to tidy his hair

the worstest beast that bores through the soil
is man with his uses for metal and oil

the worstest beast that hunts for meat
is man who kills and does not eat

the worstest beast that suckles its young
is man who's scared of nipples and dung

the worstest beast that copulates
is man who's mixed his loves and hates

the worstest beast that has warm skin
is man who stones himself with sin

he's the worstest beast because he's won
it's a master race and it's almost run

The Water-Hen

Violet Jacob

As I gaed doon by the twa mill dams i' the mornin'
The water-hen cam' oot like a passin' wraith,
And her voice ran through the reeds wi' a sound of warnin',
      'Faith – keep faith!'
'Aye, bird, tho' ye see but ane ye may cry on baith!'

As I gaed doon the field when the dew was lyin',
My ain love stood whaur the road an' the mill-lade met,
And it seemed to me that the rowin' wheel was cryin',
      'Forgie – forget,
And turn, man, turn, for ye ken that ye lo'e her yet!'

As I gaed doon the road 'twas a weary meetin',
For the ill words said yestreen they were aye the same,
And my het he'rt drouned the wheel wi' its heavy beatin'.
      'Lass, think shame,
It's no for me to speak, for it's you to blame!'

As I gaed doon by the toon when the day was springin'
The Baltic brigs lay thick by the soundin' quay
And the riggin' hummed wi' the sang that the wind was singin',
      'Free – gang free,
For there's mony a load on shore may be skailed at sea!'

When I cam hame wi' the thrang o' the years ahint me
There was naucht to see for the weeds and the lade in spate,

But the water-hen by the dams she seemed aye to mind me,
        Cryin' 'Hope – wait!'
'Aye, bird, but my een grow dim, an' it's late – late!'

Tam i' the Kirk

Violet Jacob

O Jean, my Jean, when the bell ca's the congregation
O'er valley and hill wi' the ding frae its iron mou',
When a'body's thochts is set on their ain salvation,
        Mine's set on you.

There's a reid rose lies on the Buik o' the Word afore ye
That was growin' braw on its bush at the keek o' day,
But the lad that pu'd yon flower i' the mornin's glory
        He canna pray.

He canna pray, but there's nane i' the kirk will heed him
Whaur he sits sae still his lane at the side o' the wa',
For nane but the reid rose kens what my lassie gied him –
        It and us twa.

He canna sing for the sang that his ain he'rt raises,
He canna see for the mist that's afore his een,
And a voice droons the hale o' the psalms and the paraphrases
        Crying 'Jean! Jean! Jean!'

The Neep-Fields by the Sea

Violet Jacob

Ye'd wonder foo the seasons rin
This side o' Tweed an' Tyne:
The hairst's awa'; October-month
Cam in a whilie syne,
But the stooks are oot in Scotland yet,

There's green upon the tree,
And oh! what grand's the smell ye'll get
Frae the neep-fields by the sea!

The lang lift lies abune the warld,
On ilka windless day
The ships creep doon the ocean line
Sma' on the band o' grey;
And the lang sigh heaved upon the sand
Comes pechin' up tae me
And speils the cliffs tae whaur ye stand
I' the neep-fields by the sea.

Oh, time's aye slow, tho' time gangs fast
When siller's a' tae mak',
An' deith, afore ma poke is fu'
May grip me i' the back;
But ye'll tak' ma banes an' my Sawbath braws,
Gin deith's ower smairt for mc,
And set them up amang the shaws
I' the lang rows plantit atween the wa's,
A tattie-dulie for fleggin' craws
I' the neep-fields by the sea.

Arraheids

Kathleen Jamie

See thon raws o flint arraheids
in oor gret museums o antiquities
awful grand in Embro –
Dae'ye near'n daur wunner at wur histrie?
Weel then, Bewaur!
The museums of Scotland are wrang.
They urnae arraheids
but a show o grannies' tongues,
the hard tongues o grannies
aa deid an gaun
back to thur peat and burns,

but for thur sherp
chert tongues, that lee
fur generations in the land
like wicked cherms, that lee
aa douce in the glessy cases in the gloom
o oor museums, an
they arenae lettin oan. But if you daur
sorn aboot an fancy
the vanished hunter, the wise deer runnin on;
wheesht . . . an you'll hear them,
fur they cannae keep fae muttering
ye arenae here tae wonder,
whae dae ye think ye ur?

The Queen of Sheba
Kathleen Jamie

Scotland, you have invoked her name
just once too often
in your Presbyterian living rooms.
She's heard, yea
even unto heathenish Arabia
your vixen's bark of poverty, come down
the family like a lang neb, a thrawn streak,
a wally dug you never liked
but can't get shot of.

She's had enough. She's come.
Whit, tae this dump? Yes!
She rides first camel
of a swaying caravan
from her desert sands
to the peat and bracken
of the Pentland hills
across the fit-ba pitch
to the thin mirage
of the swings and chute; scattered with glass.

Breathe that steamy musk
on the Curriehill Road, not mutton-shanks
boiled for broth, nor the chlorine stink
of the swimming pool where skinny girls
accuse each other of verrucas.
In her bathhouses women bear
warm pot-bellied terracotta pitchers
on their laughing hips.
All that she desires, whatever she asks
She will make the bottled dreams
of your wee lasses
look like *sweeties*.

Spangles scarcely cover
her gorgeous breasts, hanging gardens
jewels, frankincense; more voluptuous
even than Vi-next-door, whose
high-heeled slippers
keeked from dressing gowns
like little hooves, wee tails
of pink fur stuffed in the cleavage of her toes;
more audacious even than Currie Liz
who led the gala floats
though the Wimpey scheme
in a ruby-red Lotus Elan
before the Boys' Brigade band
and the Brownies' borrowed coal-truck;
hair piled like candy-floss;
who lifted her hands from the neat wheel
to tinkle her fingers
at her tricks
    among the Masons and the elders and the police.

The cool black skin
of the Bible couldn't hold her,
nor the atlas green
on the kitchen table,
you stuck with thumbs
and split to fruity hemispheres –
yellow Yemen, Red Sea, *Ethiopia*. Stick in
with homework and you'll be

cliver like yer faither.
But not too cliver,
no *above yersel.*

See her lead those great soft camels
widdershins round the kirk-yaird,
smiling
as she eats
avocados with apostle spoons
she'll teach us how. But first

she wants to strip the willow
she desires the keys
     to the National Library
she is beckoning
     the lasses
     in the awestruck crowd . . .

Yes we'd like to
     clap the camels,
to smell the spice,
admire her hairy legs and
bonny wicked smile, we want to take
PhDs in Persian, be vice
to her president: we want
to help her
     ask some Difficult Questions

she's shouting for our wisest man
to test her mettle:

     Scour Scotland for a Solomon!

Sure enough: from the back of the crowd
someone growls:
                    whae do you think y'ur?

and a thousand laughing girls and she
draw our hot breath
     and shout:

THE QUEEN OF SHEBA!

Mrs McKellar, Her Martyrdom
Kathleen Jamie

Each night she fills, from the fabled
well of disappointment, a kettle
for her hottie. Lying
in his apportioned bed:
Mr McKellar – annulled
beside his trouser press.

Who mentions, who defers to whom
on matters concerning
redecorating the living room,
milk delivery, the damp
stain spreading on the ceiling

when a word is a kind of touch?
Speaking of which, and they don't,
the garden needs attention
and the bedroom window frames,
exquisitely, the darkening hills,
a sky teased with mauve.

But he won't notice, or smell her burning
fix it! fix it!
won't look up the number
of Roofer and Son about that
slightly bewildering stain,

and she'll keep schtum.
Medieval in a dressing gown,
she'd rather display
toward an indifferent world
the means of her agony:
a broken toilet seat,

or die, lips sealed, regarding
the rotting window sills, that
wobbling shelf, which she could
as it happens, repair herself,
but won't, on principle.

Crossing the Loch

Kathleen Jamie

Remember how we rowed toward the cottage
on the sickle-shaped bay,
that one night after the pub
loosed us through its swinging doors
and we pushed across the shingle
till water lipped the sides
as though the loch mouthed 'boat'?

I forget who rowed. Our jokes hushed.
The oars' splash, creak, and the spill
of the loch reached long into the night.
Out in the race I was scared:
the cold shawl of breeze,
and hunched hills; what the water held
of deadheads, ticking nuclear hulls.

Who rowed, and who kept their peace?
Who hauled salt-air and stars
deep into their lungs, were not reassured;
and who first noticed the loch's
phosphorescence, so, like a twittering nest
washed from the rushes, an astonished
small boat of saints, we watched water shine
on our fingers and oars,
the magic dart of our bow wave?

It was surely foolhardy, such a broad loch, a tide,
but we live – and even have children
to women and men we had yet to meet
that night we set out, calling our own
the sky and salt-water, wounded hills
dark-starred by blaeberries, the glimmering anklets
we wore in the shallows
as we shipped oars and jumped,
to draw the boat safe, high at the cottage shore.

Old Tongue

Jackie Kay

When I was eight, I was forced south.
Not long after, when I opened
my mouth, a strange thing happened.
I lost my Scottish accent.
Words fell off my tongue:
eedyit, dreich, wabbit, crabbit,
stummer, teuchter, heidbanger,
so you are, so am ur, see you, see ma ma,
shut yer geggie, or I'll gie you the malkie!

My own vowels started to stretch like my bones
and I turned my back on Scotland.
Words disappeared in the dead of night,
new words marched in: ghastly, awful,
quite dreadful, scones said like stones.
Pokey hats into ice-cream cones.
Oh where did all my words go –
my old words, my lost words?
Did you ever feel sad when you lost a word,
did you ever try and call it back
like calling in the sea?
If I could have found my words wandering,
I swear I would have taken them in,
swallowed them whole, knocked them back.

Out in the English soil, my old words
buried themselves. It made my mother's blood boil.
I cried one day with the wrong sound in my mouth.
I wanted them back; I wanted my old accent back,
my old tongue. My dour, soor Scottish tongue.
Sing-songy. *I wanted to gie it laldie.*

Teeth

i.m. Joy Gardner

Jackie Kay

This is X who has all her own teeth.
Her mother is horrified by this.

Look into her mouth. She still has them.
Perfect pearls. Milk stones. Pure ivory.

Not a filling, no receding gums.
X was a woman with a lively

smile. Since she was a girl. No dark holes.
Her mother wore, still does, false teeth. Tusks,

badly fitted, left something unsaid –
a tiny gap between tooth and gum.

Her mum's teeth, in a glass tumbler, swam
at night: a shark's grin; a wolf's slow smirk.

What upsets her mother now, oddly,
is this: X had such beautiful lips.

This morning the men broke in – 8 a.m.
X was wearing her dressing gown, white

towelling. They came wearing her number
on their arms. *Did you know*, her mother says,

they taped my daughter's mouth to choke her
screams. They covered her mouth in white tape.

The small boy pulled at the sharp trousers.
He was soundless. The big men flung him

into that grey corner. His voice burst.
He will stand there, that height, forever, see

those minutes grab and snatch and repeat
themselves. The men in plain-clothes have claws;

they attack his mother like dogs, gagging her,
binding her, changing her into someone

else. He will watch her hands smash and thrash.
His hands making a church, then a tall

steeple. He crosses his fingers. Squeezes them.
His hands wet themselves. He is five years old.

He knows his address. He knows his name.
He has ten fingers. He counts them again.

This is X who has all her own teeth.
Came to this country with her own teeth.

Soundbites will follow. Lies will roll
tomorrow. The man with the abscess

will say she had a weak heart. High blood.
Illegal. Only doing his job.

Fill it in. Write it down. Bridge the gap.
Give him a stamp of approval: silver

or gold or NHS, she resisted arrest;
there's your cause of death. On a plate.

She was wrong. Give her a number. Think
of a number. Take away the son.

If Ye Hivni . . .

I. W. King

If ye hivni ate a cauld pie along
Sauchiehall Street ona
drizzly day
   yer no a poet
An if ye hivni been
battirt aff the side i the heid wi a
giez oor baw back Jimmie
   yer naebdy at aw
An if ye hivni stood
three hoors ina bookshop
cap in haund ti be telt
come back latir
athoot swearin
ye must i bin brocht up
   heluva posh
An if ye hivni bin telt
bi yer eldir an bettir
thit yer best poem
wisnae bad *fir a kailyairdir* bit
it didnae rhyme
    . . .
well if ye hivni . . .
. . . an ye hivni
then A'm tellin ye
an that's some'hn

In Torrett, Minorca

Norman Kreitman

A thin priest, emphatic in black,
stands like an exclamation mark
against a page of limewashed wall.
I walk past with head averted
and wonder, briefly, what he is for.

More engaging is how the hibiscus lifts
a brilliant branch over the hedge
confirming red as the colour of trumpets,
or that elegant girl boasting her figure
as though she had won it in a contest.

And everywhere the sun is bestowing
the old understanding, so that each trellis,
every warmed and crooked flowerpot
smiles in the Mediterranean light,
content in the world of huge simplicities.

Now I rejoice my very limbs, and risk
the grand gesture, a vague benediction,
yet pause at what my raised hand declares.
For how can I, naïve, say what I affirm
unless I invent a new name for a blessing?

Lizard

Norman Kreitman

A blurred grey streak and he is gone
too fast for the eye to understand.
His track rustles dead stalks, makes
the leaves to shudder; then silence
over the mound of pebbles. And silently
he is there again on the white wall.

> A tooled leather sheath
> on miniature crocodile legs;
> a fleck of granite eye
> held by a saucer's rim;
> each fluted foot
> pointing in five directions;
> a statuette of dust. Only
> the jugular flutter shows
> he has run a dark age,
> stopped instantly, and holds
> immobile in the glare.

Perfect heraldic emblem of day,
yet traveller from primaeval time;
the messenger of tombs transposed
to a stillness in sunlight.

Then the ancient head lifts slightly
in a decision. The wall is bare.

Glossy Mail

Norman Kreitman

Leaving home I left behind on the table
    a clutter of shiny letters
from Oxfam, Barnardo's, Help the Aged,
    Cancer Relief, and did I know
of Sam, 19, who has no arms? But now I was driving
    through a mist of leaves to the river,
    letting the green wash my eyes.

In this land the sky is vast with the colour
    of good fortune, clouds sit snugly
on the rounded hills, the lanes are intimate
    and their problems innocent.
But that other country has no map or signposts
    to greater or lesser pain.
    Silently the supplicants wait

face after face, confronting the way things are.
    Or perhaps there is a sea
where the blind and the grieving mothers
    are merely the surface waves.
And here I wait in this small stream, giving praise
    for flowing water,
casting a fly at the setting sun, standing
    sideways to the world.

Bonfire in April

Norman Kreitman

No emblem, this; not a ducal banner
Of pluming clouds, no circlet of gold to crown
A lord of autumn in his scarlet and brown,
Just a fire to clear junk in the laziest manner.

Old prunings with their fingers now gone brittle,
A tangle of couchgrass still sprouting in force,
Plastic bags, even half a headless wooden horse
From storybook summers when the children were little.

It must have been me who hoed round this spot,
Played father, was a man who had reasons
For inhabiting a place and marking the seasons.
Tried to raise a few plants, tossed others to rot.

Perhaps after all those flowers really mattered –
The fuschia's hats for elves, hydrangea's lace –
Which a basic husbandry brought to this space.
Their dance is lost now, their finery scattered.

I add another forkload to the pile, stoke
The spitting grey pyramid's one whispy flame
And squint through smarting eyelids to reclaim
The shape of the years in the acrid smoke.

from *An Old Guide-Book to Prague*

Frank Kuppner

1

It being my almost invariable habit
To visit a second-hand bookshop on a Saturday afternoon,
And wander among those rearranged heaps of the past,
Rearranging them myself each Saturday afternoon.

2

And surely I can afford this little book:
This little book of photographs of a city:
Almost any city, provided I can afford it:
I shall go and ask the man what price he sets on it.

3

Three days later, I read the back cover,
And discover that the book was published in June 1937;
Before that, it had hovered among the forties and fifties;
Suddenly all those people breathe on the other side of a war.

4

The River Vltava is still approaching Prague;
At tables on terraces hundreds overlook it;
An approaching war is not so easily photographed;
People are moving to and fro from the tables.

10

If the crowds were suddenly to vanish from all those tables,
Except for those who, seven years within that day,
Would have been taken away to be murdered somewhere,
A crowd would still remain, looking at the river.

11

Odd, during darkness to look at sunlight;
To look at a world without so much known history;
It is merely to indicate a busy intersection at a bridge
That these seventeen people and three and a half motor cars are
    presented.

12

Surely the absence of the Second World War
Ought to be more apparent in the quality of light;
All I see are old cars, and coats somewhat the wrong length;
I am unable to decide even what season it is.

24

I re-open the book on the next day, at last a sunlit day;
Again I observe exactly the same past sunlight;

The same brief movements still caught among the same
   architecture;
But what they did next is a little further away.

40

Such slight marks on a wide square far away
Seem too occasional to contain a whole life each;
A woman following a man following a man;
No, the one in the middle is actually a woman.

44

As I listen to a recording now twenty years old,
Although it was bought by me only two days ago,
I stare at a picture in a book bought nine days ago,
Showing two windows opened, thirty years before that clarinet.

55

There is so much sunlight in this little book,
As if ten suns were shining on that city;
I can barely remember rainfall in my dreams;
And everywhere three or four or five windows open.

56

A surprisingly narrow road outside a palace;
A flag fluttering serenely from the roof;
That car is very badly parked, on that corner;
I think the Prime Minister was killed in that building.

61

Somehow surprising that ordinary real lives should go on
In what seem such extravagantly picturesque surroundings,
Like living on a set for *Fidelio*;
A fraudulent antique pram stands in the middle of the pavement.

76

How callous architecture is – such little nostalgia for horses;
Each day for thousands hoof-clops reverberated off every one of
   those houses;
Now, above the screaming and the smell of automobiles,
Their curtains signal to each other as impassively as ever.

89

I suppose someone there is driving a car for the last time;
How much nonchalance are those small vehicles carriers of?
Or the wild joy of driving your own car for the first time,
Lost among those impassive rows of traffic.

90

That dot there will kill some people within five years;
That dot runs his eyes over a newspaper;
That dot seems to huddle wearily against a huge building;
That dot halts by a car, letting a tram pass.

92

This dot here is troubled by two of his teeth;
This dot is passionately in love with that one there;
That one there is about to buy a favourite cheese;
This dot here is the merest speck in the distance.

107

The sense of Sunday and a listless, fleeting crowd;
The familiarity of this distant scene haunting me;
Some of my German relatives must be here or hereabouts;
Oh, silver nitrate, silver nitrate, how much I have loved thee.

126

A man standing outside the Ministry of Defence
As inconspicuous as the Venus de Milo;
At the moment probably no-one is being tortured there;
Two schoolgirls are almost out of the picture.

127

Window after window on the spare clean modern building;
Is Czech being spoken behind every window?
Behind how many windows has Malay been spoken?
That one or that one or that one?

129

I sit in a library, looking at a photograph of a library;
I inspect the caught positions of the passers-by;
How resolutely they cross streets forty-five or forty-six years ago;
I hear traffic on the road outside.

140

Huge angels flutter on the roof of the theatre;
Directly below one of them, at ground level,
A woman smaller than their wings is reading a poster;
Tactfully, the angels are gazing elsewhere.

145

I feel that sort of building would surely have been familiar to
    Schubert:
It looks sufficiently old, and similar to his birthplace;
Not so familiar perhaps would be the black stain on the sky;
No doubt he often lay looking at stains upon the ceiling above him.

168

On the far side of the bridge, the neatness of a formal château;
On the near side an unkempt wilderness;
At no point does there seem to be a gate;
Doubtless there is a gate, but we do not see it.

169

I shudder to think what revels were carried on
In that odd, brutal castle, abruptly rising through foliage;
I suspect, though, that they did not involve Thai girls;
All the Thai girls who were dancing were dancing elsewhere.

172

Every twilight, the city has departed;
It has crept away into the tourists' memories,
And its quieter sister has slipped into its place;
The next day it returns, with a slight hangover.

173

Lights are on the statues, lights are on the porticoes,
Lights are on the monuments, lights are in the towers;
Lights show at most of the windows in the streets;
But it is the lights in the windows that go out first.

Sonnet 4

R. D. Laing

When I consider what you mean to me,
It is a fact I've come to realize
That you're my closest link to paradise
Despite what wise men try to make me see.

They caution us against idolatry
And tell us that we should not jeopardize
Immortal life for anything that dies:
And not be bemused by mere beauty.

It seems ungracious not to take delight
In day because it turns so soon to night.
Eternity is always here to stay:
It's only you and I who fade away.

You are my here and now, my present tense.
I hope you will excuse my diffidence.

Sonnet 16

R. D. Laing

Now all our guests have come and gone away,
And you and I can hold each other close.
No need for haste as we await the day
The night falls into. No need suppose
We've failed to find what we had lost before
We caught the gleam in one another's eyes
Which signalled hope returned, to teach us more
Than seemed our crumpled hearts could realize.
    The ghosts of youth are weary of the stage.
There's no one left to offer us a fight.
No sermons we must sit through at our age.
No passing fancies shrouding our delight.
Sweetheart, our love is true, but can't outlast
Our ruined, raddled flesh. O hold me fast.

She Said / He Said
Helen Lamb

She said – you want space?

He said – we used to be
so thin and intense
made love and devoured
slabs of bread
ripe golden cheese
in the velvet hour
before the dawn.

She said – space?
We'd be lost in it.
Space is an empty place.

He said – honesty then.

She said – I used to be
so very thin.
Never had to question.
I knew you in my bones.

He said – the thing is
you're fatter now.

Evidence
Helen Lamb

He brought her presents
each visit marked by another possession
evidence – he said – that he had been.

In her cupped palm he placed
a whorl of cool unity
a smooth speckled shell

and said – now will you tell me
how this shelter can be breached.

And then there was the mirror
he hung upon her wall
the glass fashioned to distort
so that when she looked
she only saw what he desired.

He slipped a strand of ice cold crystal
around her melting neck
and left his folded calling card
a honey-eater with bill dipped
in an origami flower.

He brought her presents
each visit marked by another possession
evidence – he said – that she belonged to him.

The Good Thief
Tom Leonard

heh jimmy
yawright ih
stull wayiz urryi
ih

heh jimmy
ma right insane yirra pape
ma right insane yirwanny us jimmy
see it nyir eyes
wanny uz

heh

heh jimmy
lookslik wirgonny miss thi gemm

gonny miss thi GEMM jimmy
nearly three a cloke thinoo

dork init
good jobe theyve gote thi lights

Feed Ma Lamz

Tom Leonard

Amyir gaffirz Gaffir. Hark.

    nay fornirz ur communists
    nay langwij
    nay lip
    nay laffn ina Sunday
    nay g.b.h. (septina wawr)
    nay nooky huntn
    nay tea-leaven
    nay chanty rasslin
    nay nooky huntn nix doar
    nur kuvitn their ox

Oaky doaky. Stick way it
– rahl burn thi lohta yiz.

At Hans Christian Andersen's Birthplace,
Odense, Denmark

Maurice Lindsay

Sunlight folds back pages of quiet shadows
against the whitewashed walls of his birthplace.
Tourists move through crowded antiseptic rooms and ponder
what row after row of glass-cased papers ought to prove.

Somehow the long-nosed gangling boy who was only
at home in fairyland, has left no clues.
The tinder-box of Time we rub
answers us each way we choose.

For kings have now no daughters left for prizes.
Swineherds must remain swineherds; and no spell
can make the good man prince; psychiatrists
have dredged up wonder from the wishing well.

The whole of this terrible, tiny world might be
dismissed as a beautiful madman's dream, but that each of us
    knows
whenever we move out from the warmth of our loneliness
we may be wearing the Emperor's new clothes.

Hurlygush

Maurice Lindsay

The hurlygush and hallyoch o the watter
skinklan i the moveless simmer sun
harles aff the scaurie mountain wi a yatter
that thru ten-thoosan centuries has run.

Wi cheek against the ash o wither't bracken
I ligg at peace and hear nae soun at aa
but yonder hurlygush that canna slacken
thru time and space mak never-endan faa:

as if a volley o the soun had brocht me
doun tae the pool whaur timeless things begin,
and e'en this endless faa'in that had claucht me
wi ilka ither force was gether't in.

'Tis Sixty Years Since

Scott's subtitle to Waverley

Maurice Lindsay

Day after day we stood in helpless fields
of southern England while the fading sun
got shuttered as a flight of bombers wields
menace towards London. Every now and then, one

birled, a twirling leaf, to hit the ground
with an exploding flash, as the spread banks
of droning wings was darted, through and round,
by fighters, puncturing the serried ranks

with spits of gunfire. Once a parachute
swung free from a hit bomber, with a white-
faced lad clutching its strings. *Don't shoot,*
I shouted. *That's not how we fight!*

Grumbling, my soldiers seized him prisoner
and passed him upwards to authority.
Odd, I thought, just how chivalrous we are
when, going on leave through London, I could see

shut streets, my taxi halted; snake-wet hose,
burnt spars from rooms torn open to the sky –
a bomb, no doubt dropped out of one of those
that briefly darkened my lost yesterday.

And as the taxi waited, picking through
the wet confusion, past tired firemen, came
a woman with her shopping bag, to queue
for life's necessities, in just the same
way she had done each day for years,
knowing we have to feed our hopes and fears.

My Rival's House

is peopled with many surfaces.
Ormolu and gilt, slipper satin,
lush velvet couches,
cushions so stiff you can't sink in.
Tables polished clear enough to see distortions in.

We take our shoes off at her door,
shuffle stocking-soled, tiptoe – the parquet floor
is beautiful and its surface must
be protected. Dust
cover, drawn shade,
won't let the surface colour fade.

Silver sugar-tongs and silver salver,
my rival serves us tea.
She glosses over him and me.
I am all edges, a surface, a shell
and yet my rival thinks she means me well.
But what squirms beneath her surface I can tell.
Soon, my rival
capped tooth, polished nail
will fight, fight foul for her survival.
Deferential, daughterly, I sip
and thank her nicely for each bitter cup.

And I have much to thank her for.
This son she bore –
first blood to her –
never, never can escape scot free
the sour potluck of family.
And oh how close
this family that furnishes my rival's place.

Lady of the house.
Queen bee.
She is far more unconscious,
far more dangerous than me.
Listen, I was always my own worst enemy.
She has taken even this from me.

She dishes up her dreams for breakfast.
Dinner, and her salt tears pepper our soup.
She won't
give up.

Liz Lochhead

The Empty Song

Liz Lochhead

Today saw the last of my Spanish shampoo.
Lasted an age now that sharing with you,
such a thing of the past is.
Giant Size. The brand
was always a compromise.
My new one's tailored exactly to my needs.
Nonspill. Protein-rich.
Feeds Body, promises to solve my problem hair.
Sweetheart, these days it's hard to care,
But oh oh insomniac moonlight
how unhoneyed is my middle of the night.
I could see you
far enough. Beyond me
how we'll get back together.
Campsites in Spain, moonlight,
heavy weather.

Today saw the end of my Spanish shampoo,
the end of my third month without you.

Poem for My Sister
Liz Lochhead

My little sister likes to try my shoes,
to strut in them,
admire her spindle-thin twelve-year-old legs
in this season's styles.
She says they fit her perfectly,
but wobbles
on their high heels, they're
hard to balance.

I like to watch my little sister
playing hopscotch,
admire the neat hops-and-skips of her,
their quick peck,
never-missing their mark, not
over-stepping the line.
She is competent at peever.

I try to warn my little sister
about unsuitable shoes,
point out my own distorted feet, the callouses,
odd patches of hard skin.
I should not like to see her
in my shoes.
I wish she could stay
sure footed,
      sensibly shod.

Noises in the Dark
Liz Lochhead

The four a.m. call to the faithful wakes us,
its three-times off-key harmony of drones and wails.
Above our head I snap the lightcord but the power fails
as usual, leaving us in the dark. Tomorrow takes us

who knows where. What ruins? What towns? What smells?
Nothing shakes us.
We touch and today's too painful sunburn sticks and sears
apart again. Faithful to something three long years,
no fear, no final foreign dark quite breaks us.

Hotel habitués,
the ritually faithful wash their feet. Old plumbing grumbles.
The tap-leak in our rust-ringed basin tickles
irritant, incessant, an inch out of the dark. Whitewash crumbles
from the wall where the brittle cockroach trickles.
Fretful, faithful, wide to the dark, can we ever forget
this shabby town hotel, the shadow of the minaret?
Human or bird or animal? What was it cried?
The dark smear across the wall still unidentified.

Yeah Yeah Yeah

Roddy Lumsden

No matter what you did to her, she said,
There's times, she said, she misses you, your face
Will pucker in her dream, and times the bed's
Too big. Stray hairs will surface in a place
You used to leave your shoes. A certain phrase,
Some old song on the radio, a joke
You had to be there for, she said, some days
It really gets to her; the way you smoked
Or held a cup, or her, and how you woke
Up crying in the night sometimes, the way
She'd stroke and hush you back, and how you broke
Her still. All this she told me yesterday,
Then she rolled over, laughed, began to do
To me what she so rarely did with you.

Vanishing

Roddy Lumsden

Inside the box, her heels escape the air.
He hears the hollow silence, turns to where
The blades are catching all eyes in the hush.
His click of fingers touches off a rush
Of cymbals. Now he holds the first blade taut
And steers its whetted edge toward the slot.
She slips out of her costume, checks her face
As he reveals the white dove in her place.
She lingers till the last of the applause,
Collects her things, while back on stage he saws
Himself in half with worry, grins with fear.
The sea of faces knows she'll reappear
Amongst them soon. She slams a backstage door.
Her heels echo in the corridor.

Prayer to Be with Mercurial Women

Roddy Lumsden

Let her never have her father
call me, saying how's about
a round of golf? Instead I'll take
the grim, forbidding monster
who inspects me for a crooked
trouser crease. And spare me too
from palmy evenings which sail by
in restaurants, on barstools,
without a storming off or two.
'Darling, you were made for me.'
I pray I'll never hear those words.
I need to feel I'm stealing
love another man would kill for.
When in sleep she curls herself
around me, may she whisper names
that are not mine. I'd prefer

to be the second best she's had.
A curse on mouths which dovetail
as if there'd been a blueprint made:
I'd rather blush and slobber.
And once a month, please let me be
a punchbag. I'll take the blame
for everything: I want to taste
the stinging of a good slap.
I hope I'll find my begging notes
crumpled, torn in half, unread,
and when I phone, I want to hear
an endless sound of ringing.
Help me avoid the kind of girl
who means things when she says them,
unless she's screeching, telling me
exactly what I am. Amen.

Shotts

George MacBeth

Grown-over slagheaps rise like burial mounds
For giant moles: the outworks of a siege
Where coal that ruled their lives fell back and failed.

Subsidence, unturned wheels. Fresh conifers
In tiny forests mark the perished seams
And ragwort flares above blown galleries.

Where shafts go down, there must lie bones of men
And dregs of anthracite, once linked by work
As at the brink of something, luck or change.

I see my father, measuring his hat
Against my little skull, day after day
Go down those shafts and frame a better future.

I was born here. Now, after sixty years,
I come back weaker to the place of launching
And drive through dirty streets, tears in my eyes.

The Ward

George MacBeth

Along that ward men died each winter night.
One in an iron lung
Used to cry out before that salving tin
Strapped round his breathing stifled him. One hung
In a strange brace
That moved his dead leg gently. And no light
Out of that blaze where Hitler in
His burning concrete died lit the cramped face

Of a boy paralysed. I in that war
Lay with cold steel on wrists
Recording how my heart beat, saved and one
With the men dying. Dark amidst the mists
Across the seas
Each night in France those armies gripped and tore
Each other's guts out, and no sun
Arched in at dawn through stiff windows to ease

Men left in pain. Sisters on morning rounds
Brought laundered sheets and screens
Where they were needed. And when doctors came
In clean coats with their talk and their machines,
Behind their eyes
Moving to help, what was there? To the sounds
Of distant gunfire, in our name,
So many men walked into death. What lies

And festers is the wastage. Here the beast
Still breathes its burning stone
And claws the entrails. And those hours of cold
When I lay waking, hearing men alone
Fight into death
Swim back and grip. And I feel rise like yeast
A sense of the whole world grown old
With no one winning. And I fight for breath.

Alsatian

George MacBeth

And yet
without exactly the
appearance of

being violent,

that heavy
tail, tucked

under the firm
hind-quarters,
occasions

doubts about the
advisability
of treating

this law-dog
as if
he was really only

a sheep
in wolf's-
clothing

Seagull

Brian McCabe

We are the dawn marauders.
We prey on pizza. We kill kebabs.
We mug thrushes for bread crusts
with a snap of our big bent beaks.
We drum the worms from the ground
with the stamp of our wide webbed feet.

We spread out, cover the area –
like cops looking for the body
of a murdered fish-supper.
Here we go with our hooligan yells
loud with gluttony, sharp with starvation.
Here we go bungee-jumping on the wind,
charging from the cold sea of our birth.
This is invasion. This is occupation.
Our flags are black, white and grey.
Our wing-stripes are our rank.
No sun can match the brazen
colour of our mad yellow eyes.

We are the seagulls.
We are the people.

Kite

Brian McCabe

So what if I'm fragile –
I continually risk my neck
just to stay where I'm not.

My life is brief, a loop-the-loop,
a figure-eight, bound to end
in a crashed catastrophe.

But my life has a purpose.
Why else does my colour's quick
tug so intently at your eye?

To gather the open sky
into your mind's shuttered room –
unravelling my rippling arrow.

I point at nothing but the vast
openness inside you. I am
a pennant of your desire.

I say play with me, play me.
I say hold me, let me go.
Hold me –

No Choice

Norman MacCaig

I think about you
in as many ways as rain comes.

(I am growing, as I get older,
to hate metaphors – their exactness
and their inadequacy.)

Sometimes these thoughts are
a moistness, hardly falling, than which
nothing is more gentle:
sometimes, a rattling shower, a
bustling Spring-cleaning of the mind:
sometimes, a drowning downpour.

I am growing, as I get older,
to hate metaphor,
to love gentleness,
to fear downpours.

Toad

Norman MacCaig

Stop looking like a purse. How could a purse
squeeze under the rickety door and sit,
full of satisfaction, in a man's house?

You clamber towards me on your four corners –
right hand, left foot, left hand, right foot.

I love you for being a toad,
for crawling like a Japanese wrestler,
and for not being frightened.

I put you in my purse hand, not shutting it,
and set you down outside directly under
every star.

A jewel in your head? Toad,
you've put one in mine,
a tiny radiance in a dark place.

Praise of a Collie

Norman MacCaig

She was a small dog, neat and fluid –
Even her conversation was tiny:
She greeted you with *bow*, never *bow-wow*.

Her sons stood monumentally over her
But did what she told them. Each grew grizzled
Till it seemed he was his own mother's grandfather.

Once, gathering sheep on a showery day,
I remarked how dry she was. Pollóchan said, 'Ah,
It would take a very accurate drop to hit Lassie.'

She sailed in the dinghy like a proper sea-dog.
Where's a burn? – she's first on the other side.
She flowed through fences like a piece of black wind.

But suddenly she was old and sick and crippled . . .
I grieved for Pollóchan when he took her a stroll
And put his gun to the back of her head.

Heron

Norman MacCaig

It stands in water, wrapper in heron. It makes
An absolute exclusion of everything else
By disappearing in itself, yet is the presence
Of hidden pools and secret, reedy lakes.
It twirls small fish from the bright water flakes.

(Glog goes the small fish down.) With lifted head
And no shoulders at all, it periscopes round –
Steps, like an aunty, forward – gives itself shoulders
And vanishes, a shilling in a pound,
Making no sight as other things make no sound.

Until, releasing its own spring, it fills
The air with heron, finds its height and goes,
A spear between two clouds. A cliff receives it
And it is gargoyle. All around it hills
Stand in the sea; wind from a brown sail spills.

Byre

Norman MacCaig

The thatched roof rings like heaven where mice
Squeak small hosannahs all night long,
Scratching its golden pavements, skirting
The gutter's crystal river-song.

Wild kittens in the world below
Glare with one flaming eye through cracks,
Spurt in the straw, are tawny brooches
Splayed on the chests of drunken sacks.

The dimness becomes darkness as
Vast presences come mincing in,
Swagbellied Aphrodites, swinging
A silver slaver from each chin.

And all is milky, secret, female.
Angles are hushed and plain straws shine.
And kittens miaow in circles, stalking
With tail and hindleg one straight line.

Double Life
Norman MacCaig

This wind from Fife has cruel fingers, scooping
The heat from streets with salty finger-tips
Crusted with frost; and all Midlothian,
Stubborn against what heeled the sides of ships
Off from the Isle of May, stiffens its drooping
Branches to the south. Each man
And woman put their winter masks on, set
In a stony flinch, and only children can
Light with a scream an autumn fire that says
With the quick crackle of its smoky blaze,
'Summer's to burn and it's October yet.'

My Water of Leith runs through a double city;
My city is threaded by a complex stream.
A matter of regret. If these cold stones
Could be stones only, and this watery gleam
Within the chasms of tenements and the pretty
Boskage of Dean could echo the groans
Of cart-wheeled bridges with only water's voice,
October would just be October. The bones
Of rattling winter would still lie underground,
Summer be less than ghost, I be unbound
From all the choking folderols of choice.

A loss of miracles – or an exchange
Of one sort for another. When the trams
Lower themselves like bugs on a branch down
The elbow of the Mound, they'd point the diagrams
Buckled between the New Town and the range
Of the craggy Old: that's all. A noun

Would so usurp all grammar no doing word
Could rob his money-bags or clap a crown
On his turned head, and all at last would be
Existence without category – free
From demonstration except as hill or bird.

And then no double-going stream would sing
Counties and books in the symbolic air,
Trundling my forty years to the Port of Leith.
But now, look around, my history's everywhere
And I'm my own environment. I cling
Like a cold limpet underneath
Each sinking stone and am the changing sea.
I die each dying minute and bequeath
Myself to all Octobers and to this
Damned flinty wind that with a scraping kiss
Howls that I'm winter, coming home to me.

Empty Vessel

Hugh MacDiarmid

I met ayont the cairney
A lass wi' tousie hair
Singin' till a bairnie
That was nae langer there.

Wunds wi' warlds to swing
Dinna sing sae sweet.
The licht that bends owre a'thing
Is less ta'en up wi't.

The Bonnie Broukit Bairn
Hugh MacDiarmid

Mars is braw in crammasy,
Venus in a green silk goun,
The auld mune shak's her gowden feathers,
Their starry talk's a wheen o' blethers,
Nane for thee a thochtie sparin',
Earth, thou bonnie broukit bairn!
– *But greet, an' in your tears ye'll droun*
The haill clanjamfrie!

The Eemis Stane
Hugh MacDiarmid

I' the how-dumb-deid o' the cauld hairst nicht
The warl' like an eemis stane
Wags i' the lift;
An' my eerie memories fa'
Like a yowdendrift.

Like a yowdendrift so's I couldna read
The words cut oot i' the stane
Had the fug o' fame
An' history's hazelraw
No' yirdit thaim.

O Jesu Parvule
Followis ane sang of the birth of Christ, with the tune of
Baw lu la law – Godly Ballates

Hugh MacDiarmid

His mither sings to the bairnie Christ
Wi' the tune o' *Baw lu la law*.
The bonnie wee craturie lauchs in His crib

An' a' the starnies an' he are sib.
  Baw, baw, my loonikie, baw, balloo.

'Fa' owre, my hinny, fa' owre, fa' owre,
A'body's sleepin' binna oorsels.'
She's drawn Him in tae the bool o' her breist
But the byspale's nae thocht o' sleep i' the least.
  Balloo, wee mannie, balloo, balloo.

Milk-Wort and Bog-Cotton
Hugh MacDiarmid

Cwa' een like milk-wort and bog-cotton hair!
I love you, earth, in this mood best o' a'
When the shy spirit like a laich wind moves
And frae the lift nae shadow can fa'
Since there's nocht left to thraw a shadow there
Owre een like milk-wort and milk-white cotton hair.

Wad that nae leaf upon anither wheeled
A shadow either and nae root need dern
In sacrifice to let sic beauty be!
But deep surroondin' darkness I discern
Is aye the price o' licht. Wad licht revealed
Naething but you, and nicht nocht else concealed.

O Wha's Been Here Afore Me, Lass?
from A Drunk Man Looks at the Thistle
Hugh MacDiarmid

O wha's the bride that cairries the bunch
O' thistles blinterin' white?
Her cuckold bridegroom little dreids
What he sall ken this nicht.

For closer than gudeman can come
And closer to'r than hersel',
Wha didna need her maidenheid
Has wrocht his purpose fell.

O wha's been here afore me, lass,
And hoo did he get in?
   – A man that deed or I was born
   This evil thing has din.

And left, as it were on a corpse,
Your maidenheid to me?
   – Nae lass, gudeman, sin' Time began
   'S hed only mair to gi'e.

But I can gi'e ye kindness, lad,
And a pair o' willin' hands,
And ye sall ha'e my breists like stars,
My limbs like willow wands,

And on my lips ye'll heed nae mair,
And in my hair forget,
The seed o' a' the men that in
My virgin womb ha'e met . . .

Lo! A Child is Born

Hugh MacDiarmid

I thought of a house where the stones seemed suddenly changed
And became instinct with hope, hope as solid as themselves,
And the atmosphere warm with that lovely heat,
The warmth of tenderness and longing souls, the smiling anxiety
That rules a home where a child is about to be born.
The walls were full of ears. All voices were lowered.
Only the mother had the right to groan or complain.
Then I thought of the whole world. Who cares for its travail
And seeks to encompass it in like lovingkindness and peace?
There is a monstrous din of the sterile who contribute nothing

To the great end in view, and the future fumbles,
A bad birth, not like the child in that gracious home
Heard in the quietness turning in its mother's womb,
A strategic mind already, seeking the best way
To present himself to life, and at last, resolved,
Springing into history quivering like a fish,
Dropping into the world like a ripe fruit in due time. –
But where is the Past to which Time, smiling through her tears
At her new-born son, can turn crying: 'I love you'?

Two Memories

Hugh MacDiarmid

Religion? Huh! Whenever I hear the word
It brings two memories back to my mind.
Choose between them, and tell me which
You think the better model for mankind.

Fresh blood scares sleeping cows worse than anything on earth.
An unseen rider leans far out from his horse with a freshly-skinned
Weaner's hide in his hands, turning and twisting the hairy slimy thing
And throwing the blood abroad on the wind.

A brilliant flash of lightning crashes into the heavens.
It reveals the earth in a strange yellow-green light,
Alluring yet repelling, that distorts the immediate foreground
And makes the gray and remote distance odious to the sight.

And a great mass of wraithlike objects on the bed ground
Seems to upheave, to move, to rise, to fold and undulate
In a wavelike mobility that extends to an alarming distance.
The cows have ceased to rest; they are getting to their feet.

Another flash of lightning shows a fantastic and fearsome vision.
Like branches of some enormous grotesque sprawling plant
A forest of long horns waves, and countless faces
Turn into the air, unspeakably weird and gaunt.

The stroke of white fire from the sky is reflected back
To the heavens from thousands of bulging eyeballs,
And into the heart of any man who sees
This diabolical mirroring of the lightning numbing fear falls.

Is such a stampede your ideal for the human race?
Haven't we milled in it long enough? My second memory
Is of a flight of wild swans. Glorious white birds in the blue
    October heights
Over the surly unrest of the ocean! Their passing is more than
    music to me
And from their wings descends, and in my heart triumphantly
    peals,
The old loveliness of Earth that both affirms and heals.

from *The Glass of Pure Water*
Hugh MacDiarmid

Hold a glass of pure water to the eye of the sun!
It is difficult to tell the one from the other
Save by the tiny hardly visible trembling of the water.
This is the nearest analogy to the essence of human life
Which is even more difficult to see.
Dismiss anything you can see more easily;
It is not alive – it is not worth seeing.
There is a minute indescribable difference
Between one glass of pure water and another
With slightly different chemical constituents.
The difference between one human life and another
Is no greater; colour does not colour the water;
You cannot tell a white man's life from a black man's.
But the lives of these particular slum people
I am chiefly concerned with, like the lives of all
The world's poorest, remind me less
Of a glass of water held between my eyes and the sun
– They remind me of the feeling they had
Who saw Sacco and Vanzetti in the death cell
On the eve of their execution.
– One is talking to God.

I dreamt last night that I saw one of His angels
Making his centennial report to the Recording Angel
On the condition of human life.
Look at the ridge of skin between your thumb and forefinger.
Look at the delicate lines on it and how they change
– How many different things they can express –
As you move out or close in your forefinger and thumb.
And look at the changing shapes – the countless
Little gestures, little miracles of line –
Of your forefinger and thumb as you move them.
And remember how much a hand can express,
How a single slight movement of it can say more
Than millions of words – dropped hand, clenched fist,
Snapping fingers, thumb up, thumb down,
Raised in blessing, clutched in passion, begging,
Welcome, dismissal, prayer, applause,
And a million other signs, too slight, too subtle,
Too packed with meaning for words to describe,
A universal language understood by all.
And the angel's report on human life
Was the subtlest movement – just like that – and no more;
A hundred years of life on the Earth
Summed up, not a detail missed or wrongly assessed,
In that little inconceivably intricate movement.

The only communication between man and man
That says anything worth hearing
– The hidden well-water; the finger of destiny –
Moves as that water, that angel, moved.
Truth is the rarest thing and life
The gentlest, most unobtrusive movement in the world.
I cannot speak to you of the poor people of all the world
But among the people in these nearest slums I know
This infinitesimal twinkling, this delicate play
Of tiny signs that not only say more
Than all speech, but all there is to say,
All there is to say and to know and to be.
There alone I seldom find anything else,
Each in himself or herself a dramatic whole,
An 'agon' whose validity is timeless.
Our duty is to free that water, to make these gestures,

To help humanity to shed all else,
All that stands between any life and the sun,
The quintessence of any life and the sun;
To still all sound save that talking to God . . .

Widdershins

Ellie McDonald

Our mither tongue wis dung doun
in Scotland bi John Knox.

Juist tae mak shair
it bided yirdit

the weans got thir licks
frae the dominie

for yasin the auld leid
but it niver dee'd, though

a hantle o fowk hae trochit
thir tongue for a pig in a poke

an a sicht mair ken nocht
but a puckle o words.

Nou, the makars scrieve
translations aneath thir poems

sae that edicatit fowk
can jalouse thir implications.

Uncle

Ellie McDonald

Sam was a family embarrassment
in down-at-the-heel shoes and muffler,
exuding a delicate aroma of fish and chips.
His infrequent visits were I suspect

vaguely connected with cash and the failure
of yet another certainty at Newbury,
but to me they were something close
to magic – for who else could find

an ace of hearts behind my ear, or build
a house of cards that never fell?
No-one else's uncle had ever held
a whole platoon of Germans in a trench

at Passchendaele, nor played the concertina
for the Kaiser. Once he let me hold his medals,
two bronze and one silver hung from coloured
ribbon on a long gold clasp.

They too belonged to the magic time.

When he died, they scattered his ashes
from the window of an overnight sleeper
as it pounded across the Tay Bridge.
His final suspension of disbelief.

Mercy o' Gode

Pittendrigh Macgillivray

I

Twa bodachs, I mind, had a threep ae day,
Aboot man's chief end –
Aboot man's chief end.
Whan the t'ane lookit sweet his words war sour,
Whan the tither leuch out his words gied a clour,
But whilk got the better I wasna sure –
I wasna sure,
An' needna say.

II

But I mind them well for a queer-like pair –
A gangrel kind,
A gangrel kind:
The heid o' the ane was beld as an egg,
The ither, puir man, had a timmer leg,
An' baith for the bite could dae nocht but beg
Nocht but beg –
Or live on air!

III

On a table-stane in the auld Kirkyaird,
They ca' 'The Houff',
They ca' 'The Houff',
They sat in their rags like wearyfu' craws,
An' fankl't themsel's about a 'FIRST CAUSE',
An' the job the Lord had made o' His laws,
Made o' His laws,
In human regaird.

IV

Twa broken auld men wi' little but jaw –
Faur better awa
Aye – better awa;
Yawmerin' owr things that nane can tell,
The yin for a Heaven, the ither for Hell;
Wi' nae mair in tune than a crackit bell –
A crackit bell,
Atween the twa.

V

Dour badly he barkit in praise o' the Lord –
'The pooer o' Gode
An' the wull o' Gode';
But Stumpie believ't nor in Gode nor man –
Thocht life but a fecht without ony plan,
An' the best nae mair nor a flash i' the pan –
A flash i' the pan,
In darkness smored.

VI

Twa dune men – naither bite nor bed! –
A sair-like thing –
An' unco thing.
To the Houff they cam to lay their heid
An' seek a nicht's rest wi' the sleepin' deid,
Whaur the stanes wudna grudge nor ony tak' heed
Nor ony tak' heed:
But it's ill to read.

VII

They may hae been bitter, an' dour, an' warsh,
But wha could blame –
Aye – wha could blame?
I kent bi their look they war no' that bad
But jist ill dune bi an' driven half mad:
Whar there's nae touch o' kindness this life's owr sad
This life's owr sad,
An' faur owr harsh.

VII

But as nicht drave on I had needs tak' the road,
Fell gled o' ma dog –
The love o' a dog:
An' tho nane wad hae me that day at the fair,
I raither't the hill for a houff than in there,
'Neth a table-stane, on a deid man's lair –
A deid man's lair –
Mercy o' Gode.

Coorie Doon
Matt McGinn

Chorus
Coorie Doon, Coorie Doon, Coorie Doon, my darling,
Coorie Doon the day.

Lie doon, my dear, and in your ear,
To help you close your eye,
I'll sing a song, a slumber song,
A miner's lullaby.

Your daddy's doon the mine my darling
Doon in the Curlby Main,
Your daddy's howking coal my darling
For his own wee wean.

There's darkness doon the mine my darling,
Darkness, dust and damp.
But we must have oor heat, oor light,
Oor fire and oor lamp.

Your daddy coories doon my darling,
Doon in a three foot seam,
So you can coorie doon my darling,
Coorie doon and dream.

The Big Orange Whale
Matt McGinn

A big orange whale came up the Clyde,
Rifol-rifol-tittyfolay
A big orange whale came up the Clyde,
Landed in Ibrox on Saturday night,
With a rifolay-tittyfolay-rifol-rifol-tittyfolay.

This bloody big whale climbed intae the park,
Where the players were trying to train in the dark,

The bloody big whale sat doon in the goal,
An' drove all the players hauf up the pole,

They went and they wakened the manager up,
'If we cannae get training we'll no win the cup',

Said he: 'It's an answer tae all o' ma prayers',
An' he ran doon an' signed the whale up for the 'Gers,

With the whale for a goalie, they set oot tae win,
An' the other ten men just heidered them in,

They won every league an' they won every cup,
An' their average score was seventeen-up,

They were top o' the league for twenty-four years,
When the whale had to go, it left them in tears,

Tae give him the sack made them sad as could be,
Bit they'd caught him one Friday with fish for his tea,

They's been in such a hurry tae sign the whale on,
They'd forgotten tae ask him: 'Whit school are ye from?',

Now the moral no doubt you'll think is a queer yin,
Rangers won't have a whale if it's not Presbyterian.

(*Tune: They say that the women are worse than the men*)

Schoolquine
Alastair Mackie

I mind ye when your hair was straucht
a lassie like the lave,
till ae day, sudden-like, ye lookt up
oot o' blue een,
sma' white fingers roond the bowl o' your face
and I thocht syne in the blink o' an ee

your ain een tellt me whit the glees lang kent
when ye gied yoursel' at nicht
and the haill room was quait,
blate and fearfu' like the beats o' your hert,
and ye saw syne your briests burgeonin'
and your body cam hame to ye wi' a saft lowe
ye cairry still the wey ye haud your heid
and your narra' fingers crook aboot your lips.

Nae quine but queen.
I stand and watch ye gang your wey
aneth the douce airches o' your poo'er.
The loons glower at your by-gaein
tint awhile as the lowe nods.

Pieta

Alastair Mackie

Her face was thrawed.
She wisna aa come.

In her spurtle-shankit airms
the wummin held oot her first bairn.
It micht hae been a mercat day
and him for sale.
Naebody stoppit to haggle.

His life-bleed cled his briest
wi a new reid semmit.
He'd hippens for deid-claes.

Aifter the bombers cleck
and the sodgers traik thro the skau
there's an auld air starts up –
bubblin and greetin.
It's a ballant mithers sing
on their hunkers in the stour

for a bairn deid.
They kenit by hert.

It's the cauldest grue i the universe
yon skelloch.
It never waukens the deid.

Primary Teachers

Alastair Mackie

My primary teachers o the Thirties
maun aa be worm-eaten skeletons by nou.
Aa weemin they were.
    The early snaw in their hair.
They tholed impetigo, flechy heids, sickness,
and bairns that couldna pey their books –
    their fathers, were on the Broo.
And yet they did learn us, yon auld wives.
We chantit tables like bairn rhymes
to keep aff the inspector or the heidie.
And when we spelled the classroom skriechit
slatey music fae oor soap-scoured slates.
Their scuds were murder – the Lochgelly soond.
'Don't turn on the water-works' they girned.
    (They spoke English)
They kent naething o Munn and Dunning
but in their fashion they were as teuch
as gauleiters, ramrods withoot briests.
They did their TCs prood.
    I salute ye nou,
Miss Smith, Miss Tough, Miss McIvor,
steam hemmers somebody maun hae loved.

Molecatcher

Albert D. Mackie

Strampin' the bent, like the Angel o' Daith,
The mowdie-man staves by;
Alang his pad the mowdie-worps
Like sma' Assyrians lie.

And where the Angel o' Daith has been,
Yirked oot o' their yirdy hames,
Lie Sennacherib's blasted hosts
Wi' guts dung oot o' wames.

Sma' black tramorts wi' gruntles grey,
Sma' weak weemin's han's,
Sma' bead-een that wid touch ilk hert
Binnae the mowdie-man's.

Newsboy

Albert D. Mackie

I heard a puir deleerit loon
Cryan papers through the nicht
Wi deil a sowl to buy.
Me aa owre, thinks I,
Singan sangs wi aa my micht
And nane to hear a sound.

After the Snow

Rayne Mackinnon

The snow's thick froth scraped off by rain,
The pale grass surfaces again
And busking sparrows tune their toil,
Eke out a living from the soil

By crowding pavements of the sky,
Importuning passers-by;
Stiffened by a bustling breeze,
Startled by the sun, the firm fields blink
Then, gazing round the world, they link
Their eyesight to the earnest trees.
Called by the sun's alarm-clock, moles
Stand on the doorway of their holes,
Sniff the air, shiver, then draw back
Back to the soil where warmth is black;
Beeches whose leaves are withered, curled,
Offer them cut-price to the world,
Finding no interest, branches mutter,
Fling them down a puddle's gutter;
Meanwhile the burns, swollen, obese,
Shed whole tons of surplus girth,
Motors add melody to peace
And snowdrops simmer in the earth.

Bruckner

Rayne Mackinnon

A simpleton, he squeezed the vastness
Of his vision within huge orchestras
And hour-long frames, and his adagios
Cover the length and breadth of Heaven. A hundred
Chopin nocturnes could rattle around
Inside one Bruckner adagio. At one
With silence, a theme will breathe
Itself into being; the instruments
At times will separate, groping for God,
Then once more the whole orchestra will turn
Over and Man is safe. Hard, wooden
Sapless violins will edge their way
Into the soul's dryness – all is static now;
And then Man's anguish, real at any time,
Is spread throughout, yet mocked by bitter brass.
Despair, though, spends itself within the peace

Known by one ageing Austrian, who heaves
The orchestra Heavenwards, holds it there
And God is known
By a hundred straining instruments.
It fades, the vision, and the soul sinks down
Into the lower strings, yet even loss
Is tranquil now, and horns unwind a peace,
To which deep silence adds the final chord.

Scotland

Rayne Mackinnon

Green-coated elms stand placidly around
And munch the fodder of the warm damp air,
While collies chase their own animal joys.
And here the breeze begins
In this small park, slowly slips
Along two dusty streets, swirling the litter
As it goes. Then it stops and hears a girl
Singing aloud
To herself, all summer in her voice.
And in the warm white living room, the clock
Has scarce the energy to tick. The breeze
Moves on subdued, but soon it leaves behind
The stifling Glasgow streets, takes to the air.
Below it sees
Hamilton, Airdrie, Motherwell spread out,
Tired towns with dying dog-tracks, shabby parks,
And factory chimneys clotted thick with soot.
It whispers all the comfort that it can
To these forgotten towns, and then turns north,
Meets other breezes, swells into a wind.
As it passes on, fields flee its sight,
And soon it reaches Perth, a city where
Small knocks and knuckles of hill are all as warm
With spruces. There it goes slack, slowed down
By simmering heat. And now the clouds take on
The colour of dull metal. Somewhere it seems,

A storm is sniffing slowly round, unlike
The spring, where busy skies grind out a few
Hard raindrops. All is motionless. But now
The wind takes heart and clips the hardness off
The heat, moves on above small farms sunk deep
In summer's peace.
Then it sees rivers melt into the sea.
The wind awash with strength rejoices, moves
Beyond Man's sight,
Searching out Norway, and beyond the Steppes.

The Cuillin

Rayne Mackinnon

When bitter passion stirred the earth,
The Cuillin first knew pangs of birth,
Tugging each way inside earth's womb,
Cracked the soil, gasped for room,
Shook off the heather and the grass
Then froze in an ungainly mass;
The lava took thought, bided its time
And then once more began to climb
Till earth had no more soot to spew;
Then in the vacuum, winds rushed back,
Sucked by the mountains' magnet, blew
And, hard as iron, filed away
The gabbro, that each storm sung black,
Until the peaks, in man's own day,
Gaptoothed, lie growling at the sky.
Thickening the darkness, I've seen them lean
Over the glen, and stamp the scene
With anger, while the hissing wind
Blows night around, and chases it
From peak to peak, until the light,
With grey fingers, gropes to find
Stray corners of the sullen range
whose iron passions never change.

Island Rose

Hamish MacLaren

She has given all her beauty to the water;
She has told her secrets to the tidal bell;
And her hair is a moon-drawn net, and it has caught her,
And her voice is in the hollow shell.

She will not come back any more now, nor waken
Out of her island dream where no wind blows:
And only in the small house of the shell, forsaken,
Sings the dark one whose face is a rose.

Rams

Alasdair Maclean

Their horns are pure baroque,
as thick at the root as a man's wrist.
They have golden eyes and roman noses.
All the ewes love them.

They are well equipped to love back.
In their prime, they balance;
the sex at one end of their bodies
equalling the right to use it at the other.

When two of them come face to face,
in the mating season,
a spark jumps the gap.
Their heads drive forward like cannon balls.
Solid granite hills splinter into echoes.
They never wrestle, as stags and bulls do.
They slug it out. The hardest puncher wins.
Sometimes they back up so far for a blow
they lose sight of one another
and just start grazing.

They are infinitely and indefatigably stupid.
You can rescue the same one
from the same bramble bush
fifty times.
Such a massive casing to guard a tiny brain!
As if Fort Knox were built to house a single penny.
But year by year those horns add growth.
The sex is outstripped in the end;
the balance tilts in the direction of the head.
I found a ram dead once.
It was trapped by the forefeet
in the dark water of a peatbog,
drowned before help could arrive
by the sheer weight of its skull.
Maiden ewes were grazing near it,
immune to its clangorous lust.
It knelt on the bank, hunched over its own image,
its great head buried in the great head facing it.
Its horns, going forward in the old way,
had battered through at last to the other side.

Question and Answer

Alasdair Maclean

'Do you love me? Do you love me?'
You keep on repeating the question.
'Say you love me. I want to hear you say it.'
I say that once, when I was very young,
I saw a rat caught in a trap,
in a wire cage, squealing and snapping.
The cage was lowered into a tank of water.
I watched the stream of bubbles
slacken and at long last cease,
and when the cage was raised to the surface
the dead rat clung to the roof,
its jaws so firmly clamped around the wire
they had to be chiselled free.
But all this I say to myself;

to you I mouth, sullenly but truthfully,
the words you want to hear.
Satisfied then, you turn your back for sleep
and I lie awake, feeling the taste of the wire
between my teeth, feeling, in the darkness,
the cold water flow over me.

After Culloden

Alasdair Maclean

When the rains came, it was cold at night
but worse in morning, sun spying out
behind the hills, and our damp plaids
sending chills through our bodies and our memories.
Somehow, in the night, we had hoped
our dreams would rearrange events and consequences –
but every morning we were anchored
by the sea – ringed by fugitive hills.
Somewhere behind us or in front of us –
our lives were being stalked;
we talked about the past – the future
lay behind the wall of hills and sea;
we talked freely, as you find you do,
when death is stalking you.

The clenched fist and the shelled emotion
can be prised or broken open.
But when the cause is fought and lost
there is no more anger, no more cost,
you give yourself up, to the ocean.

If it didn't rain, the midges came
in swarms; as intent on our blood
it seemed, as the soldiers who
were hunting us. From every friendly house
we heard rumours and reports;
sometimes there was smoke rising,
only a hill away; sometimes an encampment

we skirted in the night –
breathing quietly on the stony paths,
not to disturb their sleep.

They called me traitor when I left them –
not to my face, but in their hearts.
But I was tired of slaughter and the burnt-out houses
and the torture; and my wife and child
were left alone and undefended.
I could not see what good it would do them or me
to add another martyrdom to history –
that no-one would remember anyway –
except my woman and my child, left fatherless,
their lives would just accuse my death,
now that the dream had disappeared,
now that the cause was lost.

I found a leaky boat, and moving with
the currents and the tide, managed to stay afloat,
until I drifted to another island shore.
Of course the soldiers found me,
travelling without a pass, and locked me up
to starve – they said – the truth from me.
I made up some tale of ailing parents;
they could pin nothing on me and reluctantly,
they let me go.

I later heard the Prince escaped by sea –
but some who sheltered him were not so lucky.
I gave thanks to whatever deity had helped him.
Years later I heard rumours
that he married the lass from Bannockburn
who nursed him in his illness
before the battle of Culloden.
And that he did not treat her well.
In the end, she left him. Time will tell
us something of the story; but it won't tell mine,
because the heroes and their sacrifices,
all the glory woven into tales of murder,
imprisonment and the burnings on the hills,
counts for very little.

In my old age, I still have my loved ones
with me. Evenings are long here,
on the islands, with no gunshot to break the silence,
no smell of burning in the air.
If I fought for anything, I tell my grandchildren,
I fought for these untroubled evenings,
the sounds of curlews breaking through the air,
the waves slapping the stones at the ocean shore.

Calbharaigh

Somhairle MacGill-Eain

Chan eil mo shùil air Calbharaigh
no air Betlehem an àigh
ach air cùil ghrod an Glaschu
far bheil an lobhadh fàis,
agus air seòmar an Dùn-éideann,
seòmar bochdainn 's cràidh,
far a bheil an naoidhean creuchdach
ri aonagraich gu bhàs.

Calvary

Sorley MacLean

My eye is not on Calvary
nor on Bethlehem the Blessed,
but on a foul-smelling backland in Glasgow,
where life rots as it grows;
and on a room in Edinburgh,
a room of poverty and pain,
where the diseased infant
writhes and wallows till death.

My Een Are Nae on Calvary
Sorley MacLean
translated by Douglas Young

My een are nae on Calvary
or the Bethlehem they praise,
but on the shitten back-lands in Glesga toun
whaur growan life decays,
and a stairheid room in an Embro land,
a chalmer o puirtith and skaith,
whaur monie a shilpet bairnikie
gaes smoorit doun til daith.

Coin is madaidhean-allaidh
Somhairle MacGill-Eain

Thar na slorruidheachd, thar a sneachda,
chì mi mo dhàin neo-dheachdte,
chì mi lorgan an spòg a' breacadh
gile shuaimhneach an t-sneachda;
calg air bhoile, teanga fala,
gadhair chaola's madaidhean-allaidh
a' leum thar mullaichean nan gàradh
a' ruith fo sgàil nan craobhan fàsail
ag gabhail cumhang nan caol-ghleann
a' sireadh caisead nan gaoth-bheann;
an langan gallanach a' sianail
thar loman cruaidhe nan àm cianail,
an comhartaich bhiothbhuan na mo chluasan
an deann-ruith ag gabhail mo bhuadhan:
réis nam madadh 's nan con iargalt
luath air tòrachd an fhiadhaich
troimh na coilltean gun fhiaradh,
that mullaichean nam beann gun shiaradh;
coin chiùine caothaich na bàrdachd,

madaidhean air tòir na h-àilleachd,
àilleachd an anama 's an aodainn,
fiadh geal thar bheann is raointean,
fiadh do bhòidhche ciùine gaolaich,
fiadhach gun sgur gun fhaochadh.

Dogs and Wolves

Sorley MacLean

Across eternity, across its snows
I see my unwritten poems,
I see the spoor of their paws dappling
the untroubled whiteness of the snow:
bristles raging, bloody-tongued,
lean greyhounds and wolves
leaping over the tops of the dykes,
running under the shade of the trees of the wilderness
taking the defile of narrow glens,
making for the steepness of windy mountains;
their baying yell shrieking
across the hard barenesses of the terrible times,
their everlasting barking in my ears,
their onrush seizing my mind:
career of wolves and eerie dogs
swift in pursuit of the quarry,
through the forests without veering,
over the mountain tops without sheering;
the mild mad dogs of poetry,
wolves in chase of beauty,
beauty of soul and face,
a white deer over hills and plains,
the deer of your gentle beloved beauty,
a hunt without halt, without respite.

Tràighean
Somhairle MacGill-Eain

Nan robh sinn an Talasgar air an tràigh
far a bheil am beul mòr bàn
a' fosgladh eadar dà ghiall chruaidh,
Rubha nan Clach 's am Bioda Ruadh,
sheasainn-sa ri taobh na mara
ag ùrachadh gaoil nam anam
fhad 's a bhiodh an cuan a' lìonadh
camas Thalasgair gu sìorraidh:
sheasainn an siud air lom na tràghad
gu 'n cromadh Preiseal a cheann àigich.

Agus nan robh sinn cuideachd
air tràigh Chalgaraidh am Muile,
eadar Albar is Tiriodh,
eadar an saoghal 's a' bhiothbhuan,
dh'fhuirichinn an siud gu luan
a' tomhas gainmhich bruan air bhruain.
Agus an Uidhist air tràigh Hòmhstaidh
fa chomhair farsaingeachd na h-ònrachd,
dh'fheithinn-sa an siud gu sìorraidh,
braon air bhraon an cuan a' sìoladh.

Agus nan robh mi air tràigh Mhùideart
còmhla riut, a nodhachd ùidhe,
chuirinn suas an co-chur gaoil dhut
an cuan 's a' ghaineamh, bruan air bhraon dhiubh.
'S nan robh sinn air Mol Steinnseil Stamhain
's an fhàirge neo-aoibhneach a' tarraing
nan ulbhag is gan tilgeil tharainn,
thogainn-sa am balla daingeann
ro shìorraidheachd choimhich 's i framhach.

Shores

Sorley MacLean

translated by Iain Crichton Smith

If we were in Talisker on the shore
where the great white foaming mouth of water
opens between two jaws as hard as flint –
the Headland of Stones and the Red Point –
I'd stand forever by the waves
renewing love out of their crumpling graves
as long as the sea would be going over
the Bay of Talisker forever;
I would stand there by the filling tide
till Preshal bowed his stallion head.

And if the two of us were together
on the shores of Calgary in Mull
between Scotland and Tiree,
between this world and eternity,
I'd stand there till time was done
counting the sands grain by grain.
And also on Uist, on Hosta's shore,
in the face of solitude's fierce stare,
I'd remain standing, without sleep,
while sea were ebbing, drop by drop.

And if I were on Moidart's shore
with you, my novelty of desire,
I'd offer this synthesis of love,
grain and water, sand and wave.
And were we by the shelves of Staffin
where the huge joyless sea is coughing
stones and boulders from its throat,
I'd build a fortified wall
against eternity's savage howl.

Hallaig
Somhairle MacGill-Eain

'Tha tìm, am fiadh, an coille Hallaig'

Tha bùird is tàirnean air an uinneig
troimh 'm faca mi an Aird an Iar
's tha mo ghaol aig Allt Hallaig
'na craoibh bheithe, 's bha i riamh

eadar an t-Inbhir 's Poll a' Bhainne,
thall 's a bhos mu Bhaile-Chùirn:
tha i 'na beithe, 'na calltuinn,
'na caorunn dhìreach sheang ùir.

Ann an Screapadal mo chinnidh,
far robh Tarmad 's Eachunn Mór,
tha 'n nigheanan 's am mic 'nan coille
ag gabhail suas ri taobh an lóin.

Uaibhreach a nochd na coilich ghiuthais
ag gairm air mullach Cnoc an Rà,
dìreach an druim ris a' ghealaich –
chan iadsan coille mo ghràidh.

Fuirichidh mi ris a' bheithe
gus an tig i mach an Càrn,
gus am bi am bearradh uile
o Bheinn na Lice f' a sgàil.

Mura tig 's ann theàrnas mi a Hallaig
a dh' ionnsaigh sàbaid nam marbh,
far a bheil an sluagh a' tathaich,
gach aon ghinealach a dh' fhalbh.

Tha iad fhathast ann a Hallaig,
Clann Ghill-Eain's Clann MhicLeòid,
na bh' ann ri linn Mhic Ghille-Chaluim:
chunnacas na mairbh beò.

Na fir 'nan laighe air an lianaig
aig ceann gach taighe a bh' ann,
na h-igheanan 'nan coille bheithe,
dìreach an druim, crom an ceann.

Eadar an Leac is na Feàrnaibh
tha 'n rathad mór fo chòinnich chiùin,
's na h-igheanan 'nam badan sàmhach
a' dol a Chlachan mar o thùs.

Agus a' tilleadh as a' Chlachan,
á Suidhisnis 's á tir nam beò;
a chuile té òg uallach
gun bhristeadh cridhe an sgeòil.

O Allt na Feàrnaibh gus an fhaoilinn
tha soilleir an dìomhaireachd nam beann
chan eil ach coimhthional nan nighean
ag cumail na coiseachd gun cheann.

A' tilleadh a Hallaig anns an fheasgar,
anns a' chamhanaich bhalbh bheò,
a' lìonadh nan leathadan casa,
an gàireachdaich 'nam chluais 'na ceò,

's am bòidhche 'na sgleò air mo chridhe
mun tig an ciaradh air na caoil,
's nuair theàrnas grian air cùl Dhùn Cana
thig peileir dian á gunna Ghaoil;

's buailear am fiadh a tha 'na thuaineal
a' snòtach nan làraichean feòir;
thig reothadh air a shùil 'sa' choille:
chan fhaighear lorg air fhuil ri m' bheò.

Hallaig

Time, the deer, is in the wood of Hallaig

Sorley MacLean

The window is nailed and boarded
through which I saw the West
and my love is at the Burn of Hallaig,
a birch tree, and she has always been

between Inver and Milk Hollow,
here and there about Baile-chuirn:
she is a birch, a hazel,
a straight slender young rowan.

In Screapadal of my people
where Norman and Big Hector were,
their daughters and their sons are a wood
going up beside the stream.

Proud tonight the pine cocks
crowing on the top of Cnoc an Rà
straight their backs in the moonlight –
they are not the wood I love.

I will wait for the birch wood
until it comes up by the cairn,
until the whole ridge from Beinn na Lice
will be under its shade.

If it does not, I will go down to Hallaig,
to the Sabbath of the dead,
where the people are frequenting,
every single generation gone.

They are still in Hallaig,
MacLeans and MacLeods,
all who were there in the time of Mac Gille Chaluim:
the dead have been seen alive.

The men lying on the green
at the end of every house that was,
the girls a wood of birches,
straight their backs, bent their heads.

Between the Leac and Fearns
the road is under mild moss
and the girls in silent bands
go to Clachan as in the beginning,

and return from Clachan
from Suisnish and the land of the living;
each one young and light-stepping,
without the heartbreak of the tale.

From the Burn of Fearns to the raised beach
that is clear in the mystery of the hills,
there is only the congregation of the girls
keeping up the endless walk,

coming back to Hallaig in the evening,
in the dumb living twilight,
filling the steep slopes,
their laughter a mist in my ears,

and their beauty a film on my heart
before the dimness comes on the kyles,
and when the sun goes down behind Dun Cana
a vehement bullet will come from the gun of Love;

and will strike the deer that goes dizzily,
sniffing at the grass-grown ruined homes;
his eyes will freeze in the wood,
his blood will not be traced while I live.

Lìonmhorachd anns na speuran
Somhairle MacGill-Eain

Lìonmhorachd anns na speuran,
òr-chriathar muillionan de reultan,
fuar, fad as, lòghmhor, àlainn,
tosdach, neo-fhaireachdail, neo-fhàilteach.

Lànachd an eòlais m' an cùrsa,
failmhe an aineolais gun iùl-chairt,
cruinne-cè a' gluasad sàmhach,
aigne leatha fhèin san àrainn.

Chan iadsan a ghluais mo smaointean,
chan e mìorbhail an iomchair aognaidh,
chan eil a' mhìorbhail ach an gaol duinn,
soillse cruinne an lasadh t' aodainn.

Tumultuous Plenty in the Heavens
Sorley MacLean
translated by Iain Crichton Smith

Tumultuous plenty in the heavens,
gold-sieve of a million stars,
cold, distant, blazing, splendid,
silent and callous in their course.

Fullness of knowledge in their going,
an empty, chartless, ignorant plain.
A universe in soundless motion.
A brooding intellect alone.

It was not they who woke my thinking.
It was not the miracle of their grave
fearful procession, but your face,
a naked universe of love.

Sang
Robert McLellan

There's a reid lowe in yer cheek,
Mither, and a licht in yer ee,
And ye sing like the shuilfie in the slae,
But no for me.

The man that cam the day,
Mither, that ye ran to meet,
He drapt his gun and fondlet ye
And I was left to greit.

Ye served him kail frae the pat,
Mither, and meat frae the bane.
Ye brocht him cherries frae the gean,
And I gat haurdly ane.

And nou he lies in yer bed,
Mither, and the licht growes dim,
And the sang ye sing as ye hap me ower
Is meant for him.

Shakespeare No More
Anne MacLeod

Macbeth was never Thane of Cawdor.
Shakespeare was wrong, and yet the wood endures,
a pale cathedral, shining in the sun,
washed clean and pure.

There is no murder here, nor ever was
except the land now shattered by the gorge
burn-bruised and torn, blistered with snow-drops
pricked with holly and tourists' laughter.
The Scottish play is based on lies.
There was no murder foul, nor falsity

but battle-courage and maternal line;
Macbeth's wife had the stronger claim.
Why has she lost all public sympathy
forever banished in consumer hands
to bleak detergent fears – out, out damned spot?
She would have made a killing nowadays
floating amid the elegaic trees
beech-stained, an Ariel of the modern age,
bolder than many, branded best or worst.
Gruoch by name and nature, Boece wrote,
inventing gruesome facts to flesh the tale
ignoring southern politics; and to the end
he blames the wife, exonerates the male
the Mormaer who ruled honestly and well
with Gruoch, rightful Queen of Scotland.

Queenship has never been a sinecure.
Take Mary; impulsive, tolerant and brave
she could have won Miss World, or been Eurhythmic.
The price was wrong. She came unstuck, not down.
Misunderstood and always under-rated
(they never had the poll-tax in those days)
too beautiful, too young, she was pole-axed
wasted by Calvin and the Scottish male.
Confused, conditioned and contaminated
she tried to break the geis laid upon her
– It cam wi' a lass, and it'll pass wi' a lass
her father's words.

She died to prove they weren't meant for her.
There was no sister-feeling, intuition
Elizabeth allowed her execution
spotting an erstwhile virgin reputation
with blood that will not wash, even in Cawdor
while Mary shines as white as Cairngorm snow
fresh on the summit in the heart of spring
poised for the avalanche.

Though Scottish history is always tragic
even from tears, fresh hope will grow
wholesome and free, polyunsaturated

as Flora, who braved prison-ships and death
to help a prince who did not write to thank her.
The public did. She'd brightened up their lives
(just like a dose of Lawley did for Wogan)
adding that necessary female touch
to a sad, misdirected revolution
that ended in the death-masque of Culloden
and dies there still.
The clans were crushed, their way of life deleted
all for a few sweet songs by Rabbie Burns
and Flora, fresh with courage, emigrated
to fight a losing battle in the States
returning home to die, queen of our hearts
queen of puddings:
we cannot rise above it, yet we must.
She was not saccharine, but made from girders
no iron lady, but an iron brew
a bitter sweet that courses through the veins
a vision independent and dependable
at once good for the heart, and for the reputation
white-washed, slightly rusty at the edges.
We see her elevated by the years
above the young pretender, who dissolves
into a slurry of hard drink and mountains
till he was shipped to France and lost the mountains,
Monroes no more, nor any other clan.

And so the clans were brushed into the sea
to farm the shores and harvest kelp and sorrow
the caschrom, not the plough to till the stones
this was no land for people, only lairds.
Two women, among others, changed the highlands
fashioned a country fit for Harry Lauder
and timeshares, but for very little else:
Victoria, hiding in Balmoral heights
and Sutherland, who did not have the gaelic
to understand the suffering of her people
and thought the clearances were beneficial
leaving the land more profitable, empty
except for sheep. 'A braw bricht moonlicht nicht?'
Aye, right enough.

They did not look beyond their castle doors
but sat in towers like Ulysses' widow
spinning time, ever weaving and unpicking
they did not think, they did not see, or ask
and yet we do not censure them as harshly
as Shakespeare slated Gruoch, though the land
lies empty, ruined, fit for deer and tourists
who wonder at the 'natural' solitude
see plots of special scientific interest
not murdered land where hearts and people bled.

Shakespeare was wrong, and yet his word endures,
tossed lightly through the land, blind faith unchallenged
as slick as TV advertising slogans
as slick as any party-smart campaign
– out, out damned spot – poor Grouch's name is mud
and where there's mud, there's brass, brass-neck, no doubt
or fire.

But set the wood alight, rethink the claims
of history as it rises in the gorge
and spills beyond the banks of truth and reason
distorts perception, carries all before it
leaving no time to seek a proper balance
between the past and present prejudices.

This is not Camelot, and not Culloden
this is not Fotheringay, this wood is Cawdor
where Gruoch did not live, nor yet Macbeth.
Spring creeps through the yearning trees
a grey-green shadow on the smaller boughs
snowdrops bloomed and died two months ago.
Now bluebells struggle through the coarser grass
and now and then a violet or primrose
shines beneath our feet, but all in vain;
our eyes fly upwards to the towering trees
we grow with them, we must, burn-bruised and torn
like Flora, Mary, Gruoch, we must rise –
and if we fall, we fall.

Persephone's Daughter
Anne MacLeod

My mother never gave me pomegranates,
did not buy them, would not have them in the house
and little wonder. Were not they

the source of her undoing
deep in the underground?
Had she not tasted seven pomegranate seeds

she would have escaped, emerging fresh
from Piccadilly, sweet as violets
to Eros' tender flight.

My mother never brought me pomegranates
and I endured the lack impatiently:
misunderstanding what she did not say

till I too tasted darkly and the fruit
tinctured my flesh;
no longer free, I roam

half the year dead, endure
my black love's lust
desiring more

Leaving Scotland by Train
Hugh McMillan

It's not easy.
Near Perth there's a conspiracy
of gravity and guilt
that propels me forward in my seat
to squint at my motherland
from a foetal position,
my nose snorkelling through the coffee
and the world whirling backwards,

disappearing gaily down some Scottish plughole,
an Omphalos near Denny
where the land is conjured back
with all the sheep and the seagulls and the trees
still buttoned on it,
and broken down to formless green.

I daren't open my eyes
in case it's really done the trick
and I'm bobbing like a peeled lychee
in the gynaecological soup,
a heart pulsing in my ear
and a gentle voice saying:
'Where do you think you're going, you bastard?
Stay here. Where it's warm.'

The X Files: Bonnybridge, October '95
Hugh McMillan

Lorrayne
before you hit me with that object
shaped like a toblerone
let me explain.
We only went for a half pint and a whisky
then set off home but somehow
lost two hours on a thirty minute journey.
My mind's a blank
but Brian clearly saw
Aliens with black eyes and no lips
leading us onto a kind of craft.
I tried to lash out, explain that I was late,
but they used some kind of numbing ray on me:
it put me in this state.
Lorrayne, don't you see what it explains?
All the times I crawled home with odd abrasions.
Put that down Lorrayne,
don't you see I *have* to go again,
for the sake of future generations.

Oor Hamlet

To the tune of 'The Mason's Apron'

Adam McNaughtan

There was this king sitting in his gairden a' alane,
When his brither in his ear poured a wee tate o' henbane.
Then he stole his brither's crown an' his money an' his widow,
But the deid king walked an' goat his son an' said, 'Hey, listen,
   kiddo,
Ah've been kilt an' it's your duty to take revenge on Claudius,
Kill him quick an' clean an' show the nation whit a fraud he is.'
The boay says, 'Right, Ah'll dae it but Ah'll need to play it crafty –
So that naeb'dy will suspect me, Ah'll kid oan that Ah'm a dafty.'

So wi' a' excep' Horatio – an' he trusts him as a friend –
Hamlet, that's the boay, kids oan he's roon' the bend,
An' because he wisnae ready for obligatory killin',
He tried to make the king think he was tuppence aff the shillin'.
Took the mickey oot Polonius, treatit poor Ophelia vile,
Tellt Rosencrantz an' Guildenstern that Denmark was a jile.
Then a troupe o' travellin' actors like 7.84
Arrived to dae a special wan-night gig in Elsinore

Hamlet! Hamlet! Loved his mammy!
Hamlet! Hamlet! Acting balmy!
Hamlet! Hamlet! Hesitatin',
Wonders if the ghost's a cheat
An' that is how he's waitin'.

Then Hamlet wrote a scene for the players to enact
While Horatio an' him wad watch to see if Claudius cracked.
The play was ca'd 'The Moosetrap' – no the wan that's runnin' noo –
An' sure enough the king walked oot afore the scene was through.
So Hamlet's goat the proof that Claudius gi'ed his da the dose,
The only problem being noo that Claudius knows he knows.
So while Hamlet tells his ma that her new husband's no a fit wan,
Uncle Claud pits oot a contract wi' the English king as hit-man.

Then when Hamlet kilt Polonius, the concealed corpus delecti
Was the king's excuse to send him for an English hempen neck-tie,
Wi' Rosencrantz an' Guildenstern to make sure he goat there,
But Hamlet jumped the boat an' pit the finger oan that pair.
Meanwhile Laertes heard his da had been stabbed through the
　　arras.
He came racin' back to Elsinore tout suite, hot-foot fae Paris,
An' Ophelia wi' her da kilt by the man she wished to marry –
Eftir sayin' it wi' flooers, she committit hari-kari.

Hamlet! Hamlet! Nae messin'!
Hamlet! Hamlet! Learnt his lesson!
Hamlet! Hamlet! Yorick's crust
Convinced him that men, good or bad,
At last must come to dust.

Then Laertes loast the place an' was demandin' retribution,
An' the king says, 'Keep the heid an' Ah'll provide ye a solution.'
He arranged a sword-fight for the interestit pairties,
Wi' a bluntit sword for Hamlet an' a shairp sword for Laertes.
An' to make things double sure (the auld belt-an'-braces line)
He fixed a poisont sword-tip an' a poisont cup o' wine.
The poisont sword goat Hamlet but Laertes went an' muffed it,
'Cause he goat stabbed hissel' an' he confessed afore he snuffed it.

Hamlet's mammy drank the wine an' as her face turnt blue,
Hamlet says, 'Ah quite believe the king's a baddy noo.'
'Incestuous, treacherous, damned Dane,' he said, to be precise,
An' made up for hesitatin' by killin' Claudius twice.
'Cause he stabbed him wi' the sword an' forced the wine atween
　　his lips.
Then he cried, 'The rest is silence!' That was Hamlet hud his chips.
They firet a volley ower him that shook the topmaist rafter,
An' Fortinbras, knee-deep in Danes, lived happy ever after.

Hamlet! Hamlet! Aw the gory!
Hamlet! Hamlet! End of story!
Hamlet! Hamlet! Ah'm away!
If you think this is borin',
Ye should read the bloody play!

The Jeelie Piece Song
Adam McNaughtan

Ah'm a skyscraper wean, Ah live on the nineteenth flair,
But Ah'm no gaun oot to play any mair,
'Cause since we moved to Castlemilk Ah'm wastin' away,
'Cause Ah'm gettin' wan less meal every day.

> *Oh ye cannae fling pieces oot a twinty-storey flat.*
> *Seven hundred hungry weans'll testify to that.*
> *If it's butter, cheese or jeelie, if the breid is plain or pan,*
> *The odds against it reachin' earth are ninety-nine to wan.*

On the first day ma maw flung oot a daud o Hovis broon;
It cam skytin' oot the windae and went up instead o doon.
Noo every twinty-seven 'oors it comes back intae sight,
'Cause ma piece went intae orbit an' became a satellite.

On the next day ma maw flung me a piece oot wance again.
It went an' hut the pilot in a fast, low-flying plane.
He scraped it aff his goggles, shouting through the intercom,
'The Clydeside Reds've goat me wi' a breid-an'-jeelie bomb.'

On the third day ma maw thought she would try anither throw.
The Salvation Army baun' was staunin' doon below.
'Onward, Christian Soldiers' was the piece they should've played
But the oompah man was playin' a piece on marmalade.

We've wrote away to Oxfam to try an' get some aid,
An' a' the weans in Castlemilk've formed a 'piece brigade'.
We're gonnae march to George's Square demandin' civil rights,
Like nae mair hooses ower piece-flinging height.

Oideachadh ceart

Aonghas MacNeacail

nuair a bha mi òg
cha b'eachdraidh ach cuimhne

nuair a thàinig am bàillidh, air each
air na mnathan a' tilleadh a-nuas
às na buailtean len eallaichean frainich
's a gheàrr e na ròpan on guailnean
a' sgaoileadh nan eallach gu làr,
a' dìteadh nam mnà, gun tug, iad gun chead
an luibhe dhan iarradh e sgrios,
ach gum biodh na mnathan
ga ghearradh 's ga ghiùlain gu dachaigh,
connlach stàile, gu tàmh nam bò
(is gun deachdadh e màl às)

cha b'eachdraidh ach cuimhne
long nan daoine
seòladh a-mach
tro cheathach sgeòil
mu éiginn morair
mu chruaidh-chàs morair
mun cùram dhan tuathan,
mu shaidhbhreas a' feitheamh
ceann thall na slighe,
long nan daoine
seòladh a-mach,
sgioba de chnuimheagan acrach
paisgte na clàir,
cha b'eachdraidh ach fathann

cha b'eachdraidh ach cuimhne
là na dìle, chaidh loids a' chaiptein
a sguabadh dhan tràigh
nuair a phòs sruthan rà is chonain
gun tochar a ghabhail
ach dàthaidh an sgalag
a dh'fhan 'dileas dha mhaighstir'
agus cuirp nan linn às a' chladh

cha b'eachdraidh ach cuimhne
an latha bhaist ciorstaidh am bàillidh
le mùn à poit a thug i bhon chùlaist
dhan choinneamh am bràighe nan crait
gun bhraon a dhòrtadh

cha b'eachdraidh ach cuimhne
an latha sheas gaisgich a' bhaile
bruach abhainn a' ghlinne
an aghaidh feachd ghruamach an t-siorraidh
a thàinig air mhàrsail, 's a thill gun òrdag a bhogadh,
le sanasan fuadach nan dùirn

cha b'eachdraidh ach gràmar
rob donn
uilleam ros
donnchadh bàn
mac a' mhaighstir

cha b'eachdraidh ach cuimhne
màiri mhòr, mairi mhòr
a dìtidhean ceòlar
cha b'eachdraidh ach cuimhne
na h-òrain a sheinn i
dha muinntir an cruaidh-chàs
dha muinntir an dùbhlan

agus, nuair a bha mi òg
ged a bha a' chuimhne fhathast
fo thughadh snigheach,
bha sglèat nan dearbhadh
fo fhasgadh sglèat
agus a-muigh
bha gaoth a' glaodhaich
eachdraidh nam chuimhne
eachdraidh nam chuimhne

A Proper Schooling

when i was young
it wasn't history but memory

when the factor, on horseback, came
on the women's descent from
the moorland grazings laden with bracken
he cut the ropes from their shoulders
spreading their loads to the ground,
alleging they took without permit
a weed he'd eliminate
were it not that women cut it and carried it home
for bedding to ease their cows' hard rest;
and there was rent in that weed

it wasn't history but memory
the emigrant ships
sailing out
through a fog of stories
of landlords' anguish
of landlords' distress
their concern for their tenants,
the riches waiting
beyond the voyage,
the emigrant ships
sailing out
a crew of starved maggots
wrapped in their timbers,
it wasn't history but rumour

it wasn't history but memory
the day of the flood, the captain's lodge
was swept to the shore
when the streams of rha and conon married
taking no dowry
but david the servant
who stayed 'true to his master'
and the corpses of centuries from the cemetery

it wasn't history but memory
the day kirsty baptised the factor
with piss from a pot she took from the backroom
to the meeting up in the brae of the croft
not spilling a single drop

it wasn't history but memory
the day the township's warriors stood
on the banks of the glen river
confronting the sheriff's surly troops
who marched that far, then returned without dipping a toe,
clutching their wads of eviction orders

it wasn't history but grammar
rob donn
william ross
duncan ban
alexander macdonald

it wasn't history but memory
great mary macpherson
her melodic indictments,
it wasn't history but memory
the anthems she sang
for her people distressed
for her people defiant

and when i was young
though memory remained
under a leaking thatch,
the schoolroom slate
had slates for shelter
and outside
a wind was crying
history in my memories
history in my memories

Anochd is tu bhuam

Aonghas MacNeacail

ged a bhiodh cuairt nan reul
eadar mi is tu
cha chrìon an snàth-sìoda
a chuibhich thu rium
a cheangail mi riut,
agus a-nochd is tu bhuam
tha mi san dubhar
cur bhriathran thugad
luchd mo chridhe
faclan trom dorcha gun chruth,
foghair is connrag
a' siolachadh gu ciall,
mar a tha duilleach nan craobh
a' cromadh nan geug,
anns an doilleir
san oiteag
a' mireadh an guirme
priobadh na camhanaich

Tonight You Being From Me

although the journey of the stars
were between you and me
the thread of silk will not decay
that bound you to me
that tied me to you,
and tonight you being from me
i am in darkness
sending words to you
my heart's cargo
heavy dark words without shape,
vowel and consonant
multiplying to sense,
as the foliage of trees

bends their branches,
in darkness
in the breeze
leaves sporting their green
first flicker of dawn

Looking for 78's in the '40s

Hugh Macpherson

Concerts in those days were that much longer.
People didn't hear the music quite as often.
They wanted just as much as they could get,
wanted as much as could be played
until the orchestra was weary, until
conductor and musicians had to stagger
from the stage, dizzy from making sound.

Now, so much recorded sound is heard,
the music's harder to retain.
The occasions that provided it
blur in remembrance.
But when I hear the melodies
the pictures too return again,
and I can see the London of those war-time years,

When I'd be walking from the early trains
past shattered streets and pulsing water mains
to one more weekend sifting through the record shops,
and hear behind the tunes the hiss of the acoustics
of the rooms in Prague or Warsaw or Vienna
that musicians had lit up
with spinning cross talk of their strings and woodwind.

The pipes sprayed moisture far
across the brick dust, filling streets
with symphonies of fountain sound that
smelt of rain, and sent me out in search of Liszt
and water playing at the Villa d'Este.

The owners of the shops recited names
of famed performers, of long since vanished discs,

they remembered reverentially the concerts
in the now embattled cities.
On quiet mornings, one would put on a record
of a melancholy Bach piece, played with emotion
by an exiled pianist in London studios.
Their faces would appear, sculpted with nostalgia,
at concerts in the National Gallery.

And then, the end to fighting,
ecstatic bursts of Purcell and of Handel,
trumpets and counter tenors in Whitehall,
military bands and choirs,
records from America at unexpected parties,
the smell of hot valves and technology
in listening booths where I would sit for hours.

Now the ordered lines of records hold the memories
of distant purchase, producing chains of sound
that take me late into the night,
up to the sibilance of Thomas Tallis anthems
softly echoing about the house
and then the hiss and slow repeating click
that follows from the stylus, nodding on the final disc.

Glasgow 1956

Gerald Mangan

There's always a headscarf stooped
into a pram, nodding in time
with a plastic rattle, outside a shop
advertising a sale of wallpaper.

There's a queue facing another queue
like chessmen across the street;
a hearse standing at a petrol-pump
as the chauffeur tests the tyres,

the undertaker brushes ash off
his morning paper, and my mother,
looking down at me looking up,
is telling me not to point.

The background is a level site
where we recreate the war.
Calder Street is Calder Street,
level as far as the Clyde.

Without a tree to denote it,
the season is moot. That faint
thunder is the Cathcart tram,
and the sky is white as a trousseau

posed against blackened bricks.
A grey posy in her hands,
the bride stands smiling there
for decades, waiting for the click.

Ailsa Craig

Gerald Mangan

It bulked large above my sandcastles:
a stepping-stone from a land of giants,
with a noose of surf around its neck.

One blustery sunset, turning purple,
it reared above my father's head
as he slammed outdoors from a row,

to sulk on the fuming causeway.
Geysers of spume were spouting high
as he strode down past the warning-signs,

and the last light was a hellish red
as he dwindled, stooping into the rocks,
and drowned in my streaming eyes.

He'll be right back, my mother said.
But I saw the Irish Sea overwhelm
a rage that could shake a tenement.

He'd never looked so small, and wrong.
I never knew what drove him there,
but I saw him thrashed by a stormy God,

and he never seemed so tall again.
I'd never seen him so whole, before
I saw that tombstone over his head.

Kirkintilloch Revisited

Gerald Mangan

Crying to God, 'I fear Thee no longer'
As the blackbird does, for a few fine days.
                              Dante, *Purgatory*

1

Turning their backs on the sabbath,
the miners stamp a circle
of asphalt hard on the towpath,
and pitch up coins in the snow.

The slag-heap they threw up here
is levelled to a sports-pitch.
The pit-head is rusting
like a nail in Scotland's waist

and the church ringing for mass
rises like a new leviathan
out of the shale. It spouts
new liturgies for a new estate,

but the sabbath is as it was.
The pub is a locked pillbox,
ringed with barbs, and the gamblers
swig from a wrapped bottle.

2

This ridge between the foothills
and Glasgow was the rampart
where Rome drew the line,
between history and snow.

The white of the fells
outstared the legions,
and the empire's wall is rubble.
But the stones are in the name –

a church on a fort on a hill,
where Rome came back as a dove
and gripped like winter.
Above the sandstone school,

where they taught us Pliny and the litany
and tawsed me for disbelief,
the cross on the spire is black
as a cassock against the snow.

3

The church disgorging
a mass into the car-park
clangs its tongue at the blackbird,
for reading the season wrong

and singing, out of turn:
I fear Thy wrath no longer.
A feather of white breath
flutters at every mouth,

and a raucous synod of crows,
holding court in the tree-tops,
is taking him to task.
But he sticks to his theme:

the thaw on the Forth-and-Clyde
as it winds around the foundry,
and the crocuses open-mouthed,
like nests of fledglings.

Passchendaele

In memory of John Mackenzie (1888–1917)

Angus Martin

Hae ye cam here fae Passchendaele?
Close-mooth tae stair-heid's a trail o glar.
Ye look lik a man's been deid owerlang,
still rug in a kilt for the war.

Forgie me – A'll no invite ye in.
It's no that A'm prood o the hoose
or asham't o ma granfaither, no:
it's the state o yer claes, an yer boose.

Ye'd frichten the weans if they saw ye,
an A'm tellin ye truthfully noo –
A'm jeest a bit feart o yer look, masel,
an the guff o ye gies me the grue.

Ah weel, ye willna speak, or canna.
That A'll dae, an mair, masel.
Here's ma han – Hoo ir ye, man,
an hoo ir things in Hell?

There is nae Hell? – Ye're talkin noo!
Hell's where ye went tae dee,
blawn tae smoorach bi a shill
in the blinkin o an ee.

But ye've got yer body back thegither –
it's taen ye mair as seeventy year –
an ye're lookin for yer faimily
an tryin tae gaither up yer gear.

But we divna want tae think on war;
we haena got wan on ee noo.
We're leevin weel an sweir tae feel
aucht o the blast that ruint you.

There's aye a wheen o wars gan on
aroon the warld, an aye will be;
it's jeest yer luck if ye get struck
an sunnert fae yer faimily.

There's no a wan that minds o ye
an no a wan that cares,
sae bide a ghaist an lee us be:
A'll see ye doon the stairs.

Who Among Common Men of Their Time?
Angus Martin

Who among common men of their time
could claim such freedom? They had their boats
and could catch a wind to hell and back
and spit in the storm's black eye
from a lee of their ancestry.

And money? They had it or hadn't.
The pleuter of herring or stroke of a wandering solan
in some still bight with dusk on the water
and *there* was the flurry of notes
equal in every man's hand
and a stroke of ink through every debt-line.

You could ask them the name of a rock
the shape of the ground
five fathoms under the keel,
the meaning of this or that in nature's order,
and you'd have your answer, aye,
more than you'd asked for.

The Scrimshaw Sailor

for Desmond and Trude

Gordon Meade

In the belly of a ship
On a storm-tossed sea, a sailor
Carves out the figure of a polar bear
From the jaw-bone of a whale

Delicately, with cut-
Throat razor and sail-maker's awl,
His nimble fingers etch in the pupils
Of its eyes, the talons on

Its shaggy paws. Outside,
The ocean batters at the ship's
Stout timbers as the tempest blows.
Inside the ship's dank hold,

The man becomes, himself,
A scrimshaw sculpture, fashioned
In the sea's own image by the ship's
Thrown pitch and tumbling roll.

The Great Spotted Woodpecker

Gordon Meade

With that prodigious tongue,
Wrapped round his head and anchored
In his skull, you'd think

He'd be the greatest songbird
Of them all. And yet, he cannot sing
A single word at all.

That drumming noise, we hear,
Comes not from underneath the furrows
Of his spotted brow,

But from the rapping of his
Sharpened beak upon the features
Of some dead tree's bough.

'No song?' I hear you scoff
And start to leave. 'Well yes,' I say,
'It's true his voice is very weak.'

'But who, apart from him,
With but a single blow, could make
A fallen tree rise up and speak?'

In Eyemouth Harbour

Gordon Meade

'Ariel' is a trawler,
A trawler with a full belly,
Emptying herself onto the quay.
Roped by men, her innards
Rise in air, fall on stone.

First, the King Prawns,
Shattered armour clattering,
Jet-black eyes open, reflecting
Nothing, are lifted to the dawn.

Then, the unfrocked Monks,
Grey habits ripped open, are
Laid, face down in wooden crates.
Almost saints, they are preserved
In ice from the town's factory.

Finally, the common Haddock,
Heads clubbed, eyes staring up,

Away from unzipped bodies, are
Bundled into boxes, hoisted ashore.

'Ariel' rises lighter
On the oily water. Her morning
Sickness over, she'll sleep through
A lazy afternoon, the stretchmarks
On her empty hold tightening

In the sun. Woken, hungry
By the moon, she'll carry her
Hard-faced men, back to the sea,
And back to the harbour again.

The Crucifixion Will Not Take Place
Elma Mitchell

Gentlemen of the Press,
I'm sorry to disappoint you
By calling off the whole project.
I really *wanted* to go through with it –
My individual conscience
Kept on and on at me
(It really made me sweat)
But now I admit
I was wrong about my always being right,
I was wrong about wanting
To die for you lot.
I've come to realise
I was just being selfish –
What's the *good* of sacrifice
If it makes all the rest of you
So uncomfortable?

With my unfortunate gift of second sight
(It's kept me awake all night)
I can see, very clearly,
What my crucifixion

Would do to our nation.
Look at the trouble
It would make for the Jewish people
(Might even bring down the Temple),
Consider the bother
It would raise with all that Roman law and order,
Poor old Pilate being accused of murder
(Quite a decent fellow, really –
These colonial magistrates
Do have some terrible problems
Which admit of no simple solutions
Etcetera.)

And then my disciples
(Bless their hearts) are totally unreliable
(Over-emotional)

I don't want to show *them* up – I can simply *see* them
Doing a bunk, disowning me,
Or resorting to violence – anyway,
Saying things they'd be sorry for.
No, no, it wouldn't be fair to them.
Last but not least, dear Judas
Who has always had such faith in my ability
To do something big, to come out on top, to *prove*
I was some kind of God Almighty –
No, I can't let *him* down.
Why, a type like that might do away with himself.
I wouldn't want *that* on my conscience.
And then, all the wives and families . . .
I can't help thinking what would become of Mother.
Women can't be expected
To suffer like men. Surely we have to protect them
From the consequences of *our* one-sided idealism?

Then, looking still further ahead, (as I can't help doing)
I can see my future followers
– All these unfortunate Christians,
Eaten by lions, burning alive, crusading,
Splitting hairs, misquoting me, dressing up funny, and simply
Loathing each other,
All in my name, for my sake.

No, no, it was all a mistake.
So now, my dear fellow-humans,
Now that I know what you want (and will certainly achieve
Without any help from me)
I shall leave you to your own devices.

There is no alternative.
There might have been, but
I give up
Because you didn't want the alternative.
Tough.

Enjoy while you can
All the kingdoms of the world and the glory of them.
I have withdrawn
The terms of my extra-special offer. God
Has called it a day.

Well, thank, you, gentlemen,
I hope you all make your deadlines.
This is my first and last
Press conference.
You will not be hearing from me
Nor about me
Ever again.

What was that, at the back?
No.
There are no authorised portraits
Nor acceptable images.
No Press handouts: no official biography.
I shall not be writing my memoirs in my retirement
And anything purporting to give an account of me
– My sayings, my acts and my motives –
Was done without my authority
And is probably a fraud.

Good-night. Sleep well. I shall.
Yours, still faithfully,
God.

(Yes, if you want a quiet word,
I am always there.
Come to me by night, unobtrusively,
No politics, no publicity.
If you are who I think you are
You'll know where to find me.
But, for the love of God,
Don't tell the world.)

The Death of Adam
Elma Mitchell

I saw it coming,
The cold.
It must have been coming on a long time.
Ever since I'd known him.

Not surprising, really,
With him come up from the dust
And me from the bone.

Still, it was odd,
Watching it actually happen.
Everything sags; did you know?
I didn't know.

Teeth fall out, and then the face falls in.
Skin
Withers and wrinkles and shrivels like an apple
(Yes, like an apple)
And the top of the skull
(Where the hair and the brains keep complicated house together)
Becomes
Plain, smooth, simple,
Unoccupied by anything.

And he couldn't walk at all, nor talk at all
(We had to stop arguing about whose fault it was)

And the sun made his eyes hurt
And he had to leave the world that belonged to him
And the animals he'd given a name to
And the wife that was part of him,
To become a kind of collapse,
A remnant, something remembered,
Not all there any more.

He was always first at everything
And now
The first man ever to be dead.

Perhaps, as gardeners,
We should have learned from the leaves
What it means to be deciduous.

Will it always be just like this
For the rest of us?
Or must I look forward
To a separate, feminine, suitable
Method of disappearance?
Middle-aged, but still naked
To man-stare and God-stare,
Covering myself up with my hands and my long grey hair,
Breasts falling like apples
And the small pool of darkness
Inside me
Gone dry?

Thoughts After Ruskin
Elma Mitchell

Women reminded him of lilies and roses.
Me they remind rather of blood and soap,
Armed with a warm rag, assaulting noses,
Ears, neck, mouth and all the secret places:

Armed with a sharp knife, cutting up liver,
Holding hearts to bleed under a running tap,
Gutting and stuffing, pickling and preserving,
Scalding, blanching, broiling, pulverising,
– All the terrible chemistry of their kitchens.

Their distant husbands lean across mahogany
And delicately manipulate the market,
While safe at home, the tender and the gentle
Are killing tiny mice, dead snap by the neck,
Asphyxiating flies, evicting spiders,
Scrubbing, scouring aloud, disturbing cupboards,
Committing things to dustbins, twisting, wringing,
Wrists red and knuckles white and fingers puckered,
Pulpy, tepid. Steering screaming cleaners
Around the snags of furniture, they straighten
And haul out sheets from under the incontinent
And heavy old, stoop to importunate young,
Tugging, folding, tucking, zipping, buttoning,
Spooning in food, encouraging excretion,
Mopping up vomit, stabbing cloth with needles,
Contorting wool around their knitting needles,
Creating snug and comfy on their needles.

Their huge hands! their everywhere eyes! their voices
Raised to convey across the hullabaloo,
Their massive thighs and breasts dispensing comfort,
Their bloody passages and hairy crannies,
Their wombs that pocket a man upside down!

And when all's over, off with overalls,
Quickly consulting clocks, they go upstairs,
Sit and sigh a little, brushing hair,
And somehow find, in mirrors, colours, odours,
Their essences of lilies and of roses.

To a Fisherman with the Present of a Knife

Naomi Mitchison

When you cut the bread
Remember me
Who will be far
From ship and sea,
Whose books unread,
Whose heart unread,
Are like a star,
Remote, remote,
As such things are,
Far from your boat
A polar star.

The Scottish Renaissance in Glasgow: 1935

Naomi Mitchison

This city, builded on more hills than Rome was,
With a river bigger than Tiber, tidal and foamless,
I came to in the cold of winter of a bad trade year,
I, Scottish too, with the same hunger for knowledge laden.
Somewhere in all this bareness, these squared, grey houses
Of harsh, unweathering stone, only ill thoughts rousing,
Somewhere up grim stairs,
      steep streets of fog-greased cobbles,
In harsh, empty closes with only a dog or a child sobbing,
Somewhere among unrhythmic,
      shattering noises of tram-ways
Or by cranes and dock-yards, steel clanging and slamming,
Somewhere without colour, without beauty,
      without sunlight,
Amongst this cautious people,
      some unhappy and some hungry,
There is a thing being born as it was
      born once in Florence:
So that a man, fearful, may find his mind fixed on tomorrow.

And tomorrow is strange for him, aye,
    full of tearings and breakings,
And to the very middle he feels his whole spirit shaken.
But he goes on.

The Farm Woman: 1942

Naomi Mitchison

Why the blue bruises high up on your thigh,
On your right breast and both knees?
Did you get them in the hay in a sweet smother of cries,
Did he tease you and at last please,
With all he had to show?
Oh no, oh no,
Said the farm woman:
But I bruise easy.

Why the scratched hand, was it too sharp a grip,
Buckle or badge or maybe nail,
From one coming quick from camp or ship,
Kissing as hard as hail
That pits deep the soft snow?
Oh no, oh no,
Said the farm woman:
But I bruise easy.

There was nothing, my sorrow, nothing that need be hidden,
But the heavy dung fork slipped in my hand,
I fell against the half-filled cart at the midden;
We were going out to the land.
Nobody had to know.
And so, and so,
Said the farm woman:
For I bruise easy.

The tractor is ill to start, a great heaving and jerking,
The gear lever jars through palm and bone,
But I saw in a film the Russian women working

On the land they had made their own,
And so, and so,
Said the farm woman:
And I bruise easy.

Never tell the men, they will only laugh and say
What use would a woman be!
But I read the war news through, every day;
It means my honour to me,
Making the crops to grow.
And so, and so,
Said the farm woman:
But I bruise easy.

Nettlebed Road

Naomi Mitchison

On this road, this road,
I reap what I sowed.
Suppose, now, I had been good,
I might truly have understood
And accepted the coming of age
Without a heart of rage.
And if only I had been bad
– All women wish they had –
The golden leaves would whisper yes,
That glory, that success,
One negation less.
But being half bad, half good,
– Ah, love, who thought we could –
Between a yea and a nay
Tread the classic middle way! –
What switch of taunts and jeers,
The road twists and sneers
At an old fool, an old hurt fool,
Failed in the Final School,
Nothing, oh nothing to show for all that conniving,
I must watch my driving.

Flodden

William Montgomerie

A hawk hovering over oak trees
I watch where
by footpaths and rutted road
an army moves
in a mad migration south
slow oxen pulling the great cannon

A King's red banner and the blue banners
of two saints
beyond the hills yonder
meet the bright banners of other saints
of another King
and there's civil war in Heaven

I follow the King who passed this way
who has no royal tomb
his bones thrown into
an old waste room among rubbish
his skull in another place among skulls
of other men's skeletons

They made a song of his army
whose dead were the fodder of the four horses
in the nightmare of John Surnameless

with sword and with hunger and with death
and the beasts of the earth

Epitaph

*for 2nd Officer James S. Montgomerie of the S.S. Carsbreck,
torpedoed off Gibraltar, 24th October 1941*

William Montgomerie

My brother is skull and skeleton now
empty of mind behind the brow
in ribs and pelvis empty space
bone-naked without a face

On a draughty beach drifting sand
clawed by a dry skeleton hand
sifts in the hourglass of his head
time useless to bones of the dead

King Billy

Edwin Morgan

Grey over Riddrie the clouds piled up,
dragged their rain through the cemetery trees.
The gates shone cold. Wind rose
flaring the hissing leaves, the branches
swung heavy, across the lamps.
Gravestones huddled in drizzling shadow,
flickering streetlight scanned the requiescats,
a name and an urn, a date, a dove
picked out, lost, half-regained.
What is this dripping wreath, blown from its grave
red, white, blue and gold
'To Our Leader of Thirty years Ago' –

Bareheaded, in dark suits, with flutes
and drums, they brought him here, in procession
seriously, King Billy of Brigton, dead,
from Bridgeton Cross: a memory of violence,
brooding days of empty bellies,
billiard smoke and a sour pint,

boots or fists, famous sherrickings,
the word, the scuffle, the flash, the shout,
bloody crumpling in the close,
bricks for papish windows, get
the Conks next time, the Conks ambush
the Billy Boys, the Billy Boys the Conks till
Sillitoe scuffs the razors down the stank –
No, but it isn't the violence they remember
but the legend of a violent man
born poor, gang-leader in the bad times
of idleness and boredom, lost in better days,
a bouncer in a betting club,
a quiet man at last, dying
alone in Bridgeton in a box bed.
So a thousand people stopped the traffic
for the hearse of a folk hero and the flutes
threw 'Onward Christian Soldiers' to the winds
from unironic lips, the mourners kept
in step, and there were some who wept.

Go from the grave. The shrill flutes
are silent, the march dispersed.
Deplore what is to be deplored,
and then find out the rest.

Glasgow Green
Edwin Morgan

Clammy midnight, moonless mist.
A cigarette glows and fades on a cough.
Meth-men mutter on benches,
pawed by river fog. Monteith Row
sweats coldly, crumbles, dies
slowly. All shadows are alive.
Somewhere a shout's forced out – 'No!' –
it leads to nothing but silence,
except the whisper of the grass
and the other whispers that fill the shadows.

'What d'ye mean see me again?
D'ye think I came here jist for that?
I'm no finished with you yet.
I can get the boys t'ye, they're no that faur away.
You wouldny like that eh? Look there's no two ways aboot it.
Christ but I'm gaun to have you Mac
if it takes all night, turn over you bastard
turn over, I'll – '
  Cut the scene.
Here there's no crying for help,
it must be acted out, again, again.

This is not the delicate nightmare
you carry to the point of fear
and wake from, it is life, the sweat
is real, the wrestling under a bush
is real, the dirty starless river
is the real Clyde, with a dishrag dawn
it rinses the horrors of the night
but cannot make them clean,
though washing blows
   where the women watch
by day,
  and children run,
    on Glasgow Green.

And how shall these men live?
Providence, watch them go!
Watch them love, and watch them die!
How shall the race be served?
It shall be served by anguish
as well as by children at play.
It shall be served by loneliness
as well as by family love.

It shall be served by hunter and hunted in their endless chain
as well as by those who turn back the sheets in peace.
The thorn in the flesh!
Providence, water it!
Do you think it is not watered?
Do you think it is not planted?

Do you think there is not a seed of the thorn
as there is also a harvest of the thorn?
Man, take in that harvest!
Help that tree to bear its fruit!
Water the wilderness, walk there, reclaim it!
Reclaim, regain, renew! Fill the barns and the vats!

Longing,
      longing
                  shall find its wine

Let the women sit in the Green
and rock their prams as the sheets
blow and whip in the sunlight.
But the beds of married love
are islands in a sea of desire.
Its waves break here, in this park,
splashing the flesh as it trembles
like driftwood through the dark.

Strawberries

Edwin Morgan

There were never strawberries
like the ones we had
that sultry afternoon
sitting on the step
of the open french window
facing each other
your knees held in mine
the blue plates in our laps
the strawberries glistening
in the hot sunlight
we dipped them in sugar
looking at each other
not hurrying the feast
for one to come
the empty plates
laid on the stone together

with the two forks crossed
and I bent towards you
sweet in that air
in my arms
abandoned like a child
from your eager mouth
the taste of strawberries
in my memory
lean back again
let me love you

let the sun beat
on our forgetfulness
one hour of all
the heat intense
and summer lightning
on the Kilpatrick hills

let the storm wash the plates

The First Men on Mercury

Edwin Morgan

– We come in peace from the third planet.
Would you take us to your leader?

– Bawr stretter! Bawr. Bawr. Stretterhawl?

– This little plastic model
of the solar system, with working parts.
You are here and we are there and we
are now here with you, is that clear?

– Gawl horrop. Bawr. Abawrhannahanna!

– Where we come from is blue and white
with brown, you see we call the brown
here 'land', the blue is 'sea', and the white
is 'clouds' over land and sea, we live

on the surface of the brown land,
all round is sea and clouds. We are 'men'.
Men come –

– Glawp men! Gawrbenner menko. Menhawl?

– Men come in peace from the third planet
which we call 'earth'. We are earthmen.
Take us earthmen to your leader.

– Thmen? Thmen? Bawr. Bawrhossop.
Yuleeda tan hanna. Harrabost yuleeda.

– I am the yuleeda. You see my hands,
we carry no benner, we come in peace.
The spaceways are all stretterhawn.

– Glawn peacemen all horrabhanna tantko!
Tan come at'mstrossop. Glawp yuleeda!

– Atoms are peacegawl in our harraban.
Menbat worrabost from tan hannahanna.

– You men we know bawrhossoptant. Bawr.
We know yuleeda. Go strawg backspetter quick.

– We cantantabawr, tantingko backspetter now!

– Banghapper now! Yes, third planet back.
Yuleeda will go back blue, white, brown
nowhanna! There is no more talk.

– Gawl han fasthapper?

– No. You must go back to your planet.
Go back in peace, take what you have gained
but quickly.

– Stretterworra gawl, gawl . . .

– Of course, but nothing is ever the same,
now is it? You'll remember Mercury.

To a Shy Girl at a Party
Ken Morrice

You stand hoping that reticence will pass
for composure, uncomfortably on the edge
of things, feigning poise, fumbling with glass,
cigarette and canapé, fearing the exposure
of silence, the embarrassment of talk,
uncertain what is better –
to be noticed or to be ignored.

Once again you find yourself in baulk,
lonely, ridiculous, forgotten,
and wondering why you ever came.

I wish I could remember your name.

Crossing the Alps
Ken Morrice

Bold Hannibal himself force-marched beneath
these awesome peaks, his tireless army softening
rocks with vinegar and fire. To sight
a line of elephants now would be quite apt,
for here I sit, perched in a crowded howdah,
swaying between these towers of snow and ice.

But I campaign at ease. Fortified with gin,
plying plastic chicken with plastic fork and knife,
I nibble cheese and After Eights. Around me
no-one else seems suitably impressed. More
seasoned travellers perhaps, or hungrier than I.

The plane ascends. In my gin, as in the sky
beneath, the ice-caps melt, Lumbering hugely
the Jumbo mounts his monstrous stride
to take an airier sybaritic path to Rome.

Voyager

Ken Morrice

When at last the prow crunches on sand
and he leaps eagerly down and away
salt-lipped to Penelope,
is she still softly at her sewing,
needle pricking off her suitors?

Through weary days, restless dragging
years of absence – the lack, the yearning
of endless nights – has she succumbed
white neck to others' hot caresses?
Or does she laugh, showing sweet curve of breast,
coy still behind the tapestry, pink tongue
between her teeth, darting, teasing?

Or so prim a princess is she –
her virtuous bed as chaste as marble –
that he regrets escape from Circe
and finds return less welcome
than the hard deck and pitching sea?

Scotland 1941

Edwin Muir

We were a tribe, a family, a people.
Wallace and Bruce guard now a painted field,
And all may read the folio of our fable,
Peruse the sword, the sceptre and the shield.
A simple sky roofed in that rustic day,
The busy corn-fields and the haunted holms,
The green road winding up the ferny brae.
But Knox and Melville clapped their preaching palms
And bundled all the harvesters away,
Hoodicrow Peden in the blighted corn

Hacked with his rusty beak the starving haulms.
Out of that desolation we ere born.

Courage beyond the point and obdurate pride
Made us a nation, robbed us of a nation.
Defiance absolute and myriad-eyed
That could not pluck the palm plucked our damnation.
We with such courage and the bitter wit
To fell the ancient oak of loyalty,
And strip the peopled hill and the altar bare,
And crush the poet with an iron text,
How could we read our souls and learn to be?
Here a dull drove of faces harsh and vexed,
We watch our cities burning in their pit,
To salve our souls grinding dull lucre out,
We, fanatics of the frustrate and the half,
Who once set Purgatory Hill in doubt.
Now smoke and dearth and money everywhere,
Mean heirlooms of each fainter generation,
And mummied housegods in their musty niches,
Burns and Scott, sham bards of a sham nation,
And spiritual defeat wrapped warm in riches,
No pride but pride of pelf. Long since the young
Fought in great bloody battles to carve out
This towering pulpit of the Golden Calf.
Montrose, Mackail, Argyle, perverse and brave,
Twisted the stream, unhooped the ancestral hill.
Never had Dee or Don or Yarrow or Till
Huddled such thriftless honour in a grave.

Such wasted bravery idle as a song,
Such hard-won ill might prove Time's verdict wrong,
And melt to pity the annalist's iron tongue.

Mary Stuart
Edwin Muir

My brother Jamie lost me all,
Fell cleverly to make me fall,
And with a sure reluctant hand
Stole my life and took my land.

It was jealousy of the womb
That let me in and shut him out,
Honesty, kingship, all shut out,
While I enjoyed the royal room.

My father was his, but not my mother,
We were, yet were not, sister, brother,
To reach my mother he had to strike
Me down and leap that deadly dyke.

Over the wall I watched him move
At ease through all the guarded grove,
Then hack, and hack, and hack it down,
Until that ruin was his own.

Scotland's Winter
Edwin Muir

Now the ice lays its smooth claws on the sill,
The sun looks from the hill
Helmed in his winter casket,
And sweeps his arctic sword across the sky.
The water at the mill
Sounds more hoarse and dull.
The miller's daughter walking by
With frozen fingers soldered to her basket
Seems to be knocking
Upon a hundred leagues of floor

With her light heels, and mocking
Percy and Douglas dead,
And Bruce on his burial bed,
Where he lies white as may
With wars and leprosy,
And all the kings before
This land was kingless,
And all the singers before
This land was songless,
This land that with its dead and living waits the Judgment Day.
But they, the powerless dead,
Listening can hear no more
Than a hard tapping on the sounding floor
A little overhead
Of common heels that do not know
Whence they come or where they go
And are content
With their poor frozen life and shallow banishment.

Song

Edwin Muir

Why should your face so please me
That if one little line should stray
Bewilderment would seize me
And drag me down the tortuous way
Out of the noon into the night?
But so, into this tranquil light
You raise me.

How could our minds so marry
That, separate, blunder to and fro,
Make for a point, miscarry,
And blind as headstrong horses go?
Though now they in their promised land
At pleasure travel hand in hand
Or tarry.

This concord is an answer
To questions far beyond our mind
Whose image is a dancer.
All effort is to ease refined
Here, weight is light; this is the dove
Of love and peace, not heartless love
The lancer.

And yet I still must wonder
That such an armistice can be
And life roll by in thunder
To leave this calm with you and me.
This tranquil voice of silence, yes,
This single song of two, this is
A wonder.

Merlin

Edwin Muir

O Merlin in your crystal cave
Deep in the diamond of the day,
Will there ever be a singer
Whose music will smooth away
The furrow drawn by Adam's finger
Across the meadow and the wave?
Or a runner who'll outrun
Man's long shadow driving on,
Break through the gate of memory
And hang the apple on the tree?
Will your magic ever show
The sleeping bride shut in her bower,
The day wreathed in its mound of snow
And Time locked in his tower?

One Foot in Eden
Edwin Muir

One foot in Eden still, I stand
And look across the other land.
The world's great day is growing late,
Yet strange these fields that we have planted
So long with crops of love and hate.
Time's handiworks by time are haunted,
And nothing now can separate
The corn and tares compactly grown.
The armorial weed in stillness bound
About the stalk; these are our own.
Evil and good stand thick around
In the fields of charity and sin
Where we shall lead our harvest in.

Yet still from Eden springs the root
As clean as on the starting day.
Time takes the foliage and the fruit
And burns the archetypal leaf
To shapes of terror and of grief
Scattered along the winter way.
But famished field and blackened tree
Bear flowers in Eden never known.
Blossoms of grief and charity
Bloom in these darkened fields alone.
What had Eden ever to say
Of hope and faith and pity and love
Until was buried all its day
And memory found its treasure trove?
Strange blessings never in Paradise
Fall from these beclouded skies.

The Coming of the Wee Malkies
Stephen Mulrine

Whit'll ye dae when the wee Malkies come,
if they dreep doon affy the wash-hoose dyke,
an pit the hems oan the sterrheid light,
an play wee heidies oan the clean close-wa,
an bloo'er yir windae in wi the baw,
missis, whit'll ye dae?

Whit'll ye dae when the wee Malkies come,
if they chap yir door an choke yir drains,
an caw the feet fae yir sapsy weans,
an tummle thur wulkies through yir sheets,
an tim thur ashes oot in the street,
missis, whit'll ye dae?

Whit'll ye dae when the wee Malkies come,
if they chuck thur screwtaps doon the pan,
an stick the heid oan the sanit'ry man;
when ye hear thum shauchlin doon yir loaby,
chantin, 'Wee Malkies! The gemme's a bogey!'
Haw, missis, whit'll ye dae?

Hey, Jock, Are Ye Glad Ye 'Listed?
Neil Munro

Hey! Jock, are ye glad ye 'listed?
O Jock, but ye're far frae hame!
What d'ye think o' the fields o' Flanders?
Jockey lad, are ye glad ye came?
Wet rigs we wrought in the land o' Lennox,
When Hielan' hills were smeared wi' snaw;
Deer we chased through the seepin' heather,
But the glaur o' Flanders dings them a'!

This is no' Fair o' Balloch,
Sunday claes and a penny reel;
It's no' for dancin' at a bridal
Willie Lawrie's bagpipes squeal.
Men are to kill in the morn's mornin';
Here we're back to your daddy's trade;
Naething for't but to cock the bonnet,
Buckle on graith and kiss the maid.

The Cornal's yonder deid in tartan,
Sinclair's sheuched in Neuve Eglise;
Slipped awa wi' the sodger's fever,
Kinder than only auld man's disease.
Scotland! Scotland! little we're due ye,
Poor employ and skim-milk board.
But youth's a cream that maun be paid for,
We got it reamin', so here's the sword!

Come awa, Jock, and cock your bonnet,
Swing your kilt as best ye can;
Auld Dumbarton's Drums are dirlin',
Come awa, Jock, and kill your man!
Far's the cry to Leven Water
Where your fore-folks went to war,
They would swap wi' us to-morrow,
Even in the Flanders glaur!

The Heather

Neil Munro

If I were King of France, that noble fine land,
And my gold was elbow-deep in the iron chests;
Were my castles grey and scowling o'er the wine-land,
With towers as high as where the eagle nests;
If harpers sweet, and swordsmen stout and vaunting,
My history sang, my stainless tartan wore,
Was not my fortune poor with one thing wanting,
      The heather at my door?

My galleys might be sailing every ocean,
Robbing the isles and sacking hold and keep,
My chevaliers go prancing at my notion,
To bring me back of cattle, horse and sheep;
Fond arms be round my neck, the young heart's tether,
And true love-kisses all the night might fill,
But oh! *mochree*, if I had not the heather,
            Before me on the hill!

A hunter's fare is all I would be craving,
A shepherd's plaiding and a beggar's pay,
If I might earn them where the heather, waving,
Gave grandeur to the day.
The stars might see me, homeless one and weary,
Without a roof to fend me from the dew,
And still content, I'd find a bedding cheery
            Where'er the heather grew!

In Prison

From the French of Paul Verlaine

Neil Munro

Outside the window, stanchion-barred,
A gean-tree's wavin',
Through the blue lift abune the yard
The sun gangs stavin'.

Saft frae the ancient steeple falls
The toon-bell's ringin',
In good men's gardens ower the walls
A bird is singin'.

My God! how simple life may be –
Tranquil, slow-glidin',
There where the folk are douce and free,
An' law-abidin'.

Oh! you that in the cauld tolbooth
Greet, broken-hearted,
What hae ye done wi' your braw youth,
That's now departed?

Gin I Was God

Charles Murray

Gin I was God, sittin' up there abeen,
Weariet nae doot noo a' my darg was deen,
Deaved wi' the harps an' hymns oonendin' ringin',
Tired o' the flockin' angels hairse wi' singin',
To some clood-edge I'd daunder furth an', feth,
Look owre an' watch hoo things were gyaun aneth.
Syne, gin I saw hoo men I'd made mysel'
Had startit in to pooshan, sheet an' fell,
To reive an' rape, an' fairly mak' a hell
O' my braw birlin' Earth, – a hale week's wark –
I'd cast my coat again, rowe up my sark,
An', or they'd time to lench a second ark,
Tak' back my word an' sen' anither spate,
Droon oot the hale hypothec, dicht the sklate,
Own my mistak', an', aince I'd cleared the brod,
Start a'thing ower again, gin I was God.

Charon's Song

Charles Murray

Another boat-load for the Further Shore,
Heap them high in the stern;
Nae ane o' them ever has crossed before
An' never a ane 'll return.
Heavy it rides sae full, sae full,
Deep, deep is the River,
But light, light is the backward pull,
The River flows silently on.

A cargo o' corps that are cauld I trow –
They're grippy that grudge the fare –
An' the antrin quick wi' his golden bough
That's swappin' the Here for There.
Heavy it rides sae full, sae full,
Slow, slow is the River,
But light, light is the backward pull,
The River flows silently on.

In vain will they look wha seek for a ford,
Where the reeds grow lank an' lang:
This is the ferry, an' I am the lord
An' King o' the boat an' stang.
Heavy it rides sae full, sae full,
Black, black is the River,
But light, light is the backward pull,
The River, my River, flows on.

The Whistle

Charles Murray

He cut a sappy sucker from the muckle rodden-tree,
He trimmed it, an' he wet it, an' he thumped it on his knee;
He never heard the teuchat when the harrow broke her eggs,
He missed the craggit heron nabbin' puddocks in the seggs,
He forgot to hound the collie at the cattle when they strayed,
But you should hae seen the whistle that the wee herd made!

He wheepled on't at mornin' an' he tweetled on't at nicht,
He puffed his freckled cheeks until his nose sank oot o' sicht,
The kye were late for milkin' when he piped them up the closs,
The kitlin's got his supper syne, an' he was beddit boss;
But he cared na doit nor docken what they did or thocht or said,
There was comfort in the whistle that the wee herd made.

For lyin' lang o' mornin's he had clawed the caup for weeks,
But noo he had his bonnet on afore the lave had breeks;
He was whistlin' to the porridge that were hott'rin' on the fire,

He was whistlin' ower the travise to the baillie in the byre;
Nae a blackbird nor a mavis, that hae pipin' for their trade,
Was a marrow for the whistle that the wee herd made.

He played a march to battle, it cam' dirlin' through the mist,
Till the halfin' squared his shou'ders an' made up his mind to 'list;
He tried a spring for wooers, though he wistna what it meant,
But the kitchen-lass was lauchin' an' he thocht she maybe kent;
He got ream an' buttered bannocks for the lovin' lilt he played.
Wasna that a cheery whistle that the wee herd made?

He blew them rants sae lively, schottisches, reels, an' jigs,
The foalie flang his muckle legs an' capered ower the rigs,
They grey-tailed futt'rat bobbit oot to hear his ain strathspey,
The bawd cam' loupin' through the corn to 'Clean Pease Strae';
The feet o' ilka man an' beast gat youkie when he played –
Hae ye ever heard o' whistle like the wee herd made?

But the snaw it stopped the herdin' an' the winter brocht him
    dool,
When in spite o' hacks an' chilblains he was shod again for
    school;
He couldna sough the catechis nor pipe the rule o' three,
He was keepit in an' lickit when the ither loons got free;
But he aften played the truant – 'twas the only thing he played,
For the maister brunt the whistle that the wee herd made!

An Incomplete History of Rock Music
in the Hebrides
Donald S. Murray

Peewits quiffed like Elvis reel from rocks,
their sheen of feathers like blue suede
the breeze buffs in the midday air.
'He loves ewe. Meah! Meah! Meah!'
bleat a Fat Four of blackface sheep
beneath mop-tops of unshorn hair.

Jagged stalks of thistles strut,
flashing menace in the evening light
before a group of timeworn stones.
Spangled with glitter, starlings soar
and oystercatchers sport red lips
while herons stalk on platform soles.

Each fulmar packs its pistol.
There's anarchy on cliff-tops
as they reel and spit on rocks below.
Then a riff is played on marram grass,
shells syncopate on shorelines as
night downs its curtain on the show.

A Celtic History

William Neill

I'm tellt the auncient Celts collectit heids
like some fowks gaither stamps,
an gin ye were their guest wad shaw ye kists
fou o their latest prizes.
Nou we're delivirt frae sic ugsome weys
we scrieve lists o the scunnersomely deid
prentit in black and white.
Yon's faur mair hygienic and forbye
ye can get a lot mair in than ye can in a kist.

I'm tellt the auncient Celts focht in bare scud . . .
Man . . . *yon's* a mark o unco determination.
Ye've shairly got tae ken whit ye're fechtin *fur*
tae tak the haill Roman Empire on in yir buff.
Gin they'd taen Hitler, Napoleon and aa the lave
o the born leaders o sufferan mankind
and gart thaim fecht in nocht but their drawers and semmits
yon wad hae been a solid move towards peace.

Lark

William Neill

Lark sings as she has always done
over the thorn hedge of the spring meadow.
Now my time's very nearly run . . .
long gone the day of the coarse fellow
who heard the song and indifferently whistled
and thought of beef and beer and fun and girls,
ignoring warnings of his careless heading.

Now Lark has a deal more of attention:
a careful leaning on the broken gate.
I think of the subject we try not to mention,
former abstractions of our certain fate,
cold speculations on threescore years and ten.
Sing Lark, sing Lark to me and then
perhaps the scented hour will seem less late.

Are You There, Mr Punch?

William Neill

Down on the beach, the Punch and Judy show
contained within its horrid, scary plot
a simple foretaste of the human lot.
The red-nosed tyrant of the squeaky crow
gave us male-chauvinistic-piggery blow by blow;
killed hangman, death's head, devil, on the trot;
like all true rogues, for all his sins, uncaught.
We pondered, naughty children down below.

Oh, crafty Punchinello, nose and chin
touching each other, velvet suit and bells;
our dreams were haunted by your wicked smile.

How could we know the world we'd venture in
more frightful yet, for all your gleeful yells,
than skeleton, policeman, hangman, crocodile.

Steel Yourself
Siùsaidh NicNèill

He said my eyes were misty grey;
soft as the morning light

on the head of Marsco
or the heron rising.

And now they are steel.

clank
clank

steel shutters down.

What made it so?
Brittle and hard.
Unrequited in love,
perhaps?
Or just a vacuum –
where love should be?

Gone the silver smile.
Now it's lined with lead.

clank
clank

For Eric Blair
Siùsaidh NicNèill

Our generation had no Spain,
no romantic fight to draw
the passions forth,
and commit us for life
to the Cause.

Bandolero Rosso, Bandolero Rosso.
We lifted our voices in fervent song
aching for a fight
that our minds had out-grown.

Immersed now in Highland comforts,
collectors of those things we despised,
how easily our youthful dreams are mislaid
when the bellow of suffering has died.

Bandolero Rosso, Bandolero Rosso.
We can only lift a chant for a Chile or Nicaragua
now that our sword is blunted
on the soggy edge of talk.

The Young Men of Blackburn

Dennis O'Donnell

They swagger through the village like Capulets –
cropped heads, shades, stubble, ear-rings,
jackets over one shoulder, torero-style.
They give each other extravagant aliases,
stage-names too baroque for the common place:
Cue-Ball, Lockjaw, Silver, The Louse.

Taciturn, not their style
the callow yowling of other cubs.
Theirs is the hauteur of Prussian junkers,
curtly acknowledging passers-by:
'Peter', 'Samson', 'Mrs Pearce',
like God giving names to the animals.

Drunk as dragoons, I've seen them
with duelling scars from their latest skirmish
with the young blood of Whitburn, or the police.
And, though they refuse to go on in the roles
of their fathers – fools from a history play –
their moves have all been blocked in advance.

The Crab

Dennis O'Donnell

Rills of cool water curtained the windows;
the saltwater scent from the fishmonger's shop
lured me in from the broiling streets.
It was a secret cavern behind a waterfall.
'Bring something nice for the tea', she'd said.

I bought a crab the size of a dustbin-lid,
ludicrously big, too big to be wrapped,
and carried it like a discus home,
at every step the legs and claws
clicking and snapping together like claves.

My wife of a month was not impressed.
She frisbeed it out of our second-floor window.
It took the air, a ceramic kite
and wheeled, like a stricken helicopter,
far over the heads of playing children,
then smacked on the road and burst like a shell.
The mess was as obscene as cancer.
We had beans on toast.

In the morning, all that remained
once the gulls had ripped away the flesh,
was red and brown shrapnel, scattered limbs.

Even Solomon

Dennis O'Donnell

Coal, shale, iron and steel –
the lives of the people for generations
was the heavy reality of work.
Now it's the heavy reality of none.

But they're still working men.
They still do the things they always did –
tend gardens, race doo's, play bowls and drink beer.
They don't piss about with ideology –
they know for a fact there are no certainties
in this life or any other.

When Wullie Gardner's old man died,
they put in the coffin beside the stiff,
a bottle of rum, a packet of fags
and a deck of cards.
                    Just in case.

Wine and Wooing

Donny O'Rourke

I wasn't the first one
I wasn't the worst one
You called me your baleful boy
After all the losers
And cynical users
There was no cause to be coy
So what you wanted you named and took
And the name you chose was mine
Yours was the first grown woman's look
That I knew to be love's sign

You taught me wine and wooing
I learned by candlelight
To do what needed doing
To do it slow, and right?

It was your proud prime
And my first time
You wept but wouldn't say
What joys or fears
Had caused the tears
As the dark spring night turned grey –

Again that look, but what you took
Was your loving leave of me
That callow shallow lad mistook
How a woman's heart comes free

You taught me wine and wooing
I learned by candlelight
To do what needed doing
To do it slow, and right?

On other nights
When brighter lights
Glow in younger eyes
Older now and bolder now
Still waiting to be wise
All I know and show of love
was learned that night we shared
Long ago in Glasgow
When you looked at me and dared.

A Letter From My Father

Donny O'Rourke

It's extant only on official forms –
the wee coiled writing of my father.

His copperplate chalked on corporation
slate was lyric, legible, neat.

On tax returns its furls and curlicues
were daintier far than Carolingian Minuscule.

Yet he hated writing and many's the chit
or docket I penned for him

in the naïve scrawl that prints these lines.
Through all my journeyings, small triumphs

and reverses
I never had a note from him; whatever

needed telling, he was more inclined to say.
Slicing through the post these mornings

how I crave a letter from my father,
paternal greetings in a flawless script.

The Intellectual

Janet Paisley

Intelligence
That's whit ah'm luikin fur in a fella.
Sumdy thit's akchully read Plato,
mibbe recites Trouvère in bed,
likes Poussin, kens the difference
atween Ormazd an Ahriman,
his trimeter fae his tercepts,
an even unnerstauns Brecht.
Weel, ye kin hoap. Ah mean, Archimedes,
see whin ye're in the bath thegither,
displacemint, best if ye ken.
Saves the flair. Cue fur Coleridge therr
an wha waants that. Big turn aff.
Last guy ah went oot wi, daft? Ken the kind
– open thur mooth ye git a draft.
A jiner, he wis. Energy, bit.
Nae finesse. Mind oan wan track.
Ah says twa hunner an twelve BC
Archimedes inventit the screw.
Ah um regretting it noo.
See ma back. Rubbed raw.
Naw, ah waant a man wi mair up here
thin doon there. Brains no brawn.
Nae wey ah'm fawin fur the Chippindale type
– like ripplin muscles – aw that ile.
Slip oot yer hauns, win't they. Din't they?

Wan squeeze – and skoosh, thur awa.
An jist think, could ye go aw that
ap-pli-cation – pittin the poalish oan
they hard is a rock biceps,
shinin up thur knock on em pecs,
smoothin it in they groovy choaclit block
abdominals . . . rubbin it richt roon . . .
aw here, ah'll needtae awa an sit doon.

Feminist

Janet Paisley

Dae ye think there is nae saftness in ma breist?
Am I as hard as a bed oan the moor?
Cauld as an ice-frigid watterfaw?
Is it a man I should be havin tae thaw me oot?
I ken ma ain needs, the ebb an flow
ae the tide in me. Ice an fire.
Oh, I am no easy won.
Whit man truly kens, kin gie the saftest touch,
the haudin back, the wettest gentlin,
kin fan the lowes an keep me . . . oh, keep me . . .
Whit man wid draw ma pleisure oot
ower aw the hoors I kin, whit man
hus onything tae add baur the thrust.

The Turning

Janet Paisley

Did you pass that old man on the stair?
An empty wind whistled through his hair
and in his ghostly eyes the icy glare
froze hard enough to crackle in my ear.

He was here, I tell you. He was here.

And was he leaving? Oh don't turn and stare
for he lifted from the hook just over there
that overcoat of loneliness he wears.
Is that the drag of his returning I can hear?

He is near, I tell you. He is near.

What is that pungent perfume on the air?
The sour ageing in your lack of care
that beggars wanton love to raw despair
and cracks the door to draw in haunting fear.

He is here, you tell me. He is here.

The Trans-Siberian Express

for Eva

Don Paterson

One day we will make our perfect journey –
the great train smashing through Dundee, Brooklyn
and off into the endless tundra,
the earth flattening out before us.

I follow your continuous arrival,
shedding veil after veil –
the automatic doors wincing away
while you stagger back from the buffet

slopping Laphroaig and decent coffee
until you face me from that long enfilade
of glass, stretched to vanishing point
like facing mirrors, a lifetime of days.

The Eyes

Don Paterson

When his beloved died
he decided to grow old
and shut himself inside
the empty house, alone
with his memories of her
and the big sunny mirror
where she'd fixed her hair.
This great block of gold
he hoarded like a miser,
thinking here, at least,
he'd lock away the past,
keep one thing intact.

But around the first anniversary,
he began to wonder, to his horror,
about her eyes: Were they brown or black,
or grey? Green? Christ! I can't say . . .

One Spring morning, something gave in him;
shouldering his twin grief like a cross,
he shut the front door, turned into the street
and had walked just ten yards, when, from a dark close,
he caught a flash of eyes. He lowered his hat-brim
and walked on . . . yes, they were like that; like that . . .

Exilics: Leaving Lochboisdale, 1919

Walter Perrie

Scatters of eider and shelduck ride
the rocking swell. A raven banner
tattered, faded, blesses the blood-tide
freighting out the island's fever.

Confused into a ceilidh atmosphere
some younger gallants call-out to the shore

some whiskeyed-up from fear of their own fear.
Their wild sea-wedding calls for jig and reel;
and each tune answered from the beach, four
hands set parallel in chanter-thrall.

Anchors weigh as the sun's death raises a wind.
And from Beinn Ruigh Choinnich the bonfire
peats in solemn conflagration spark and send
their open arms out wide, the island's answer.

An older hand takes up the pipes, their gospel
from Dunara Castle and The Marloch's rail;
cha till, cha till, the old, throat-gripping wail
far out beyond their rocking cradle-shore
tears salt from seas that never cried before.

Ascending Strathbraan

Walter Perrie

Leaving lower earth the long thorn hedgerow
gives way to hip-high labour of dry-stane
snake-sidling upwards till the landscape shift again:
no fences this high up among the ling
even bracken surrenders far below.

I have come to know these sculpted moorland hills
hills made of buzzard *pieow* and hare:
even on the kindest summer's day they
never wholly smile. Always a question curls
their slopes. Our presence tolerated only
where the earth confronts the Blue with no more
than lichen, dwarf willow, juniper cover.

December, when the struggle between
earth and sky slogs to aphelion
this is no place for the casual visitor;
here hostile Absolutes confront each other
and only the dedicated partisan
would share their buffetings of grace and pain.

Season on season, rain for rain, this thin soil
leaches particles of precious metal:
binding our bodies to the earth with atom
of gold and iron, long chains of chromium
chaining earth to the forges of heaven:
who choose but one Absolute are not forgiven.

A Favourite Stretch of Disused Railway

Dalbeattie to Dumfries line

Tom Pow

I

Turn sharp right off the forestry track.

You're on a path of large granite chips
shrouded by silver birch. This will lead you
onto the viaduct. Here the birch become
glossy saplings, the stones one long rockery
for wild strawberry, for the palest green tree shoots.

From here you can see how well-appointed
the big houses are; their stables boarded up now
and windows broken, but your eye led to them
by the fold of the landscape, by the command
of trees, as surely as in any Claude.

A hawk skims the variegated tops
of an arboretum – cyprus, copper beech,
improbable monkey puzzle. Your spirit
goes with it – for you are halfway
to flying here, riding these great arcs of air
with only a mane of rough red stone to hold onto.

II

At the end of the viaduct, a broken grey stile.
The path weeps into a green baize, stitched
with tiny white stars. A moped, clogged with rust,

stands alone; the garish flowers on its petrol tank
almost fading as you look. Playful ghosts
crowd in on you. Old beech trees
spread their arms in perfect planes.

III

When the path becomes a path again,
it is a sodden mud-track, a fine silt
of rootless earth, whose depth you could not judge,
if not aware of that broken vertebrae beneath.
One pool, clear of the choking tagliatelle of algae,
still shows the sharp edges of a few pinkish pieces
of granite. Everywhere else, marsh marigolds
sway imperiously on teased-out stems.

IV

This vegetable world delivers you
into a dark valley of blasted rock, where the ghosts
of a hundred dead wills feel exotic. The purest water
drips down a dank face to be caught on the tip
of each asterisk of moss and become – up close –
a reredos of opalescent drops. Green railings
of nettles crowd the base of this achievement:
sycamore, birch, ash stubbornly cling.

V

As I see it, passing through this gorge,
when the carriage was cast into shadow, a passenger –
one bull-necked, ruddy-complexioned, studying
the market-price of lambs – sighed dust and smoke
up spidery nostrils, laid his paper on his lap
and glanced up at the blur of rock, so that

when it was past, his blinking eyes just caught
the sun hitting the heraldic bank of wild rose
and giant daisy. And, as the perfect landscape
opened out before him, he heard the auctioneer's
breathless chanting become the sound
of a speeding train.

The Years
Tom Pow

Sometimes to get their own back
our years forget us. They uncouple
and trundle off, one by one,
down gentle gradients into sidings
overgrown by giant hogweed,
there to become their own
secret memorials.

Strange creatures take up residence
in the dusty old carriages –
shiny black beetles, tenacious fungus, a dwarf.
In faded photographs, seaside towns shift
mysteriously abroad.

Still – if you're lucky – rendezvous
can take place. Behind the mighty
blind engines of passion
may come tenderness – the freight
of the years.

Horseshoe Crab in Flagrante Delicto
Richard Price

Full moon and a grey piece of the moon
slips out of the restlessness, the sea.
Say a million years, say four hundred,
and begin with her again:
life is lisping in the water,
the Earth is just rising.

As usual, she's lugging her man,
gaining the globby sand.

She'll let him do what she likes,
bury it, and get back.

An abstract spider,
she'll re-enter the fusses of the foam,
see the glint in the deep
and head for that struggling moon,
the moon in the ocean's web,
the moon's mime and its warning.

On, Off, Over
Richard Price

I love you,
and you,
and you

now sleeping, top on
from slipped off, finally,
over your shoulders,

now sleeping, not one
thought for me,
rightly,

now sleeping, right,
not a thought.
You were wrong.

I love you.

The Organist Confesses to His Mirror
John Purser

God knows, I've looked in you enough;
bride after bride has walked into my eye;
I've held them, hurried them, desired them
too in all unholy ways; but you are wise
to turn a blind eye to your back
for here from pedal-board to flues
I've played out more than fantasies
and fugues. I've spurned disasters
in the choir, old hymns for old souls,
ageing anthems, unannounced
I've made my alterations to their sense,
twisted progressions and, in extremis,
let the bellows roar full organ impious
extravagance of wind and reed – nature,
true nature, is an appetite for living and,
by Christ, I've put that shudder
to their limbs and stirred the church
from gratings between pews
to the fan-vaulting boss. Ah, yes –
but I have held the quiet like a thread,
a note so long that there was time
to trace it through the transepts, down the aisles,
mirrored and echoing, while I
half sit and slide upon my bench,
feet pattering like puppets on the wood,
fingers precise; – expression here
is executing notes, each digit lifted,
knowing when to stop. Switch off. Switch out
the lights. On leaving, look behind and check –
my life is scattered here in whisperings,
broken cobwebs – lock the door.

Love Poem
John Purser

No nightfall in June,
only a hot bird-hush –
exhaustion tucked
into a feather bed –
favours abandoned
in the sweet heat of sweat:
the inside of my thigh
slid on the neck
of your two limbs and then
held close, a tense meniscus
of new moons, our surface
drawn up at the sides
like wings, or eyes
half-open, half-asleep.

Crabbit Angels
David Purves

A've heard it said that bairns
is ill ti hae but waur ti want.
The same is true o ocht A ken
in aw the warld that's wurth a gant.

Ye canna hae ae syde the coin
athout, forby, the tither ane,
or prie a joy or pleisir, lyke,
athout ye thole a hantil pain.

The'r nae sic wyfe that isna baith
ane angel an a crabbit randie.
The man that downa mell the twa
maun leeve in Hell, or hochmagandie.

Cleikit

David Purves

An nou ye staun transmogrified;
licht glimmerin in yeir hair
an ilka move ye care ti mak
or wird ye care ti say
ti me, a pleisir an a thrill,
ferr ben inouth ma hert.
Sum meisterie haes merk't ye out
apairt frae ither weimen
ti synd awa aw fashiousness
an hael ma hattert sowl.
Lyke maivises in Spring, whas herts
gangs stoundin lyke ti burst,
whan mornin licht brichtens the warld,
A hae been blisst bi God.

To My Mountain

Kathleen Raine

Since I must love your north
Of darkness, cold, and pain,
The snow, the lonely glen,
Let me love true worth,

The strength of the hard rock,
The deafening stream of wind
That carries sense away
Swifter than flowing blood.

Heather is harsh to tears
And the rough moors
Give the buried face no peace
But make me rise,

And oh, the sweet scent, and purple skies!

Maire Macrae's Song
Kathleen Raine

The singer is old and has forgotten
Her girlhood's grief for the young soldier
Who sailed away across the ocean,
Love's brief joy and lonely sorrow:
The song is older than the singer.

The song is older than the singer
Shaped by the love and the long waiting
Of women dead and long forgotten
Who sang before remembered time
To teach the unbroken heart its sorrow.

The girl who waits for her young soldier
Learns from the cadence of a song
How deep her love, how long the waiting.
Sorrow is older than the heart,
Already old when love is young:
The song is older than the sorrow.

Highland Graveyard
From Eileann Chanaidh
Kathleen Raine

Today a fine old face has gone under the soil;
For generations past women hereabouts have borne
Her same name and stamp of feature.
Her brief identity was not her own
But theirs who formed and sent her out
To wear the proud bones of her clan, and live its story,
Who now receive back into the ground
Worn features of ancestral mould.

A dry-stone wall bounds off the dislimned clay
Of many an old face forgotten and young face gone

From boundless nature, sea and sky.
A wind-withered escallonia like a song
Of ancient tenderness lives on
Some woman's living fingers set as shelter for the dead, to tell
In evergreen unwritten leaves,
In scent of leaves in western rain
That one remembered who is herself forgotten.

Many songs they knew who now are silent.
Into their memories the dead are gone
Who haunt the living in an ancient tongue
Sung by old voices to the young,
Telling of sea and isles, of boat and byre and glen;
And from their music the living are reborn
Into a remembered land,
To call ancestral memories home
And all that ancient grief and love our own.

First Thaw

Tessa Ransford

Hills lie quilted in snow;
the river runs black and harsh;
sheep are fed by hand.

Next day a flicker of doves
streams over the rooftops, the church
and circles down to the river.

A sprinkle of snowdrops beside the flood
and a pair of dippers play dive and seek.
The heron flies low upstream.

A cat crouches on the wall
which sparkles with favoured moss.
A girl leads her pony along the street.

We walk slowly arm in arm
over the bridge, along the river
and imagine ourselves in the picture.

A Stable Relationship
Tessa Ransford

In a stable relationship one person
is often the horse, the other the owner.

One person is kept in the stable
and taken out only in harness.

The stable door is divided and
allows the horse to look out.

The harness gives freedom of movement
but none of direction or speed.

Horse and owner often enjoy
the deepest trust and intimacy.

But horses have been known
to break out of the stable

and to bolt away, dangling
an end of broken halter.

Viewpoint
Tessa Ransford

*Why can't they give these damn mountains
proper names?* Their names are
in our language. The mountains
understand it and know each other
by these proper Gaelic names.

Why can't they be spelt so we can
pronounce them? – like Ben Nevis
or Ring of Bright Water?
The spelling is the way it works
and makes everything real.

I can't remember these names.
What does 'Sgurr' mean?
Steep, high, impenetrable peak
that divides our minds, our speech
and our understanding.

Here's one I can say: Ben Tee.
And here is Gleouraich, Gairich,
Spidean Mialach, Sgurr na Ciche.

(Mist and clouds are swirling
as an eagle soars and falls.)

What is that range called, that
you see and then it fades?
Knoydart. It means Rough Bounds!
Dear, far, near, fearsome
rough bounds of our being.

Propinquity

is the province of cats. Living by accident,
lapping the food at hand, or sleeking down
in an adjacent lap when sleep occurs to them,
never aspiring to consistency
in homes or partners, unaware of property,
cats take their chances, love by need and nearness
as long as the need lasts, as long as the nearness
is near enough. The code of cats is simply
to take what comes. And those poor souls who claim
to own a cat, who long to recognize
in bland and narrowing eyes a look like love,
are bound to suffer should they expect

cats to come purring punctually home.
Home is only where the food and the fire are,
but might be anywhere. Cats fall on their feet,
nurse their own wounds, attend to their own laundry,
and purr at appropriate times. O folly, folly
to love a cat, and yet
we dress with love the distance that they keep,
the hair-raising way they have, and easily blame
all the abandoned litters and torn ears
on some marauding tiger. Well, no matter;
cats do not care.
  Yet part of us is cat. Confess –
love turns on accident, and needs
nearness; and the various selves we have
all come from our cat-wanderings, our chance
crossings. Imagination prowls at night,
cat-like among odd possibilities.
Only our dog-sense brings us faithfully homeward,
makes meaning out of accident, keeps faith,
and, cat-and-dog, the arguments go at it.
But every night, outside, cat-voices call
us out to take a chance, to leave
the safety of our baskets, and to let
what happens, happen. 'Live, live!' they catcall.
'Each moment is your next! Propinquity,
propinquity is all!'

Alastair Reid

Scotland
Alastair Reid

It was a day peculiar to this piece of the planet,
when larks rose on long thin strings of singing
and the air shifted with the shimmer of actual angels.
Greenness entered the body. The grasses
shivered with presences, and sunlight
stayed like a halo on hair and heather and hills.
Walking into town, I saw, in a radiant raincoat,

the woman from the fish-shop. 'What a day it is!'
cried I, like a sunstruck madman.
And what did she have to say for it?
Her brow grew bleak, her ancestors raged in their graves
as she spoke with their ancient misery:
'We'll pay for it, we'll pay for it, we'll pay for it!'

Weathering

Alastair Reid

I am old enough now for a tree
once planted, knee high, to have grown to be
twenty times me,

and to have seen babies marry, and heroes grow deaf –
but that's enough meaning-of-life.
It's living through time we ought to be connoisseurs of.

From wearing a face all this time, I am made aware
of the maps faces are, of the inside wear and tear.
I take to faces that have come far.

In my father's carved face, the bright eye
he sometimes would look out of, seeing a long way
through all the tree-rings of his history.

I am awed by how things weather: an oak mantel
in the house in Spain, fingered to a sheen,
the marks of hands leaned into the lintel,

the tokens in the drawer I sometimes touch –
a crystal lived-in on a trip, the watch
my father's wrist wore to a thin gold sandwich.

It is an equilibrium
which breasts the cresting seasons but still stays calm
and keeps warm. It deserves a good name.

Weathering. Patina, gloss, and whorl.
The trunk of the almond tree, gnarled but still fruitful.
Weathering is what I would like to do well.

The Manse

Alastair Reid

The house that shored my childhood up
razed to the ground? I stood, amazed,
gawking at a block of air,
unremarkable except
I had hung it once with crazy
daywish and nightmare.

Expecting to pass a wistful
indulgent morning, I had sprung the gate.
Facing me was a wood
between which and myself
a whole crow-gabled and slated
mythology should have stood.

No room now for the rambling
wry remembering I had planned;
nor could I replant
that plot with a second childhood.
Luck, to have been handed
instead a forgettable element,

and not to have had to meet
regretful ghosts in rooms of glass.
That house by now is fairytale
and I can gloss it over
as easily as passing
clear through a wall.

The Horse-Mill

Robert Rendall

Beside the heavenly meadows daisied with stars
The planets yoked in team – Uranus, Mars,
Jove, Neptune, Venus, Mercury, Saturn, Earth –
Not saddled now to run with tightened girth,
But to the mill's unwieldy lever bound,
Wheel their enormous burden round and round.
Linked to the trees, harnessed with hame and trace,
They stumble round the tracks of cosmic space,
With slow hard step, necks bent, and flanks a-sweat
Turning yon beam, the sun for axle set.
To grind what corn in what celestial mill
Move these great Titans, shouldering onward still?

Angle of Vision

Robert Rendall

But, John, have you seen the world, said he,
Trains and tramcars and sixty-seaters,
Cities in lands across the sea –
Giotto's tower and the dome of St Peter's?

No, but I've seen the arc of the earth,
From the Birsay shore, like the edge of a planet,
And the lifeboat plunge through the Pentland Firth
To a cosmic tide with the men that man it.

Antenor

After A. P. Rossiter, on Troilus and Cressida
for Marshall

Alan Riach

When I was told once, long ago, to write an essay on
'The character in Shakespeare you'd most like to talk to'
I'd never heard of Antenor. Now, he'd be my man. Perhaps
you haven't noticed him? Never mind. You will,
next time you read the play. Five times he enters, maybe six.
And five times he goes out, as silent as he came.
He never speaks a line. He never utters a word.
And when the others talk of him, they talk as if he isn't there
and he doesn't object.

I see him in a dark prophetic outline:
the profile of a good man caught in war.
He didn't choose the world he's in,
and can't get out or reach beyond its limits.
Nor is he scandalized. No protest would be adequate, he knows.
He simply will not use his voice
when speech is so corrupted.
He is a strong and silent man.
Shakespeare's only one.

Sankey Hymns

Alan Riach

What did they know of reverence,
the sailors' congregation? In Stornoway
they gathered, an hour before
the regular service
began, and filled the wooden pews and raised
their voices in mass praise. Resolve
of hardihood was theirs. Let reverence be left
to those more pious worshippers
who occupied the space left vacant when these men
went down to the sea to their ships, once again.

It's not a skill that's needed, catching fish.
Accuracy, yes. And strength. A physical fact so prevalent
the eyes and voices of these men reveal it
every moment. Thinking was too slow for them,
reverence unhelpful.
                              Let them stand in Stornoway,
and sing for God to help them live and work.

Melt (Twa)

J'ai plus de souvenirs que si j'avais mille ans . . .

James Robertson

translated from the French of Charles Baudelaire

If I wis a thoosan, I cudna mind mair nor whit I mind nou.

An enormous kist – its drawers stappit fou
Wi bank statements, birthday cairds, manuscripts, fliers,
Mementoes, luve letters, letters frae lawyers –
Hauds fewer secrets nor ma sorry heid.
It's a muckle Maes Howe, a laich-hoose, a pyramid –
Corps in a mass grave arena packed in sae ticht.
I am a kirkyaird, laithsome tae munelicht,
Whaur the wurms o remorse are aye haein a taste
O the dear depairtit that I cared for maist.
An auld boudoir am I, that's seen faur better days,
A bourach o dune flouers an ootmoded claes . . .
Sniff as ye pass the fadin Jessie King prints –
Ye mey catch a whiff o whit I wis yince.

There's naethin sae dreich as the lang lourd deval,
The boued-doun, hirplin, wearisome craal
O boredom, thon wersh fruit o blin indifference
As it growes intae somethin that transcends existence.
Live flesh, yer coat's on a shoogly nail,
Ye're oot o time, ye've drapped aff the scale,
Ye're a granite stane smoored wi Saharan saun,
Ye're a sphinx that deep in a dwam has fawn,
An only the settin sun's straiks are strang
Eneuch tae lunt the breeze o yer sang.

Royalty

from Stirling Sonnets

James Robertson

Not when at Falkirk in the English camp
I ate with bloody hands my people's blood;
not when upon the altar of my God
I cut the wick of Comyn's too bright lamp;
not when at Scone the countess took the gold
and pressed its weight of kingship on my ears;
not after Methven, nor the choking years
before we loosed the English stranglehold –
but now, as on this field, this little horse,
I stand high in the stirrups and I swing
my battleaxe to split this knight clean through,
and know myself filled with some greater force
than ever filled mere man: *I am a king* –
I feel it, and my people feel it too.

George Buchanan in Old Age

from Stirling Sonnets

James Robertson

He thrashed the royal *erse* so that the *heid*
would learn that kings are not above the law.
He justified tyrannicide, foresaw
where stupid Stewart vanity would lead.
De Jure Regni was his masterpiece:
no earthly power he feared, but God alone.
'The sliddriest place to sit upon's a throne'?
Buchanan of Killearn supplied the grease.
Well-wishers, calling in his dying days,
found him, far from complacency or sleep,
teaching a servant how to read, and still
the intellect flashed in his icy gaze:
'Far better this,' says he, 'nor stealing sheep,
or sitting idle, which I count as ill.'

Affair of Kites

Robin Robertson

I sit, astonished by the pink kite:
its scoop and plunge, the briefness of it;
an escaped blouse, a pocket of silk
thumping like a heart
tight above the shimmering hill.
The sheer snap and plummet
sculpting the air's curve, the sky's chambers.
An affair with the wind's body;
a feeling for steps in the rising air, a love
sustained only by the high currents
and the hopeless gesture of the heart's hand.

The kitemaster has gone, invisible
over the hard horizon;
wind walks the grass between us.
I see the falling,
days later feel the crash.

Flags of Autumn from *Camera Obscura*

Robin Robertson

Thorn grows flat against the flank of Calton Hill,
wind grooming the close wall
has disinclined the snappers
in the tour-coach below; they stay inside.
The empty lanyards slap against the poles.

To the south, the castle, Arthur's Seat:
basalt wedges, door-stops
holding open history.
Skeins of the tour-guide's commentary
ravel past the rock
in snatches; the lone piper
tugs on a cigarette

and marches back to his car:
gonfalons of Gold Leaf
fray and separate behind.

To the north, the bright regalia
of the panel-beaten Firth.
A squall lifts the gorse
at the brink of the sea-fall:
the sky's film turned to fast-forward
as clouds bloom
like milk in water.
The rabbits scud and veer
through the flattening grass
and disappear with summer.

Put up like kites in the pulling rain, gulls
skirl their greeting over the stones.
And where we sat, stunned, that day,
those months ago: crows strut. Their black flags
flare and gutter in the gale.

Desire becomes sorrow
just as night follows day
and today becomes tomorrow.

The Pawkie Duke

David Rorie

There aince was a very pawkie Duke,
Far kent for his jookerie pawkerie,
Who owned a hoose wi' a grand out-look,
A gairden and a rockery.
Hech! Mon! A pawkie Duke!
Hoot! Ay! And a rockery!
A bonnet laird wi' a sma' kail yaird
Is naethin' but a mockery.

He dwalt far up a Heelant glen,
Where the foamin' flood and the crag is;
He dined each day on the usquebae,
And he washed it doon wi' haggis.
Hech! Mon! A pawkie Duke!
Hoot! Ay! And a haggis!
For that's the way the Heelanters dae
Where the foamin' flood and the crag is!

He wore a sporran and a dirk,
And a beard like besom bristles.
He was an elder o' the kirk,
And he hated kists o' whistles.
Hech! Mon! A pawkie Duke!
And doon on kists o' whistles!
They're a' red-heidit fowk up North,
Wi beards like besom bristles.

Syne ilka four hoors through the day
He took a muckle jorum,
And when the gloamin' gathered grey
Got fou wi' great decorum.
Hech! Mon! A pawkie Duke!
Blin' fou wi' great decorum;
There ne'er were males amang the Gaels
But lo'ed a muckle jorum.

His hair was red as only rose,
His legs were lang and bony;
He had a hoast and a rubbin'-post,
And a buskit cockernony.
Hech! Mon! A pawkie Duke!
And a buskit cockernony;
Ye ne'er will ken true Heelantmen
Who'll own they hadna ony.

And aye afore he socht his bed
He danced the Gillie Callum,
Then wi's Kilmarnock owre his neb
Nae evil could befall him.
Hech! Mon! A pawkie Duke!

What evil could befall him,
When he cast his buits and soopled his cuits
Wi' a guid-gaun Gillie Callum?

Noo, if he met a Cockney loon
A-tour in Caledonia,
He garred him lilt in a cotton kilt
Till he had an acute pneumonia.
Hech! Mon! A pawkie Duke!
And a Sassenach wi' pneumonia;
He lat him feel that the land o' the leal
Is gey near Caledonia.

But they brocht a joke – they did indeed!
Ae day for his eedification,
And they needed to trephine his heid,
So he deed o' the operation.
Ochone! The pawkie Duke!
Wae's me for the operation!
For weel-a-wot this typical Scot
Was a michty loss to the nation!

Queen Bee

Dilys Rose

When she'd squeezed what she could
From her loyal industrious crew –

They'd plundered the sweetest blooms
Buzzed home, loudly announcing
A bumper crop, industriously
Dumping their spoils at her feet –

When she'd sweated from workers
Their last drops of toil
She summoned the housebees
To sweep out the dead.

The orgy over, her helpers
Helpless on the floor

The silence thickens around her
Like dust. She forgets herself
Ungraciously knocks back
The last of the mead.

Through gleaming corridors
Between the polyhedrons
Of her waxed and polished cell
She totters and crawls

Drunkenly weeping
Bittersweet, regal tears.

Figurehead
Dilys Rose

The fog thickens.
I see no ships.
The gulls left days ago

Ebbing into the wake
Like friends grown tired
Of chasing failure.

I miss their uncouth snatch and grab
Their loud insatiable hunger.
I see nothing but fog.

Before my ever-open eyes
The horizon has closed in
The world's end dissolved.

I lumber on, grudging my status –
I'm purpose-built to dip and toss
My cleavage, crudely carved

To split waves
My hair caked with salt
My face flaking off.

The Empty Glen
R. Crombie Saunders

Time ticks away the centre of my pride
Emptying its glen of cattle, crops, and song,
Till its deserted headlands are alone
Familiar with the green uncaring tide.

What gave this land to gradual decay?
The rocky field where plovers make their nest
Now undisturbed had once the soil to raise
A happy people, but from day to day

The hamlets failed, the young men sought the towns,
Bewildered age looked from the cottage door
Upon the wreck of all they'd laboured for,
The rotting gate, the bracken on the downs;

And wondered if the future was so black
The children would have stayed but did not dare,
Who might, they hoped, be happy where they are.
And wondered, Are they ever coming back?

Scotched

Alexander Scott

Scotch God
Kent His
Faither.

Scotch Religion
Damn
Aa.

Scotch Education
I tellt ye
I tellt ye.

Scotch Queers
Wha peys wha
– For what?

Scotch Prostitution
Dear,
Dear.

Scotch Presbyterianism
Blue
Do.

Scotch Glasgow-Irish
God
Weirs a green jersey.

Scotch Orangeman
Bully
For Billy.

Scotch Liberty
Agree
Wi me.

Scotch Equality
Kaa the feet frae
Thon big bastard.

Scotch Fraternity
Our mob uses
The same razor.

Scotch Optimism
Through a gless,
Darkly.

Scotch Pessimism
Nae
Gless.

Scotch Modernity
Auld
Lang syne.

Scotch Initiative
Eftir
You.

Scotch Generosity
Eftir
Me.

Scotch Co-operation
Pou thegither
– My wey.

Scotch Geniuses
Deid
– Or damned.

Scotch Sex
In atween
Drinks.

Scotch Passion
Forgot
Mysel.

Scotch Love
Barely
A bargain.

Scotch Free-Love
Canna be
Worth much.

Scotch Lovebirds
Cheap
Cheap.

Scotch Fractions
A hauf
'n' a hauf.

Scotch Troubles
Monie a pickle
Maks a puckle.

Scotch Political-Parties
Monie a puckle
Maks a pickle.

Scotch Gaeldom
Up the
Erse.

Scotch Astronomy
Keek at
Uranus.

Scotch Astrology
Omen
In the gloamin.

Scotch Soccer
Robbery
Wi violence

Scotch Waverley-Novels
Tales anent
Trains.

Scotch Exiles
Love ye
Further.

Scotch Charity
Ends
At hame.

Scotch Self-Sacrifice
Saxpence
– On Sundays.

Scotch Unionism
Wallace bled but
Here's their transfusion.

Scotch Socialism
Reid
– Indeed?

Scotch Liberalism
Pink
Kink.

Scotch Nationalism
Tartan
Scartan.

Scotch Conservatism
Lowse
Grouse.

Scotch Afternoon-Tea
Masked
Pot.

Scotch Labour
Nine months
Hard.

Scotch Drink
Nip
Trip.

Scotch England
Dam'
Nation!

Scotch Poets
Wha's the
T'ither?

Continent o Venus

Alexander Scott

She liggs ablow my body's lust and luve,
A country dearlie-kent, and yet sae fremd
That she's at aince thon Tir-nan-Og I've dreamed,
The airt I've lived in, whar I mean tae live,
And mair, much mair, a mixter-maxter warld
Whar fact and dream are taigled up and snorled.

I ken ilk bay o aa her body's strand,
Yet ken them new ilk time I come tae shore,
For she's the unchartit sea whar I maun fare
Tae find anither undiscovered land,
Tae find it fremd, and yet tae find it dear,
Tae seek for't aye, and aye be bydan there.

Calvinist Sang

Alexander Scott

A hunder pipers canna blaw
Wir trauchled times awa,
Drams canna droun them out, nor sang
Hap their scarecraw heids for lang.

Gin aa the warld was bleezan fou
Whit gowk wad steer the plou?
Gin chiels were cowpan quines aa day
They'd mak, but niver gaither, hay.

Pit by yir pipes and brak yir gless,
Gie ower yir gallusness,
The day ye need a hert and harns
Dour as the diamant, cauld as the starns.

The Sodgers

Alexander Scott

Nae wi the gallus captains
That niver jinkit war
But socht for glory's wildfire lowe
As wise men aince for anither star –

And nae wi the ramstam colonels
That leuch at the din o the drum
And skirled for the bleeze o battle's Inferno
As saunts micht skirl for Kingdom Come –

But aye wi the sweirt sodgers
That niver wished tae dee
And anelie marched the *forrart* road
Sen onie *back* they cudna see –

Near blind wi the reek o wappins
And the reek o leean words,
But niver near sae blind wi bluid
As faa in luve wi guns and swords.

Auld Sanct-Aundrians: Brand the Builder

Tom Scott

On winter days, aboot the gloamin hour,
When the nock on the college touer
Is chappan lowsin-time,
And ilka mason packs his mell and tools awa
Under his banker, and bien forenenst the waa
The labourer haps the lave o the lime
Wi soppan sacks, to keep it frae a frost, or faa
O suddent snaw
Duran the nicht;
When scrawnie craws flap in the shell-green licht
Towards yon bane-bare rickle o trees
That heeze
Up on the knowe abuin the toun,
And the red goun
Is happan mony a student frae the snell nor'easter,
Malcolm Brand, the maister,
Seean the last hand through the yett
Afore he bars and padlocks it,
Taks yae look aroond his stourie yaird
Whaur chunks o stane are liggan
Like the ruins o some auld-farrant biggin;
Picks a skelf oot o his baerd,
Scliffs his tackey buits, and syne
Clunters hamelins doun the wyn'.

Doon by the sea
Murns the white snaw owre the wrack ayebydanlie.

The main street echoes back his fuitfaas
Frae its waas
Whaur owre the kerb and causeys, yellow licht
Presses back the mirk nicht
As shop fronts flude the pavin-stanes in places
Like the peintit faces whures pit on, or actresses,
To please their different customers.

Aye the nordren nicht, cauld as rumour,
Taks command,
Chills the toun wi his militarie humour,
And plots his map o starns wi felloun hand.

Alang the shore
The greinan white sea-stallions champ and snore.

Stoopin through the anvil pend
Gaes Brand,
And owre the coort wi the twa-three partan creels,
The birss air fu
O the smell o the sea, and fish, and meltit glue;
Draws up at his door, and syne
Hawkan his craig afore he gangs in ben,
Gies a bit scart at the grater wi his heels.

The kail-pat on the hob is hotteran fu
Wi the usual hash o Irish stew,
And by the grate, a red-haired beauty frettit thin,
His wife is kaain a spurtle roond.
He swaps his buits for his baffies but a soond.

The twa-three bairns ken to mak nae din
When faither's in,
And sit on creepies roond aboot.
Brand gies a muckle yawn
And howks his paper out.

Tither side the fire
The kettle hums and mews like a telephone wire.

'Lord, for what we are about to receive
Help us to be truly thankful – Aimen;
Woman, ye've pit ingans in't again!'

'Gae wa ye coorse auld hypocrite,
Thank the Lord for your meat, syne grue at it!'

Wi chowks drawn ticht in a speakless sconner
He glowers on her,

Syne on the quate and strecht-faced bairns:
Faulds his paper doun aside his eatin-airns,
And, til the loud tick-tockin o the nock,
Sups, and reads wi nae ither word nor look.

The warld ootside
Like a lug-held seashell, sings wi the rinnan tide.

The supper owre, Brand redds up for the nicht,
Aiblins there's a schedule for to price
Or somethin nice
On at the picters – secont hoose –
Or some poleetical meetin wants his licht,
Or aiblins, wi him t-total aa his life
And no able to seek a pub for relief frae the wife,
Daunders oot the West Sands 'on the loose'.
Whatever tis,
The waater slorps frae his elbucks as he synds his phiz.

And this is aa the life he kens there is?

Fulmars

Charles Senior

When it comes to sea cliffs
I am scared to go
too close to their edges,
the long drop below
would draw me down
from the sheer pleasure of vertigo:
such a fearful thrill
sucks like a groundswell
at the most thrawn will.

Trepidatious with ifs
I inch forward on wary toe
to see on sandstone ledges
unfledged chicks of arctic snow,

lose my fear and frown
feasting eyes on feathered show,
for parent fulmars revel
in their winkle spiral
between foam and nesting sill.

The Shooting of Dan McGrew

Robert Service

A bunch of the boys were whooping it up in the
    Malamute saloon;
The kid that handles the music-box was hitting a
    rag-time tune;
Back of the bar, in a solo game, sat Dangerous
    Dan McGrew,
And watching his luck was his light-o'-love, the
    lady that's known as Lou.

When out of the night, which was fifty below,
    and into the din and the glare,
There stumbled a miner fresh from the creeks,
    dog-dirty and loaded for bear.
He looked like a man with a foot in the grave,
    and scarcely the strength of a louse,
Yet he tilted a poke of dust on the bar, and he
    called for drinks for the house.
There was none could place the stranger's face,
    though we searched ourselves for a clue;
But we drank his health, and the last to drink
    was Dangerous Dan McGrew.

There's men that somehow just grip your eyes,
    and hold them hard like a spell;
And such was he, and he looked to me like a
    man who had lived in hell;
With a face most hair, and the dreary stare of a
    dog whose day is done,
As he watered the green stuff in his glass, and
    the drops fell one by one.

Then I got to figgering who he was, and wondering
    what he'd do,
And I turned my head – and there watching him
    was the lady that's known as Lou.

His eyes went rubbering round the room, and he
    seemed in a kind of daze,
Till at last that old piano fell in the way of his
    wandering gaze.
The rag-time kid was having a drink; there was
    no one else on the stool,
So the stranger stumbles across the room, and
    flops down there like a fool.
In a buckskin shirt that was glazed with dirt he
    sat, and I saw him sway;
Then he clutched the keys with his talon hands –
    my God! but that man could play!

Were you ever out in the Great Alone, when the
    moon was awful clear,
And the icy mountains hemmed you in with a
    silence you most could *hear*;
With only the howl of a timber wolf, and you
    camped there in the cold,
A half-dead thing in a stark, dead world, clean
    mad for the muck called gold;
While high overhead, green, yellow, and red, the
    North Lights swept in bars –
Then you've a haunch what the music meant . . .
    hunger and night and the stars.

And hunger not of the belly kind, that's banished
    with bacon and beans;
But the gnawing hunger of lonely men for a home
    and all that it means;
For a fireside far from the cares that are, four
    walls and a roof above;
But oh! so cramful of cosy joy, and crowned
    with a woman's love;
A woman dearer than all the world, and true as
    Heaven is true –

(God! how ghastly she looks through her rouge, –
    the lady that's known as Lou.)

Then on a sudden the music changed, so soft that
    you scarce could hear;
But you felt that your life had been looted clean
    of all that it once held dear;
That some one had stolen the woman you loved;
    that her love was a devil's lie;
That your guts were gone, and the best for you
    was to crawl away and die.
'Twas the crowning cry of a heart's despair, and
    it thrilled you through and through –
'I guess I'll make it a spread misere,' said Danger-
    ous Dan McGrew.

The music almost died away . . . then it burst
    like a pent-up flood;
And it seemed to say, 'Repay, repay,' and my
    eyes were blind with blood.
The thought came back of an ancient wrong, and
    it stung like a frozen lash,
And the lust awoke to kill, to kill . . . then the
    music stopped with a crash,
And the stranger turned, and his eyes they burned
    in a most peculiar way;
In a buckskin shirt that was glazed with the dirt he
    sat, and I saw him sway;

Then his lips went in a kind of grin, and he
    spoke, and his voice was calm;
And, 'Boys,' says he, 'you don't know me, and
    none of you care a damn;
But I want to state, and my words are straight,
    and I'll bet my poke they're true,
That one of you is a hound of hell . . . and that
    one is Dan McGrew.'

Then I ducked my head, and the lights went out,
    and two guns blazed in the dark;

And a woman screamed, and the lights went up,
    and two men lay stiff and stark;
Pitched on his head, and pumped full of lead, was
    Dangerous Dan McGrew,
While the man from the creeks lay clutched to
    the breast of the lady that's known as Lou.

These are the simple facts of the case, and I guess
I ought to know;
They say that the stranger was crazed with
    'hooch', and I'm not denying it's so.

I'm not so wise as the lawyer guys, but strictly
    between us two –
The woman that kissed him and – pinched his
    poke – was the lady that's known as Lou.

Poem

Burns Singer

Now absence is a habit it is time
To pack the splendid images away
And send them off in buses that can climb
Up ladders or down snakes as must they may.

For absence is a habit hard to learn
And those who have it haven't much to say.
Their small advice: they live on what they earn
And put the wounded images away.

'The Local Ogres Are Against Me Here . . .'

Burns Singer

The local ogres are against me here.
They do not like the way I brush my teeth.
My dog annoys them as it slinks beneath
Their neat defences to a pint of beer.
They cannot stand the way I stand alone
As though they weren't there, as though I knew
Their clauses, causes, didn't have a clue
And that their best case was to throw a stone.

Intellect I admire, and always have,
But this is different, this is halfway there,
And all the other half is lost as were
The herd's first sheep before he taught them love.

These people are like boats beside a pier
Who cannot journey since they cannot steer.

A Poem About Death

Burns Singer

Thinking how thin the glutton's skeleton
Will one day, none too soon, be hid away
Though worms drip down from it like long saliva
I walked in Germany one year today.

Thinking how cheaply that whore's legs would open
To the damp stones that mix with reddish clay
In the last darkness of the flower and fungus
I slid through Paris eighteen months today.

Thinking how soon the bibber's mouth goes dry
Under an alphabet of stones that pray
God, the devout, to have high mercy now
I hid in London two years to this day.

Thinking how soon the glib professor's tongue
Would let obituaries have their say
And churchmen sprout like speeches round his coffin
I sat in schoolrooms thirty years today.

And long before all that I saw the smile
Slow and self-confident when lips go grey
With which old death fulfils his promises.
I was not born at all till that first day.

And since that time there has been something tight
Clasped deep within me aching like a knife
To cut me up with hands that are not mine
Till I determine to achieve my life.

Poem of Lewis

Iain Crichton Smith

Here they have no time for the fine graces
of poetry, unless it freely grows
in deep compulsion, like water in the well,
woven into the texture of the soil
in a strong pattern. The have no rhymes
to tailor the material of thought
and snap the thread quickly on the tooth.
One would have thought that this black north
was used to lightning, crossing the sky like fish
swift in their element. One would have thought
the barren rock would give a value to
the bursting flower. The two extremes,
mourning and gaiety, meet like north and south
in the one breast, milked by knuckled time,
till dryness spreads across each ageing bone.
They have no place for the fine graces
of poetry. The great forgiving spirit of the word
fanning its rainbow wing, like a shot bird
falls from the windy sky. The sea heaves

in visionless anger over the cramped graves
and the early daffodil, purer than a soul,
is gathered into the terrible mouth of the gale.

John Knox
Iain Crichton Smith

That scything wind has cut the rich corn down –
the satin shades of France spin idly by –
the bells are jangled in St Andrew's town –
a thunderous God tolls from a northern sky.
He pulls the clouds like bandages awry.
See how the harlot bleeds below her crown.
This lightning stabs her in the heaving thigh –
such siege is deadly for her dallying gown.

A peasant's scythe rings churchbells from the stone.
From this harsh battle let the sweet birds fly,
surprised by fields, now barren of their corn.
(Invent, bright friends, theology, or die.)
The shearing naked absolute blade has torn
through false French roses to her foreign cry.

Old Woman
Iain Crichton Smith

And she, being old, fed from a mashed plate
as an old mare might droop across a fence
to the dull pastures of its ignorance.
Her husband held her upright while he prayed

to God who is all-forgiving to send down
some angel somewhere who might land perhaps
in his foreign wings among the gradual crops.
She munched, half dead, blindly searching the spoon.

Outside, the grass was raging. There I sat
imprisoned in my pity and my shame
that men and women having suffered time
should sit in such a place, in such a state

and wished to be away, yes, to be far away
with athletes, heroes, Greeks or Roman men
who pushed their bitter spears into a vein
and would not spend an hour with such decay.

'Pray God,' he said, 'we ask you, God,' he said.
The bowed back was quiet. I saw the teeth
tighten their grip around a delicate death.
And nothing moved within the knotted head

but only a few poor veins as one might see
vague wishless seaweed floating on a tide
of all the salty waters where had died
too many waves to mark two more or three.

Returning Exile
Iain Crichton Smith

You who come home do not tell me
anything about yourself, where you have come from,
why your coat is wet, why there is grass in your hair.

The sheep huddle on the hills as always,
there's a yellow light as if cast by helmets,
the fences made of wire are strung by the wind.

Do not tell me where you have come from, beloved stranger.
It is enough that there is light still in your eyes,
that the dog rising on his pillar of black knows you.

Two Girls Singing

Iain Crichton Smith

It neither was the words nor yet the tune.
Any tune would have done and any words.
Any listener or no listener at all.

As nightingales in rocks or a child crooning
in its own world of strange awakening
or larks for no reason but themselves.

So on the bus through late November running
by yellow lights tormented, darkness falling,
the two girls sang for miles and miles together

and it wasn't the words or tune. It was the singing.
It was the human sweetness in that yellow,
the unpredicted voices of our kind.

Elegy V from *Under the Eildon Tree*

Sydney Goodsir Smith

Here I ligg, Sydney Slugabed Godless Smith,
The Smith, the Faber, ποιητής and Makar,
And Oblomov has nocht til lear me,
Auld Oblomov has nocht on me
Liggan my lane in bed at nune
Gantan at gray December haar,
A cauld, scummie, hauf-drunk cup o tea
At my bedside,
Luntan Virginian fags
– The New World thus I haud in fief
And levie kyndlie tribute. Black men slave
Aneath a distant sun to mak for me
Cheroots at hauf-a-croun the box.
Wi ase on the sheets, ase on the cod,
And crumbs o toast under my bum,
Scrievan the last great coronach

O' the westren flickeran' bourgeois world.
Eheu fugaces!
Lacrimae rerum!
Nil nisi et cetera ex cathedra
Requiescat up your jumper.

O, michtie Stalin i the Aist!
Coud ye but see me nou,
The type, endpynt and final blume
O' decadent capitalistical thirldom
– It took five hunder year to produce me –
Och, coud ye but see me nou
What a sermon coud ye gie
Furth frae the Hailie Kremlin
Bummlan and thunderan owre the Steppes,
Athort the mountains o Europe humman
Till Swack! at my front door, the great Schloss Schmidt
That's Numéro Cinquante (пятьдеся́т, ye ken)
I' the umquhile pairk o Craigmillar House
Whar Marie Stewart o the snawie blee
Aince plantit ane o a thousand treen.

Losh, what a sermon yon wad be!
For Knox has nocht on Uncle Joe
And Oblomov has nocht on Smith
And sae we come by a route maist devious
Til the far-famed Aist-West Synthesis!
Beluved by Hugh that's beluved by me
And the baith o us loe the barley-bree –
But wha can afford to drink the stuff?
Certies no auld Oblomov!
– And yet he does! Whiles!
But no as muckle as Uncle Joe – I've smaa dout!
На здоро́вье, then, auld Muscovite!

Thus are the michtie faaen,
Thus the end o a michtie line,
Dunbar til Smith the Slugabed
Whas luve burns brichter nor them aa
And whas dounfaain is nae less,
Deid for a ducat deid
By the crueltie o his ain maistress.

Ye Mongers Aye Need Masks for Cheatrie
Sydney Goodsir Smith

Delacroix pentit Chopin's heid
No lik ithers a jessie hauf deid
But true, wi a neb lik a eagle's beak,
Een lik levin frae the thunner's crack,
His rasch face sterk wi pouer an daith
And aa the agonie o Poland's skaith.

Wha'll pent trulie Scotland's heid
Nae couthy gloam but mirk and reid?
Skail yir myth o the Union year
Saw mob and riot but deil a cheer?
Syne an Empire's biggit wi Scottis bluid
– But wha'd hae gane gin hame was guid?

Ye mak a myth o a cheated land
As Chopin's made a lilly man;
But truth wull screich an Scotland rid
Ye mongers as the Irish did;
The bluid ye drave til ilka airt
Sall feed its ain reid sleepan hert.

Philomel
Sydney Goodsir Smith

The hushed world o midnicht
Stude strucken still,
Still were aa the simmer sternes,
The mune slept on the hill.

The void whispered in my hert,
The tuim airts were filled
As throu the nichtit wuid I heard
The dervish rossignel.

The firmament was opened wide
And aa the waters melled,
The reid tod stude by the dyke –
O Youth! O Luve! O Philomel!

Largo

Sydney Goodsir Smith

Ae boat anerlie nou
Fishes frae this shore
Ae black drifter lane
Riggs the crammasie daw,
Aince was a fleet, and nou
Ae boat alane gaes out.

War ir Peace, the trawler win
An the youth turns awa
Bricht wi baubles nou
An thirled tae factory or store;
Their faithers fished their ain,
Unmaistered; – ane remains.

And never the clock rins back,
The free days are owre;
The warld shrinks, we luik
Mair t'our maisters ilka hour –
Whan yon lane boat I see
Daith an rebellion blind ma ee!

When You See Millions of the Mouthless Dead

Charles Hamilton Sorley

When you see millions of the mouthless dead
Across your dreams in pale battalions go,
Say not soft things as other men have said,
That you'll remember. For you need not so.

Give them not praise. For, deaf, how should they know
It is not curses heaped on each gashed head?
Nor tears. Their blind eyes see not your tears flow.
Nor honour. It is easy to be dead.
Say only this, 'They are dead.' Then add thereto,
'Yet many a better one has died before.'
Then, scanning all the o'ercrowded mass, should you
Perceive one face that you loved heretofore,
It is a spook. None wears the face you knew.
Great death has made all his for evermore.

The Philosophic Taed

William Soutar

There was a taed wha thocht sae lang
On sanctity and sin;
On what was richt, and what was wrang,
And what was in atween –
That he gat naething düne.

The wind micht blaw, the snaw micht snaw,
He didna mind a wheet;
Nor kent the derk'nin fae the daw,
The wulfire frae the weet;
Nor fuggage frae his feet.

His wife and weans frae time to time,
As they gaed by the cratur,
Wud haut to hae a gowk at him
And shak their pows, or natter:
'He's no like growin better.'

It maun be twenty year or mair
Sin thocht's been a' his trade:
And naebody can tell for shair
Whether this unco taed
Is dead, or thinks he's dead.

The Gowk
William Soutar

Half doun the hill, whaur fa's the linn
Far frae the flaught o' fowk,
I saw upon a lanely whin
A lanely singin' gowk:
Cuckoo, cuckoo;
And at my back
The howie hill stüde up and spak:
Cuckoo, cuckoo.

There was nae soun': the loupin' linn
Hung frostit in its fa':
Nae bird was on the lanely whin
Sae white wi' fleurs o' snaw:
Cuckoo, cuckoo;
I stüde stane still;
And saftly spak the howie hill:
Cuckoo, cuckoo.

The Tryst
William Soutar

O luely, luely, cam she in
And luely she lay doun:
I kent her be her caller lips
And her breists sae sma' and roun'.

A' thru the nicht we spak nae word
Nor sinder'd bane frae bane:
A' thru the nicht I heard her hert
Gang soundin' wi' my ain.

It was about the waukrife hour
When cocks begin to craw
That she smool'd saftly thru the mirk
Afore the day wud daw.

Sae luely, luely, cam she in
Sae luely was she gaen;
And wi' her a' my simmer days
Like they had never been.

Who Are These Children?
William Soutar

With easy hands upon the rein,
And hounds at their horses' feet,
The ladies and the gentlemen
Ride through the village street.

Brightness of blood upon the coats
And on the women's lips:
Brightness of silver at the throats
And on the hunting whips.

Is there a day more calm, more green
Under this morning hour;
A scene more alien than this scene
Within a world at war?

Who are these children gathered here
Out of the fire and smoke
That with remembering faces stare
Upon the foxing folk?

The Permanence of the Young Men
William Soutar

No man outlives the grief of war
Though he outlive its wreck:
Upon the memory a scar
Through all his years will ache.

Hopes will revive when horrors cease;
And dreaming dread be stilled;
But there shall dwell within his peace
A sadness unannulled.

Upon his world shall hang a sign
Which summer cannot hide:
The permanence of the young men
Who are not by his side.

Winter Beauty
William Soutar

Even in winter earth is lovely still,
Bared almost to the bone:
The clean anatomy of tree and hill;
The honesty of stone:

In ultimate endurance under the touch
Of fingering wind and frost:
Withered into a beauty beyond smutch
When all but all is lost:

An incorruptible and patient grace
From bravery forsworn:
The steadfastness upon an aged face
Out of long sufferance born.

We Were Not Expecting the Prince To-day
Muriel Spark

As stated above, we were not expecting . . .
All the same, you had better show him the sleeping
Beauty upstairs with her powder still intact,
While the whole court on sentry duty, believe it,

Propped in their wigs a century exact,
Deplore her blunder, or rather, misconceive it.

And you had better and better deliver
The bat from her tresses, dispose for a kiss
That bluff on her webby mouth, for suppose he should call it,
And give her a nudge, and she takes the hint, and this
Beauty be a cloud of powder over her pallet?

The Yellow Book
Muriel Spark

They did not intend to distinguish between the essence
Of wit and wallpaper trellis. What they cared
Was how the appointments of the age appeared
Under the citron gaslight incandescence.

Virtue was a vulgar, sin a floral passion
And death a hansom at the door, while they
Kept faith with a pomaded sense of history
In their fashion.

Behind the domino, those fringed and fanned
Exclusive girls, prinked with the peacock's eye
Noted, they believed, the trickle of a century
Like a thin umbrella in a black-gloved hand.

Portrait of Mary Stuart, Holyrood
Lewis Spence

Wauken by nicht, and bydand on some boon,
Glaumour of saul, or spirituall grace,
I haf seen sancts and angells in the face,
And like a fere of seraphy the moon;
But in nae mirk nor sun-apparelled noon,

Nor pleasaunce of the planets in their place,
Of luve devine haf seen sae pure a trace
As in yon shadow of the Scottis croun.

Die not, O rose, dispitefull of hir mouth,
Nor be ye lilies waefu at hir snaw;
This dim device is but hir painted sake;
The mirour of ane star of vivand youth,
That not hir velvets nor hir balas braw
Can oueradorn, or luve mair luvely make.

Capernaum

St Matthew xi, 23

Lewis Spence

If aa the bluid shed at thy Tron,
Embro, Embro,
If aa the bluid shed at thy Tron
Were sped into a river,
It wad caa the mills o Bonnington,
Embro, Embro,
It wad caa the mills o Bonnington
For ever and for ever.

If aa the tears that thou has grat,
Embro, Embro,
If aa the tears that thou has grat
Were shed into the sea,
Whaur wad ye find an Ararat,
Embro, Embro,
Whaur wad ye find an Ararat
Frae that fell flude to flee?

If aa the psalms sung in thy kirks,
Embro, Embro,
If aa the psalms sung in thy kirks
Were gaithered in a wind,

It wad shog the taps o Roslin birks,
Embro, Embro,
It wad shog the taps o Roslin birks
Till time was out o mynd.

If aa the broken herts o thee,
Embro, Embro,
If aa the broken herts o thee
Were heapit in a howe,
There wad be neither land nor sea,
Embro, Embro,
There wad be neither land nor sea
But yon reid brae – and thou!

The Calvinist

Kenneth Steven

The heron is a Presbyterian minister,
Standing gloomy in his long grey coat,
Looking at his own reflection in a Sabbath loch.

Every now and again, pronouncing fire and brimstone,
He snatches at an unsuspecting trout
And stands with a lump in his throat.

The congregation of midges laughs at him in Gaelic.
He only prays for them, head bent into grey rain,
As a lark sings psalms half a mile above.

The Long Silence
Kenneth Steven

On Iona the last Gaelic speaker has died.
Last winter when the gales battled each roof and window
He was blown out and into the wind.

Once upon a time he was a tall man,
Leaning at the porch of his weaver's cottage,
His eyes like pools of the sea.

Now in the summer when the tourists come
You will hear the languages fast and loud –
But never a word of Gaelic there.

All over the western islands, the last ones are going
Like candles tonight, falling across the wind,
Their last words drowned and lost in time.

But everyone is talking, busy talking,
The radios and televisions are loud all night
And no-one is listening to the long silence.

Lamb
Kenneth Steven

I found a lamb
Tugged by the guyropes of the wind
Trying so hard to get up.

It was no more than a trembling bundle
A bag of bones and wet wool
A voice made of crying, like a child's.

What a beginning, what a fall,
To be born on the edge of the world
Between the sea and America.

Lamb, out of this island of stone
Yellow is coming, golden promises,
The buttery sunlight of spring.

Edge
Kenneth Steven

If you come here in summer
It is islands and islands as far west as America.
Sudden thunderings of cloud,
Light blessing the sea,
Orchids blowing across every moorland.
Sometimes a seal bumps off rocks;
The air is raucous and torn with birds.
Out on the edges of headlands, here and there,
Like chinks of gold, men and women
With Gaelic in their tongues –
Psalms in their voices.

'On With the Dance!
Let Freud Be Unconfined!'
William J. (Bill) Tait

No more we search our heart of hearts
Or rack our brains, by fits and starts,
To find why we did this or that,
Conscience and conscious both left flat.
Instead, to get the right result,
We've all been taught we must consult
Those not so deeply hidden springs,
The nasty mess that pulls the strings
And knows the answer every time,
Subliminal if not sublime.

But, if all-knowing, won't it know
That we've got wise to it, and so
Confound us with a double bluff,
Which, after all, is simple stuff
Beside the lightning calculations
And complex ratiocinations
With which we freely credit it?
And, if we grant it so much wit
And so discount it, might it not,
Again omniscient, slyly spot
Our new access of acumen,
And start the whole damned thing again?

The Contracting Universe

William J. (Bill) Tait

Mount Palomar's parabola,
Swinging its pole-wide span,
Finds in a reddening spectral light,
Launched before time began
Across five thousand million years,
The proper scale for man.

But I have held the farthest star
Within my elbow's crook;
And bathed in pure galactic seas
Without let or rebuke;
And seen the last sun gutter out
In one tormented look.

Adjustan Mysel tae the Situation
William J. (Bill) Tait

Hi, Torquemada! Dinna fash yersel!
Sen that I'm here, I'll rax my back tae fit
Yon rack o happy mem'ries. You, Procrustes!
Sen that I've made my bed, an sae maun lie,
Reck me yon axe: I'se hain ye ae nicht's darg.
Thir feet o mine ower aft hae taen this gait.

Gin Captain Carpenter had had my wit,
He could hae bidden at hame an hained his breath,
And fed his innards tae the kites his-sel.

Am bodach-ròcais
Ruaraidh MacThomais

An oidhch' ud
thàinig am bodach-ròcais dhan taigh-chèilidh:
fear caol àrd dubh
is aodach dubh air.
Shuidh e air an t-sèis
is thuit na cairtean ás ar làmhan.
Bha fear a siud
ag innse sgeulachd air Conall Gulban
is reodh na faclan air a bhilean.
Bha boireannach 'na suidh' air stòl
ag òran, 's thug e 'n toradh ás a' cheòl.
Ach cha do dh'fhàg e falamh sinn:
thug e òran nuadh dhuinn,
is sgeulachdan na h-àird an Ear,
is sprùilleach de dh'fheallsanachd Geneva,
is sguab e 'n teine á meadhon an làir
's chuir e 'n tùrlach loisgeach nar broillichean.

Scarecrow
Derick Thomson

That night
the scarecrow came into the cèilidh-house:
a tall, thin black-haired man
wearing black clothes.
He sat on the bench
and the cards fell from our hands.
One man
was telling a folktale about Conall Gulban
and the words froze on his lips.
A woman was sitting on a stool,
singing songs, and he took the goodness out of the music.
But he did not leave us empty-handed:
he gave us a new song,
and tales from the Middle East,
and fragments of the philosophy of Geneva,
and he swept the fire from the centre of the floor
and set a searing bonfire in our breasts.

Stèidhichean làidir
Ruaraidh MacThomais

Tha do stèidhichean làidir
anns a' mhuir shàthach sin tha bualadh
's a' suathadh 's a' bragail,
cnap muil air clàr creige.
Do bhallachan air an eagadh
's air a snaidheadh
le locair na mara,
le cruaidh na gaoithe,
Sitheanan a' fàs orra,
blàth air a' chreig,
is bileagan milis feòir.
Tha do chlachan-oisinn daingeann:
An Rubha Dubha, A' Chàbag, An Gallan;

tha do fhreiceadain-cuain 'nan dùisg.
Nuair a dh' fhuilig thu spòltadh nan tonn sin
fuiligidh tu obair mhic-an-duine,
teampall is eaglais is mosque;
thog Nàdur a mhinaret ort,
tha na tuinn ag ùmhlachd aig altair do stallachan,
tha 'n fhaoileag a' frithealadh na h-èifhreann,
tha 'n ùrnaigh air a slechdadh ann an cop a' chladaich.

Lewis

Derick Thomson

Your foundations are strong
in that thrusting sea that thuds
and strokes and cracks,
pebble mass on level rock.
Your walls are notched
and carved
by the plane of the sea,
the chisel of the wind.
Flowers grow on them,
blossom on the rock,
and blades of sweet grass.
Your corner-stones stand firm;
Tolsta Head, Càbag, Gallan Head;
Your sea-watchmen are awake.
Having withstood the mauling of these waves
you can suffer man's work,
temple and church and mosque;
Nature has built on you its minaret,
the waves kneel at the altar of your cliffs,
the seagull celebrates the mass,
the prayer is prostrated in the foam on the shore.

Coimhthional Hiort
Ruaraidh MacThomais

Tha na fulmairean air Stac an Armainn
beò ann an carthannas,
na h-uighean a' leantainn ris a' chreig,
dannsairean air an corra-biod,
's an t-sìorraidheachd ag at
aig bun nan stalla.

Tha 'n t-sùlaire air Sòdhaigh
a' cionacraich amhaich a' ghuga,
a sùil direach air fànas,
a gob a' teagasg nan cosamhlachdan,
gach tè air a nead fhèin.

'S tha na fachaich air oir a' phalla
'nan lèintean geala,
le'n guib dhathach;
mas breug bhuam e 's breug
thugam e: 'sann dhan Eaglais Easbaigich tha 'n treubh.

St Kildan Congregation
Derick Thomson

The fulmars are on Stac an Armainn,
living in comradeship,
their eggs keep their hold on the rock,
dancers on tip-toe,
and eternity wells up
at the foot of the rock-cliffs.

The solan on Soay
fondles the gannet's throat,
its eye stares straight into space,
its beak teaches the Parables,
each one on its own nest.

And the puffins are at the edge of the rock-ledge
in their white surplices,
with their coloured beaks;
I've heard, but don't know whether to believe it,
they're Episcopalians. Well, take it or leave it.

An dàrna eilean

Ruaraidh MacThomais

Nuair a ràinig sinn an t-eilean
bha feasgar ann
's bha sinn aig fois,
a' ghrian a' dol a laighe
fo chuibhrig cuain
's am bruadar a' tòiseachadh ás ùr.

Ach anns a' mhadainn
shad sinn dhinn a' chuibhrig
's anns an t-solas gheal sin
chunnaic sinn loch anns an eilean
is eilean anns an loch,
is chunnaic sinn
gun do theich am bruadar pìos eile bhuainn.

Tha an staran cugallach
chon an dàrna eilein,
tha a' chlach air uideil
tha a' dion nan dearcag,
tha chraobh chaorainn a' crìonadh,
fàileadh na h-iadhshlait a' faileachdainn oirnn a-nis.

The Second Island
Derick Thomson

When we reached the island
it was evening
and we were at peace,
the sun lying down
under the sea's quilt
and the dream beginning anew.

But in the morning
we tossed the cover aside
and in that white light
saw a loch in the island
and an island in the loch,
and we recognised
that the dream had moved away from us again.

The stepping-stones are chancy
to the second island,
the stone totters
that guards the berries,
the rowan withers,
we have lost now the scent of the honeysuckle.

Birds of Passage
Valerie Thornton

Up on Partickhill
from the space where a house has been
you can eyeball the cranes
and the frosted meniscus
of the gasometer
and read the high flats
like bar charts across the city.

Backs to the Atlantic
the foolish cranes
drooling chains and hooks
stare in rigid unison
up the shipless river.

The weathercock on the steeple
abandoned by last week's westerly
cannot avert his metallic eye
gazing down the lower reaches
of the vacant estuary.

Across the twilight
a swarm of starlings
draws its skein
dancing a dotted veil
over their rusting kin.

Personal History

for my son

Ruthven Todd

O my heart is the unlucky heir of the ages
And my body is unwillingly the secret agent
Of my ancestors; those content with their wages
From history: the Cumberland Quaker whose gentle
Face was framed with lank hair to hide the ears
Cropped as a punishment for his steadfast faith,
The Spanish lady who had seen the pitch lake's broth
In the West Indian island and the Fife farmers
To whom the felted barley meant a winter's want.

My face presents my history, and its sallow skin
Is parchment for the Edinburgh lawyer's deed:
To have and hold in trust, as feoffee therein
Until such date as the owner shall have need
Thereof. My brown eyes are jewels I cannot pawn,
And my long lip once curled beside an Irish bog,

My son's whorled ear was once my father's, then mine;
I am the map of a campaign, each ancestor has his flag
Marking an advance or a retreat. I am their seed.

As I write I look at the five fingers of my hand,
Each with its core of nacre bone, and rippled nails;
Turn to the palm and the traced unequal lines that end
In death – only at the tips my ancestry fails –
The dotted swirls are original and are my own:
Look at this fringed polyp which I daily use
And ask its history, ask to what grave abuse
It has been put: perhaps it has curled about the stone
Of Cain. At least it has known much of evil,

And perhaps as much of good, been tender
When tenderness was needed, and been firm
On occasion, and in its past been free of gender,
Been a hand of a mother holding the warm
Impress of the child against her throbbing breast,
Been cool to the head inflamed in fever,
Sweet and direct in contact with a lover.
O in its cupped and fluted shell lies all the past;
My fingers close about the crash of history's storm.

In the tent of night I hear the voice of Calvin
Expending his hatred of the world in icy words;
Man less than a red ant beneath the towering mountain,
And God a troll more fearful than the feudal lords;
The Huguenots in me, flying Saint Bartholomew's Day,
Are in agreement with all this, and their resentful hate
Flames brighter than the candles on an altar, the grey
Afternoon is lit by catherine wheels of terror, the street
Drinks blood and pity in death before their swords.

The cantilever of my bones acknowledges the architect,
My father, to whom always the world was a mystery
Concealed in the humped base of a bottle, one solid fact
To set against the curled pages and the tears of history.
I am a Border keep, a croft and a solicitor's office,
A country rectory, a farm and a drawing-board:
In me, as in so many, the past has stored its miser's hoard,

Won who knows where nor with what loaded dice.
When my blood pulses it is their blood I feel hurry.

These forged me, the latest link in a fertile chain
With ends that run so far that my short sight
Cannot follow them, nor can my weak memory claim
Acquaintance with the earliest shackle. In my height
And breadth I hold my history, and then my son
Holds my history in his small body and the history of another,
Who for me has no contact but that of flesh, his mother.
What I make now I make, indeed, from the unknown,
A blind man spinning furiously in the web of night.

About Scotland, &C.
Ruthven Todd

I was my own ghost that walked among the hills,
Strolled easily among the ruined stones of history;
The student of geography, concerned with fells
And screes rather than with the subtle mystery
Of action's causes – the quickly overbalanced rock
Upon the passing victim, the stab in the back.

Why did this burn run that way to the sea,
Digging a cutting through stone, moss and peat,
And so become ingredient of whisky?
Why was this glen the cause of a defeat,
The silver bullet in the young man's lung,
The devil's puppet and hero of a song?

That queen herself was lorded by the weather,
And Knox drew sustenance from poverty,
The sharp east wind, the sickle in the heather.
The reiver was cornered in the sudden sortie
Of armoured men lying hidden in the bracken,
And a royal line was by sea-storm broken.

This way the landscape formed the people,
Controlled their deeds with cairn and gully;
And no pretender or well-favoured noble
Had power like dammed loch or empty valley.
Their history's origins lie in rock and haze
And the hero seems shorter than his winter days.

This my ghost saw from the deserted keep
And the left paper-mill forgotten in the slums,
This he saw south among the soft-fleshed sheep
And north-west where the Atlantic drums.
Then, since he'd made no claim to be an apostle,
He left, his trophy a neglected fossil.

The Falls of Falloch

Sydney Tremayne

This white explosion of water plunges down
With the deep-voiced rush of sound that shakes a city.
A fine cold smoke drifts across dripping stone
And wet black walls of rock shut in the scene.

Now thought hangs sheer on a precipice of beauty
Lifting with leaping water out from the rock.
A gasp of time, flung clear in a weight of falling,
Bursts like a bud above the deep pool's black
Parted and curled back under by the shock
Where light's bright spark dives to the dark's controlling.

But the brilliance is not extinguished. The heart leaps up,
The heart of the fall leaps up, an eternal explosion,
Force without spending, form without fetter of shape.
And at the pool's edge wavelets scarcely lap
Where drifted spume clings with a soft adhesion.

North of Berwick
Sydney Tremayne

Slowly the sea is parted from the sky:
The light surprises, crinkling on the water.
The white sun hardens; cliffs solidify.
A long coast of red rock where three swans fly
Engraves itself in calm, deceptive weather.

Three swans fly north, a diesel thumping south
Draws out of sight along the rusting railway,
All windows clouded with a communal breath.
Fields flash in the sunlight, far beneath
The sea turns in its scales, well in a seal's way.

No boat invades that shining emptiness.
Because the waves are distant, the sky windless,
That pale line round the shore looks motionless.
Hearing such border warfare lost in space
You say the breathing of the sea is endless.

What is the one thing constant? Can you say?
The loneliness that we are born to merges
Perhaps with such a place on such a day.
No stones cry out because we cannot stay.
Through all our absences the long tide surges.

Mixed Weather
Sydney Tremayne

The holly leaves are glinting in the sun.
Thumped by the wind half senseless we come in,
Into our wits and out of part of our senses,
To watch how the light dances
And lie to ourselves that the long winter's done.

The naked trees roll wildly. Hedges lean
Ready to take off smartly from the scene.
Shadows, dead leaves and flurries of snow are flying.
All fixity's for denying
And wind blurts at the door like a trombone.

Forty-foot cherry trees lie on the ground
Roots raised like horns, no more to be earthbound.
The sky is blue and white and dark and glowing.
A rock in the tide's flowing,
The hill is hit by wave upon wave of sound.

At last the sun goes down, an orange blaze,
And night takes over with a darker noise.
My collie dog who wags his tail in sleeping
Feels he is in safe keeping
Lacking the fearful forethought we call wise.

Lock the door, trusting that it won't blow in.
Hear how the world's alive. The haring moon
Breaks cover and goes tearing into space,
Space that is like packed ice
With all the furies yelling out of tune.

For Whose Delight
Gael Turnbull

For whose delight
do we perform these feats

under the spangled big-top
of the turning sphere,

thronging the arena
with our dreams and needs,

jumping through flaming hoops,
striding on wires across the air,

spurred by a cracking whip, a sugar lump,
of fear, desire

when we hear no cheers
or laughter from out there

in the banked darkness
where the audience should be?

And I Think It Yours
Gael Turnbull

That place
where a fold of hillside
scoops sun and shelter
from a mountain wind

or that
where a clear spring
pours out refreshment
never holding back

or that
where a steep track
veers unexpectedly
then opens on a crest

from where a traveller may see
far out beyond
which road to take –
all these

and all such places
have their names
but in the language of the heart
only one name.

Medusa

Anne Turner

The ageing woman combs her hair
much as she did when, in her prime,
fashion and custom captured her.
And all her thought reflects that time.

Thought reflects that time for her
is a hair-spring; is defeat
spirally within the coils
of static movement, self-deceit.

Movement, self-deceit, surrounds
the car, the clothes, the views expressed.
One moment between youth and age
matured, and prophesied the rest:

prophesied the rust, the dust –
the last mutations in her veins.
She struggles, prisoner of whims
which no platonic lust sustains.

Must so stains the well-dressed act
that *why* is lost beneath what seems.
A ghost virginity presides
wistfully over dyes and creams.

Cries and dreams, corroding cares,
wrinkle the mask to mock despair:
a myth that shames the mirror where
the ageing woman combs her hair.

Full Supporting Programme
W. Price Turner

Just at the most exciting part
of the film, as the secret agent
hiding in the coffin pushed up the lid –
suddenly behind us a woman screaming!
We followed the direction, turned heads miming
disgust: she had ruptured our paid-for dream.
Meanwhile, back on the screen, sinister
extras lurked in the vaults that took
half a day to light. We saw what a crude
bit of cutting did for a poor script.
But she was at it again: 'Help
me! I think my husband's dead!'
Sure enough, there was a dark
heap in the seat beside her. What
a way to go, before you even
know what's on next week. But there was little
we could do; it was the manager's
problem. Bad for business, that. The actors
were leaping out on one another. Behind,
a nice part for a Nightingale usherette.
Luckily the heroine in a bikini
appeared in time to save her lover, because
there were only five minutes left to blow
up the castle and sell us ice-cream.
Next time I thought about it
a boy who looked too young to see
the main feature sat where the shrieker
had been. We left while a priest was easing
into the corpse's seat, his folded coat
carefully trailing across the lap
of the mesmerised boy, as more
death and seduction began.

Homely Accommodation, Suit Gent
W. Price Turner

In that repository of auction pots and post-Ark
furniture, stepping over the creaking board
you always sprang another, setting Mrs Hagglebroth
ready to intercept you with her pleated smile
and plucked eyebrows up, while conducting her
wallpaper centenary festival with a stick of feathers.

In that saddlesoap atmosphere, there was no music
after Mozart, and no smoking in the dining-room.
Sunlight was discouraged: it fades the draperies.
Sunday papers she detested, like all dirt. Even
the bought earth was sterilised before the bulbs,
one to a pot, were planted; God rest their souls.

But the remarkable strain of slaughterhouse fly
that bloated its dipstick in her best insecticide
always escaped her notice, though she stiffened
at irregular movements of bedsprings, and blushed
when the cistern gargled openly. Somehow her gentlemen
kept moving on, though she prayed for them all.

It was as if, when the seed stirred in them, they
thought of her with rubber gloves on, oiling her shears,
and fled, a week overpaid. Behind her back, when
she went to church, talk about wart-hogs in war-togs,
they called her Brothelhag, bartering sniggers,
and the sweat chilled on them in case she knew.

One lay awake at night sheeted in terror, when
the Hagglebroth bloomers billowing from the line
rose in binocular glory and loomed at his window
like a zeppelin. He left. They all left. Even
the glutted fly. Finally Mrs Hagglebroth herself
left, in a brand-new box sealed against sunlight.

So we have here the Hagglebroth effects. The souls
of miscellaneous gentlemen, welded to wicker chairs.

The fears of young men and the dread of old, potted
in antique brass. Several conscience racks, disguised
as beds. Connoisseur stuff all of it. So come now,
ladies, you have your catalogues . . . What am I bid?

Scottish Mythology
Raymond Vettese

Hades withoot an Elysium,
Blessed Isles runked o joy;
nae water o mercy washes oot memory.

We chose the wrang gods –
or the wrang gods chose us.
We maun caa doon sae muckle
but that I doot Prometheus only wad daur,
and suffer for't. See him,
chained til Schiehallion,
howked at by guid hame-bred Scottish carrion
skreichin: 'Ye cuid fare waur!'

Photograph
Raymond Vettese

Nae muckle love in that dour look:
a braw face for cauld weather,
a thraw-gabbit winter-tholin face
wi nae time for lauchin or blether.

And yet I mind whaun his wife deed
hoo he grat and I, wha shuid hae seen
this rauch auld man in a new licht,
turnt awa, as gawkit as he'd ae been.

Scottish Names

Raymond Vettese

I love the names o Scotland:
Ecclefechan, Auchenblae,
Fordoun, Gourdon, Forfar, Kirkcudbright,
Dunnichen, Echt, Panadram, Drumtochty,
and wha could ignore Auchtermuchty?

I love the names o Scotland:
hoo they dirl thro me, the stounds
o consonants, nieves o soonds
that dunt on the map; ilka ane redoonds
wi stickit pride: these are my boonds!

I love the names o Scotland:
Friockheim, Fettes, Pittenweem, Pitcaithly,
Dunnottar, Dunfermline, Aberdower, Invertay,
Catterline, Corstorphine, Craigmillar, Cruden Bay,
and wha could ignore Clachnaharry?

I love the names o Scotland:
hoo e'en the prosaic is owreset
intil a ferlie ye canna forget,
tho it's aiblins but a place whaur burns aince met
or a wee wuid fort wis, and is yet,

but only in the name. Oor past's
chairted for us, oor history's here,
in Balmaha, Birnam, Dunblane, Ardersier;
the names clash oot, tirl on the ear,
and wha could ignore braw Durisdeer?

I love the names o Scotland,
the names that are oors, and tho Wounded Knee
is fine and fair and sad, it's no Fyvie,
and gin Montrose, whaun I dee, winna hae me:
bury my hairt in the cricket-pitch o Freuchie!

Clearing Out
Val Warner

Now she was ready, in an aura of moth-balls.
The turning-out had been finished, almost.
The oldest batch of receipts
Meticulously kept for seven years, had been destroyed.
Few for each year, and getting fewer.
Sparse personal letters held together by a rubber band.
A pack of playing cards whose forties' box
Had finally collapsed rehoused in an economy size match box.
And the spare Book of Common Prayer re-covered.
Each drawer lined with fresh newspaper.
Their contents so slight they rattled when opened
Except the clothes' drawers, though almost as bare,
With pale satin bags of lavender.
Nothing out of place; not much
To tidy this time. The annual shrinking bundle
For the Oxfam shop is nearly tied.
Not many clues as to identity for next of kin.
Only the clichéd yellow photo
Tucked in an envelope, a young officer's peaked face
And a rarely subjective sigh
Seeping through the two rooms the sea through a wreck
What a terrible Martha.

Is This Man, Martin Bormann?
Roderick Watson

In the country of Guatemala
they talked to me of genocide
I did not say much;
        living the way I have
one becomes reserved,
and what could I have said?

I was always good with my hands
so I became a carpenter
and carried the boards myself
        after the donkey died
of old age, or the beatings,
it hardly matters now.

'Why shouldn't you
die for the Jews?'
I could not think of a suitable reply
        and we are known by deeds
not talk, they say:
so they took my fingerprints away.

People argue in paper-shops
'The hair-line is somewhat similar
certainly he is older
        and of course much thinner
but even changed in face and name
isn't he still the same?'

But one becomes reserved,
and soon it is too late
to explain how it was
        for an odd job man
who did not always use
the very best materials.

Brandan's Last Voyage

Kenneth White

1

Entendez ci de saint Brandent
Que fu nez devers occident
Que VII ans erra par la mer
Por plus douter Dieu et amer . . .

2

It was a stony kingdom
on the West coast of Ireland
with the wind wailing
and the roaring of Atlantic breakers
with strange men wandering and murmuring:
is é mo drui Crist mac Dé
'my druid is Christ the son of God'.

3

One had always wished to wander farther
Brandan by name and a name it was
that had the sea in it,
the breaking of waves and the memory of a poem
the old men would speak on winter nights:
'Bran thinks a great marvel it is
to sail a boat on the clear sea
Bran's eyes see the waves of the sea
the sea waves shine in summer
as far as the eyes of Bran can see
Bran loves to look upon the sea
the white sea broken by oars.'

4

There are men who are always ready
to throw everything to the winds
men who can look on life coldly
and stake everything on a gesture
Brandan was one of those
God for him was the great gesture
that had set everything in motion
also a great idea sailing through space
brighter than the sun and the moon.

5

Brandan built him a boat

he built it of seventeen places
making first a framework of pliant wood
covering it with bull hides tanned in oak
smearing the hides with grease and resin –
a boat light as a bird to ride the sea!

when the boat was ready, firm and true
he gathered men about him, saying:
'this will be no pleasure cruise
rather the wildest of wild goose chases
around the rim of the world or farther
a peregrination in the name of God
and the promise of white martyrdom'.

6

They pulled away from Ireland, heading North
oars dipping into blue water
amid a caterwauling of gulls

the going was good and the rhythm sure

to the East was the land of the white hills
and they passed by Islay, and the Isle of Tiree
then Barra, the Uists, till they came to Lewis

at the isle of Lewis they went ashore
walked round the ancient stones of Callernish
then headed again for the open sea.

7

The weather went grey and the sea grew gurly
long days of rain, snow, sleet and wind
(surely this must be the very mouth of hell)
Brandan at the prow, crying into the greyness
is é mo drui Crist mac Dé!
the words lost in the grey wastes

never letting up his holy chanting
he kept his eyes skinned for another island.

8

Brandan's mind was full of islands
he had been born and raised among islands
the Hebrides he knew by heart
the Orkneys and the Faeroes too

the world for him was all islands
and weren't the heavens themselves so made?

he was looking for an island now
but so far North he'd never come
the world here was at an end
here there was only sea and wind

at length he let loose one of his crows
and the crow made straight for the Island of Birds.

9

Ka! kaya gaya! keeya! keeya!
branta branta! branta branta!
graak! graak! graak!

that island was noisier than a church
all the birds of the ocean had foregathered there
gulls and redshanks and cormorants
kittiwakes, terns and guillemots
geese and gannets and skuas
some perched on pinnacles of rock
others flying wildly about
ah, it was a goodly sight
and music in Brandan's ears

they pulled up the boat on the bit of beach
and turning it into a shelter
settled down for the night.

10

When Brandan awoke in the morning
he was looking a skua in the eye
and it looked for all the world
like his old teacher, Mernok
away back there in Munster

'Excuse me, Skua', he said, 'can you tell me
how far we are from Paradise?'

the skua gave a sturdy beat of its wings
and stalked silently off
'I thought so', said Brandan.

11

Ah, it was beautiful, the northern blue
and the clear white curling of the surf!
every mile was a broad blue page of vellum
and Brandan was working out the words

he thought in Latin and he thought in Gaelic
murmuring *'farspag'*, *'in deserto'*, *'muir'*
trying for a freshness never found before

Brandan the voyager would be Brandan the poet
only if he could write a poem
brighter and stronger than all other poems
a poem full of the rough sea and the light

oh, the words for it, the words for a dawning!

to build a boat is good
to sail the faraway seas is good
but to write a poem on which
the minds of men could sail for centuries
that was his ambition now
with a long lifetime behind him.

12

'Brandanus laboriosus' they had called him
when he was a busy abbot of monasteries
true, he had always worked like ten
Brandan the Worker, Brandan the Mariner
he had his reputation, sure
but he'd felt it over there on Iona
when he'd been in talk with that Columba
the one who spouted poetry like a book
that somehow he was out beyond the pale
beyond the pale of the literary folk
lacking their polish, their finesse

Columba the Dove and Brandan the Crow

well, it wasn't polish and finesse he wanted
it was a freshness and a force
and a beauty that they'd never know!

13

Farther and farther they pulled away
into the white unknown.

Song of the Coffin Close
Kenneth White

Have you heard of the Coffin Close, boys
have you heard of the Coffin Close
it's one of life's rare joys, boys
it smells like a summer rose
yes, it smells like a summer rose

Have you ever climbed up the stair, boys
have you ever climbed up the stair
where the lavvy-pan overflows, boys
and gives you a whiff of rotten air
yes, a whiff of rotten air

Have you ever fallen down the stair, boys
have you ever fallen down the stair
and buried your sensitive nose, boys
in the filth and muck which is there
yes, the filth and muck which is there

Have you ever come up at night, boys
have you ever come up at night
when the burner throws its rays, boys
you see many a ghastly sight
yes, many a ghastly sight

Have you ever seen Bill McNeice, boys
have you ever seen Bill McNeice
lying dead to the world, boys
and a cat being sick in his face
yes, a cat being sick in his face

Have you ever seen Mary Cape, boys
have you ever seen Mary Cape
she often hangs there on the stairs, boys
coughing her insides up
coughing her insides up

You all know the Coffin Close, boys
you all know the Coffin Close
if I bother you all with my noise, boys
it's all for a very good cause
yes, it's all for a very good cause

I live in the Coffin Close, boys
I live in the Coffin Close
very soon they'll be taking me out, boys
and my head will come after my toes
yes, my head will come after my toes.

McTaggart

Kenneth White

What was he after there at Machrihanish
this man whose painting
the little critics said had no finish?

(that sense of windswept space
sea and sky in multiple movement
landscape seen as mindscape
the human figures
more and more transparent
till they disappeared)

if the question had been put to him directly
he would have made no answer
simply walked a little farther along the shore.

Satori in Fauldhouse

Colin Will

The great sage came to the vile West
and asked 'Who is your wisest man?"
'That would be Big Shuggie', said the villagers.
'Go then, and fetch Big Shuggie,
that we may engage in discourse
on the nature of Buddhahood.'
But the people returned, saying,
'Big Shuggie is on the bevvie
and will not come.'

'Go again, and tell him I desire to know
the sound of one hand clapping.'
The emissaries returned in sorrow, reporting,
'Big Shuggie says he'll clap yer lug in a meenit.
He's on a roll at the dominoes,
Ma Johnson's 80-shillin' is going down a treat,
an' he's just had the nod for later
from wee Senga, whose man
has neutered himself
with much lager. Bugger Buddha! he says.'
So spoke the spokesperson, apologetically,
for such was his role.

'Truly, Big Shuggie is wise in the ways of Zen',
said the sage,
'I will return to the mystic East,
            for I can learn him nothin.'

Pruning

Jim C. Wilson

I dock the dead, the damaged and diseased;
the gnarled and dry come tumbling from the heights
until I stand knee-deep in bits, well-pleased
I've put a few square yards of world to rights.
I clip and crop, encouraging new growth.
My fingers start to ache but still I snap
my Homebase secateurs. I grin as both
the gleaming silver blades expose more sap.
I deftly make the kindest cuts, and take
the part of surgeon, Adam, God. But mend
myself, I cannot. No sharp shears will make
me sprout, or slow my geriatric trend.
So, wrinkling, stiffening, stooping, short of breath,
I spend my weekends saving plants from death.

Death in Venice

Jim C. Wilson

Von Aschenbach thinks as the tide comes in,
'This is not the Ganges delta.' His lips
close round a strawberry. (It's *such* a sin,
that luscious, dead-ripe fruit.) He sees the hips,
the milky skin of Tadzio. That boy
is perfect classical grace: Greek ideal,
a thing one might aspire to. Oh, what joy
to wait, to watch. And is such beauty real?
In dark back streets, a hot wind stifles. Stone
is sluiced down with disinfectant. A man
is observed; he's powdered and rouged. Alone
he returns to the sand, refines his plan.
Close by his chair a tiger waits to spring.
The tide goes out, a woman starts to sing.

The Fear
Andrew Young

How often I turn round
To face the beast that bound by bound
Leaps on me from behind,
Only to see a bough that heaves
With sudden gust of wind
Or blackbird raking withered leaves.

A dog may find me out
Or badger toss a white-lined snout;
And one day as I softly trod
Looking for nothing stranger than
A fox or stoat I met a man
And even that seemed not too odd.

And yet in any place I go
I watch and listen as all creatures do
For what I cannot see or hear,
For something warns me everywhere
That even in my land of birth
I trespass on the earth.

Field-Glasses
Andrew Young

Though buds still speak in hints
And frozen ground has set the flints
As fast as precious stones
And birds perch on the boughs, silent as cones,

Suddenly waked from sloth
Young trees put on a ten years' growth
And stones double their size,
Drawn nearer through field-glasses' greater eyes.

Why I borrow their sight
Is not to give small birds a fright
Creeping up close by inches;
I make the trees come, bringing tits and finches.

I lift a field itself
As lightly as I might a shelf,
And the rocks do not rage
Caught for a moment in my crystal cage.

And while I stand and look,
Their private lives an open book,
I feel so privileged
My shoulders prick, as though they were half-fledged.

The Falls of Glomach
Andrew Young

Rain drifts forever in this place
Tossed from the long white lace
The Falls trail on black rocks below,
And golden-rod and rose-root shake
In wind that they forever make;
So though they wear their own rainbow
It's not in hope, but just for show,
For rain and wind together
Here through the summer make a chill wet weather.

Suilven
Andrew Young

It rose dark as a stack of peat
With mountains at its feet,
Till a bright flush of evening swept
And on to its high shoulders leapt

And Suilven, a great ruby, shone;
And though that evening light is dead
The mountain in my mind burns on,
As though I were the foul toad, said
To bear a precious jewel in his head.

Culbin Sands

Andrew Young

Here lay a fair fat land;
But now its townships, kirks, graveyards
Beneath bald hills of sand
Lie buried deep as Babylonian shards.

But gales may blow again;
And like a sand-glass turned about
The hills in a dry rain
Will flow away and the old land look out;

And where now hedgehog delves
And conies hollow their long caves
Houses will build themselves
And tombstones rewrite names on dead men's graves.

The Ballant o' the Laird's Bath

Douglas Young

In Switzerland lang syne befell
a deed o great renoun,
i the Whyte Buik o Sarnen
was trulie scryveit doun.

Alzellen's Laird rade out his lane
ae simmer mornan early;
midmaist the wuids of Uri
he sune gat wandert fairlie.

He's socht the wey baith aist and wast,
but canna win back hame;
the shelt grows mair disjeskit aye,
the Laird mair wud wi grame.

Near lowsin-time he cam at last,
aa clortit owre wi stour,
til a bonnie bit hous in a gair o park,
and breenged intil the bouer.

'Guidwife,' quo he, 'gae fetch to me
a tassie o caller wine,
and thraw a fat hen's craig about.
Alzellen's Laird maun dine.

'But saft . . . I pray thee pardon, dame,
I suldna been sae reoch,
nou that I see your bonnie blee,
your weel-faur'd breist and hough.

'Anither thochtie I hae thocht
Fair dame, I'ld speir at thee,
mak het a chaudron a clear watter
and syne come bath wi me.'

The douce guidwife was michtilie fleggit
at sic an orra demand,
the mair that she kent Alzellen's Laird
was a sair man to withstand.

Nocht answeran him she brocht the wine,
pit on the pat to boil,
syne threw a pullet's craig about,
and prayed a prayer the while:

'O Mary, mither o charitie,
ressave me frae this shame;
haud back the Laird frae his intent
whill my guidman wins hame.'

She's plied the Laird wi monie a tass
o the sweet Riesling wine,
and staad his wame wi dentie meats
fit for King Charlemagne.

Syne she's duin aff his braw sword-belt,
wi gentie mien and douce,
his cordinant shuin and the lave o his claes,
and taen them ben the hous.

He's lowpit intil the warm watter,
crouse as the Deil was he;
then bydan on that dame's return
he sings fou lustilie.

Thon randy ballant echoes loud
amang the wuids of Uri,
the guidman's heard it frae the byre,
and hame cam he in a furie.

He's breenged inby wi birsslan baird,
swingan his cleaver-axe;
he's chappit the naukit Laird in twa,
and syne in eichty-sax.

The wan watter i the bress chaudron
rins reid wi bree o bluid.
Let that be a lesson to Lairds and the lave
nae to get tint in a wuid.

For a Wife in Jizzen
Douglas Young

Lassie, can ye say
whaur ye ha been,
whaur ye ha come frae,
whatna ferlies seen?

Eftir the bluid and swyte,
the warsslin o yestreen,
ye ligg forfochten, whyte,
prouder nor onie queen.

Albeid ye hardly see me
I read it i your een,
sae saft blue and dreamy,
mindan whaur ye've been.

Anerly wives ken
the ruits o joy and tene,
the march o daith and birth,
the tryst o luve and strife

i the howedumbdeidsunsheen,
fire, air, water, yirth
mellan to mak new life,
lauchan and greetan, feiman and serene.

Dern frae aa men
the ferlies ye ha seen.

For the Old Highlands
Douglas Young

That old lonely lovely way of living
in Highland places, – twenty years a-growing,
twenty years flowering, twenty years declining, –
father to son, mother to daughter giving
ripe tradition; peaceful bounty flowing;
one harmony all tones of life combining, –
old wise ways, passed like the dust blowing.

That harmony of folk and land is shattered, –
the yearly rhythm of things, the social graces,
peat-fire and music, candle-light and kindness.
Now they are gone it seems they never mattered,
much, to the world, those proud and violent races,
clansmen, and chiefs whose passioned greed and blindness
made desolate these lovely lonely places.

Last Lauch
Douglas Young

The Minister said it wald dee,
the cypress buss I plantit.
But the buss grew til a tree,
naething dauntit.

It's growan stark and heich,
derk and straucht and sinister,
kirkyairdie-like and dreich.
But whaur's the Minister?

Notes on Poets

Helen Adam (1909–93)
Born in Scotland in 1909, Adam spent many years in America and was an influential figure in the San Francisco Renaissance. Her dark, timeless tales of doomed love and emotional revenge are hauntingly crafted into traditional ballad forms. Thanks to publication in magazines and anthologies and personal readings at universities, theatres and poetry centres, she had an enthusiastic following in the USA. Fellow poet Robert Duncan described her as 'this poet who cares nothing for opinions but all for the life of the imagination'. Her *Selected Poems and Ballads* were published in 1974.

Margot Robert Adamson (1898–unknown)
Author of several books of poetry, including *Up the Hill of Fairlight* (1925) and *Northern Holiday: Poems* (1928), Adamson also rendered poems from the *Bannatyne Manuscript* into modern English, published as *A Treasury of Middle English Verse* (1930).

James Aitchison (b. 1938)
Aitchison was born in Stirlingshire and studied at Glasgow and Strathclyde Universities, doing a doctorate on Edwin Muir at the latter. He has worked as a copywriter, information officer and lecturer and received an Eric Gregory Award for poetry in 1968. His publications include *Brain Scans* (1998) and the earlier *Sounds Before Sleep* (1971), *Spheres* (1975) and *Second Nature* (1990).

Marion Angus (1866–1946)
Born in Sunderland, the daughter of a United Presbyterian Kirk minister, Marion Angus grew up in Arbroath, and later lived in Aberdeen, Edinburgh and Helensburgh, dying in Arbroath. *The Lilt and Other Verses* appeared in 1922, to be followed by *Sun and Candlelight* (1927), *The Singin' Lass* (1929) and *Lost Country, and Other Verses* (1937). Maurice Lindsay edited her *Selected Poems* in 1950.

J. K. Annand (1908–93)

Born in Edinburgh and educated at Edinburgh University, Annand was a vigorous champion of Scots, best known for his bairn rhymes, *Sing It Aince for Pleisure* (1965) and two further collections. See Janet Campbell's *The Bairn Rhymes of J. K. Annand* (*Akros* No. 26). His adult poems include translations of Bavarian folksongs and of *Carmina Burana*.

Meg Bateman (b. 1959)

Born in Edinburgh in 1959, Bateman teaches at the Gaelic College in Skye. Her bilingual collection in English and Gaelic, *Aotromachd agus Dain Eile / Lightness and Other Poems*, was published in 1997 and she features in many anthologies and both editions of *Dream State: The New Scottish Poets*.

D. M. Black (b. 1941)

South African born Black, the son of a Scottish academic, was educated at Trinity College, Glenalmond, and Edinburgh and Lancaster Universities. He is a London-based psychoanalyst. His collections include *With Decorum* (1967), *The Educators* (1969), *The Happy Crow* (1974), and *Gravitations* (1979). His *Collected Poems* were published in 1991.

Sheena Blackhall, née Middleton (b. 1947)

Born and educated in Aberdeen, Blackhall was fellow in creative writing at the Elphinstone Institute, Aberdeen University, from 1998 to 2003 and is engaged in fostering creative writing, mainly in the vernacular. Her 1995 anthology *Stagwyse* draws on eight earlier collections; subsequent publications include *The Singing Bird* (poems in English and Scots, 2000). To date, she has published 40 poetry books, 10 short story collections and two Scots novellas.

Captain Hamish Blair (dates and life unknown)

Alan Bold (1943–98)

Poet, biographer, critic, and editor, Bold was born in Edinburgh and educated at Broughton High School and Edinburgh University. On the staff of the *Times Educational Supplement* from 1966 to 1967, he then became a full-time writer. His many books include the collections *A Perpetual Motion Machine* (1969), *In This Corner: Selected Poems 1963–1983* and *Summoned by Knox* (1985). His biography of MacDiarmid won him the McVitie Scottish Writer of the Year Award in 1989. His other critical works include *The Ballad* (1979) and *Modern Scottish Literature* (1983).

Deric Bolton (1908–93)

Paisley-born Bolton was a chemist and had a long involvement with the Poetry Association of Scotland. From 1937 he lived in Edinburgh. His works include *Glasgow Central Station* (1972), *A View from Ben More* (1972), *The Wild Uncharted Country* (1973), *Grown over with Green-ness* (1976) and his selected poems, *August Morning on Tweed* (1991).

Kate Y. A. Bone (1896–1985)

Born Kate Dryburgh in Kirkcaldy, Fife, Bone married William Bone around 1938–9. They settled in Colinton, Edinburgh. She first published *Thistle By-Blaws* in 1956 and used the same title for two subsequent pamphlets.

James Bridie / O. H. Mavor (1888–1951)

Doctor and dramatist, Bridie graduated in medicine at Glasgow University in 1914, spent the First World War in the RAMC, and retired from a distinguished medical career in 1938, though he rejoined the RAMC in 1939. From his first play, *Sunlight Sonata* (1928) to his last, *The Baikie Charivari* (1952), he wrote a series of plays that captivated audiences in London as well as Glasgow. Although he wrote an autobiography that captures the spirit of his times and some verse, of which the piece anthologised is a student example, he was essentially a playwright with his own distinctive voice. He also founded the Citizens' Theatre and was influential in the founding of the Edinburgh Festival and the School of Drama at the Royal Scottish Academy of Music and Drama. He held a CBE and an LLD.

George Mackay Brown (1921–96)

Born in Stromness, Orkney, of an Orcadian father and Highland mother, Brown was a protégé of Edwin Muir's at Newbattle Abbey. He outshone the older poet in public profile, though he rarely travelled from his Orcadian home. His vision of the Northern Isles was stamped indelibly on his readers' imaginations through plays, films, novels and especially volumes of poetry, from the early *Fishermen with Ploughs* (1971) to the posthumous *Following a Lark* (1996) and *Travellers* (2001). His autobiography, *For the Islands I*

Sing, also published after his death (1997), throws less light on the creative forces animating him than might have been expected. His novel *Beside the Ocean of Time* was short-listed for the Booker Prize. He was the recipient of an OBE and various honorary degrees. His *Collected Poems* appeared in 2005.

Hamish Brown (b. 1934)
Writer, lecturer and photographer with a special interest in Scottish affairs, the outdoors and travel, Brown is an authority on Morocco's Atlas Mountains and has written, edited and contributed to some thirty books, including *Time Gentlemen* (1983) (collected poems), *The Bothy Brew* (short stories) and the outdoors classic, *Hamish's Mountain Walk*. He edited *Poems of the Scottish Hills* and *Speak to the Hills* (twentieth-century British and Irish poems). His awards include a D.Litt. from St Andrews University (1997) and the MBE (2001). He lives in Burntisland, Fife.

Margaret Gillies Brown (b. 1929)
Margaret Gillies Brown was born near Edinburgh and now lives in Perthshire. She had seven children by her first husband, Ronald Gillies, and after his death married Henry Brown. She trained as a state registered nurse at Dundee Royal Infirmary; describes her politics as 'changeable'; and her religion as 'Protestant'. Her books include *Hares on the Horizon* (1981), *Footsteps of the Goddess* (1994) and *Of Rowan and Pearl* (2000).

George Bruce (1909–2002)
Bruce, educated in his native Fraserburgh and at Aberdeen University, taught at Dundee High School before becoming an arts producer for the BBC in Aberdeen (1946–56) and arts and features producer in Edinburgh (1956–70). Subsequently he was a writer-in-residence at Glasgow University and a professor at several American universities. His volumes of poetry included *Collected Poems* (1971) and *Pursuit* (winner of the Saltire Book of the Year 1999) which have been superseded by his 2001 volume *Today Tomorrow*. He also collaborated with the artists John Bellany (*Woman of the North Sea*, 2001) and Dame Elizabeth Blackadder (*Through the Letterbox*, 2003) and was joint editor of the anthology series *Scottish Poetry* (1966–72) and co-editor of *A Scottish Postbag* (1986 and 2002). His distinctions included an OBE and honorary degrees from Wooster College, Ohio, and Aberdeen University.

Tom Bryan (b. 1950)

Born in Canada of a Canadian father and Scots mother, Bryan has long lived in Scotland, and is a widely published poet, fiction, and non-fiction writer. He now works as Arts Development Officer in Caithness. He was a writing fellow, Aberdeenshire, 1994–97, and for the Scottish Borders, 1998–2001. Publications include *North-East Passage* (1996), *Wolfwind* (1996) and *Wolfclaw Chronicles* (2000). He edited *North Words*, 1992–97.

John Buchan / Lord Tweedsmuir of Elsfield (1875–1940)

As well as being a prolific writer of thrillers, a biographer, publisher, journalist and editor, Perth-born Buchan had a high-profile public life, from 1901 when he joined the staff of Lord Milner in the reconstruction of South Africa after the Boer War to his final appointment as Governor-General of Canada in 1935. Educated at Hutchesons' Grammar School and Glasgow University, he subsequently studied at Brasenose College, Oxford, and thereafter immersed himself in the wider world of the English Establishment. In his poetry, however, he never forgot his Scottish, and in particular Borders, roots and language. His *Poems, Scots and English*, appeared in 1917, and in 1924 he edited *The Northern Muse*, an anthology of verse in Scots.

Tom Buchan (1931–95)

Glasgow-born Buchan was educated at Jordanhill School and Balfron High School. He taught at Denny High School before becoming a lecturer at Madras University, India (1957–58), a teacher at Irvine Royal Academy (1963–65), a senior lecturer at Clydebank Technical College (1967–70), and a director of festivals at Craigmillar and Dumbarton. His best-known collection is *Dolphins at Cochin* (1969). Three others followed, as well as a novel, *Makes You Feel Great*. He also wrote five plays.

Elizabeth Burns (b. 1957)

Burns worked in bookselling and publishing and lived in Edinburgh but moved to Lancaster to raise her family. Her poems have appeared in many publications. *Ophelia and Other Poems* was published in 1991; *The Gift of Light* in 1999.

John Burnside (b. 1955)

Burnside is a Reader in Creative Writing at St Andrews University. He won the Geoffrey Faber Prize for his collection *Feast Days* in

1994, and the Whitbread Poetry Award for *The Asylum Dance* in 2000. His ninth, and latest, collection is *The Good Neighbour*. He has also written five works of fiction, including *The Dumb House* and, most recently, *Living Nowhere*.

Ron Butlin (b. 1949)

Born in Edinburgh and educated at Dumfries Academy and Edinburgh University, Butlin has had a varied career as footman, model, computer operator, security guard, barnacle scraper, labourer and city messenger, before holding academic appointments at New Brunswick, Edinburgh, Stirling and St Andrews. His collections include *Stretto* (1976), *Creatures Tamed by Cruelty* (1979), *Ragtime in Unfamiliar Bars* (1985), *Histories of Desire* (1995) and *Without a Backward Glance* (2005).

John M. Caie (1878–1949)

The son of a minister, Caie was born at Banchory-Devenick and educated at Milne's Institute, Fochabers, subsequently studying at Aberdeen University and the North of Scotland College of Agriculture. He lectured in agriculture in Ireland, Edinburgh and Aberdeen, and was latterly a senior civil servant in the Department of Agriculture. His two books of poetry, mostly in Scots, reflect his rural roots. They are *The Kindly North: Verse in Scots and English* (1934) and *'Twixt Hills and Sea* (1939).

Janet Caird (1913–92)

Born in Nyasaland (now Malawi), where her father was a missionary, Caird was educated at Dollar Academy and Edinburgh University. Married to J. B. Caird, formerly Inspector of Schools for Ross and Cromarty, she lived in Inverness and wrote several novels and short stories as well as poems. Her collections include *Some Walk a Narrow Path* (1977) and *John Donne, You Were Wrong* (1988).

Sir Alec Cairncross (1911–98)

Alec Cairncross, born in Lesmahagow, was Chancellor of Glasgow University from 1972 until his death and Master of St Peter's College, Oxford, in the 1970s. As an economics student at Cambridge he studied under Keynes and after periods alternating between academic life at Glasgow University and government service, was latterly the first head of the Government Economic

Service in the 1960s. His poems in his little volume *Snatches* (1980) were written in the late 1930s and during and immediately after the Second World War (when he wryly observed the Allies wrangling in Berlin over German reparations) and reflect the events of the times and their impact on a sentient young man.

Angus Calder (b. 1942)
Calder is an Edinburgh-based historian, academic, journalist and commentator on world literature. His first poetry collection *Waking in Waikato* (1997) was, in his own words, 'published comparatively late in life'. *Horace in Tollcross: Eftir Some Odes of Q. H. Flaccus* appeared in 2000. Calder has had two Scottish Arts Council Book Awards and was founding convenor of the Scottish Poetry Library. He was awarded an Scottish Arts Council writer's bursary in 2002 to complete further books – *Colours of Grief* (2003) and *Dipa's Bowl* and *Sun Behind the Castle* (both 2004).

Robert R. Calder (b. 1950)
Born in Burnbank, Lanarkshire, and educated at Hamilton Academy and Glasgow and Edinburgh Universities, Calder writes in English and Scots and freelances between Scotland and Germany. He has written numerous essays on philosophy and literary and cultural criticism and has edited *Chapman* and *Lines Review*. A trained singer, he is staff music writer for *PopMatters*, the Chicago 'journal of global culture'. His *Serapion* (1996) collects poems from over twenty years.

Gerry Cambridge (b. 1959)
A former freelance journalist and natural history photographer, Cambridge edits the Scottish-American poetry magazine *The Dark Horse*, and was the 1997–99 writing fellow at Hugh MacDiarmid's former home of Brownsbank, near Biggar. His collections include *The Shell House* (1995), *Nothing But Heather!: Scottish Nature in Poems, Photographs and Prose* (1999), and *Madame Fi Fi's Farewell* (2003). His pamphlet *Blue Sky, Green Grass: A Day at Lawthorn Primary* won the Callum Macdonald Memorial Award in 2004.

Kate Clanchy (b. 1965)
Kate Clanchy was born in Glasgow and grew up in Edinburgh. Her three poetry collections, *Slattern* (1996), *Samarkand* (1999), and *Newborn* (2004) have brought her critical acclaim and several

literary awards, including the Somerset Maugham, Forward and Saltire Prizes. She lives in Oxford with her family and works as a teacher, broadcaster and journalist.

W. D. Cocker (1882–1970)

Cocker was born in Rutherglen into a family of Glasgow merchants. After the First World War he joined the accounts department of the *Daily Record* newspaper and was its amateur drama critic until he retired in 1956. His enduringly popular verse can be found in *Poems, Scots and English* (1932) and *Further Poems, Scots and English* (1935).

Stewart Conn (b. 1936)

Born in Glasgow, Stewart Conn was educated at Kilmarnock Academy and Glasgow University. He was head of radio drama for BBC Scotland, 1977–92. His poetry collections include *In the Kibble Palace* (1987) and *Stolen Light: Selected Poems* (1999). He has received Scottish Arts Council, Poetry Book Society and other awards and in 2002 was appointed Edinburgh's official Makar. His latest volume, *Ghosts at Cockcrow*, appeared in 2005.

James Copeland (1918–2002)

Born in Helensburgh, Copeland was an aircraft engineer, water bailiff and policeman before emerging as an actor and writer. His career encompassed film, stage and television work. His poetry weaves social comment and pathos with satire. His wit is evident in the introduction to his *Shoogly Table Book of Verse* (1983): 'Copeland the man is a renowned rhymer-cum-raconteur who, at a recent BNS sitting, was found to have one of the highest intellects in the United Kingdom.' BNS stands for Ben Nevis Summit.

Robert Crawford (b. 1959)

Bellshill born and educated at Hutchesons' Grammar School, Glasgow, Crawford subsequently studied at Glasgow and Oxford Universities, and is now Professor of Modern Scottish Literature at St Andrews University. His first full-length collection, *A Scottish Assembly*, appeared in 1990. Four of his collections have received Poetry Book Society recommendations. His most recent collection, *The Tip of My Tongue*, was published in 2003. He also shared a volume, *Sharawaggi*, with W. N. Herbert in 1990.

Helen B. Cruickshank (1886–1975)

Often bracketed with Marion Angus and Violet Jacob, Helen B. Cruickshank was a lass o' pairts who for economic reasons had to leave school in Angus at 15 rather than pursue the higher education which her talents merited. She made her living as a civil servant in London for 10 years and subsequently in Edinburgh, where she was much involved in the lively cultural scene. For seven years she was honorary secretary of the Scottish Centre of PEN (the international association of writers). Her first collection, *Up the Noran Water*, was published in 1934, *Sea Buckthorn* in 1954, *The Ponnage Pool* in 1968, and her *Collected Poems* in 1971. Her self-styled *Octobiography* was published posthumously in 1976.

Jenni Daiches (b. 1941)

Though of Scottish parentage, Daiches was born in Chicago and educated in America and England. Following degrees at Cambridge and London Universities, she took up a career in teaching and freelance writing. From 1968 to 1971 she lived in Kenya, teaching for a year at the University of Nairobi. She has lived in Scotland since 1971, though she has travelled and lectured in the USA, Africa, China and Europe. Married from 1963 to 1982 to Angus Calder, she has published more than a dozen books (as Jenni Calder) on English, Scottish and American literature and history. *Mediterranean* (1995) is her first collection of poetry. She worked at the National Museums of Scotland from 1978 until 2001.

John Davidson (1857–1909)

Barrhead-born Davidson was brought up in Greenock and taught in Crieff and Glasgow before launching himself on a literary career in London. He became a *Yellow Book* contributor, but could not make a living even with his stream of novels and poetry collections. In 1909 in the mistaken belief that he had cancer he walked into the sea at Penzance and drowned himself. His novels and plays have sunk without trace but his poems were collected in two volumes in 1973.

Christine De Luca (b. 1947)

Christine De Luca is a Shetlander living in Edinburgh. She writes in Shetlandic and English and has had three collections published by the Shetland Library: *Voes and Sounds* (1994), *Wast wi da Valkyries* (1997) and *Plain Song* (2002). In 2004 she published a sequence of poems based on the lives of eight generations of her father's family, *Drops in Time's Ocean*.

Kirkpatrick Dobie (1909–99)

A grain merchant in Dumfries, Dobie focused much of his poetry on local places and people. His collections include *That Other life* (1980), *Against the Tide* (1985) and *Selected Poems* (1992). See also the article by Ann Karkalas in *The Dark Horse* No. 1 and obituary in *The Herald* (13.02.1999).

Keith Douglas (1920–44)

Douglas first came to the attention of poetry-readers during the Second World War, in which he was killed in Normandy at the age of 24, three days after D-Day. His background was Scots and Scots-Canadian on his father's side. His *Collected Poems* were first published in 1951, one of the editors being G. S. Fraser. He was regarded by Robert Nye as 'the finest poet to come out of the Second World War'.

Adam Drinan (1903–84)

Adam Drinan is the pen-name of Joseph MacLeod, who achieved celebrity as a BBC wartime announcer. His Highland poem sequences in English, *The Men of the Rocks* (1942) and *The Ghosts of the Strath* (1943), convey something of the 'feel' of life in the Highlands.

Carol Ann Duffy (b. 1955)

Born in Glasgow, Duffy was educated at St Joseph's Convent, Stafford, and Liverpool University. She was widely tipped to become the first woman Poet Laureate after Ted Hughes's death. Her collections include *Standing Female Nude* (1985), *Selling Manhattan* (1987), *The Other Country* (1990) and *Mean Time* (1993). Her *Selected Poems* appeared in 1994, *The World's Wife* in 1999 and *Feminine Gospels* in 2002. Her *New Selected Poems, 1984–2004*, were published in 2004.

Lesley Duncan (joint editor)

The daughter of artists, Duncan was educated at Marr College, Troon, Glasgow University (where inspirational teachers included the poets Edwin Morgan and Francis Scarfe), and Pennsylvania State University, USA. She has held various editorial posts on *The Herald* newspaper and is now its poetry editor. Much of her own poetry on current affairs and issues has been published by *The Herald*. Her study of the watercolour artist James Miller was commissioned by the Royal Scottish Academy and published in 1990.

Douglas Dunn (b. 1942)

Born in Inchinnan, Renfrewshire, Dunn was educated locally and at Hull University. After holding various jobs as a librarian, he became fellow in creative writing at Hull (1974–75) and Dundee University (1981–82). Since 1991 he has been Professor of English at St Andrews University. He has received doctorates from Hull and Dundee Universities and has won many awards, including the 1985 Whitbread Book of the Year for his sixth collection, *Elegies*. He is a fellow of the Royal Society of Literature (1981). His *Selected Poems* were published in 1986 and *The Year's Afternoon* in 2000. His *New Selected Poems 1964–2000* (2003) reflect the range of his work. He received an OBE in 2003.

Alison Fell (b. 1944)

Born in Scotland and raised in villages in the Highlands and Borders, Alison Fell moved to London in 1970 to work with the Women's Street Theatre Group. She has published seven novels. Her first volume of poems, *Kisses for Mayakovsky*, won the Alice Hunt Bartlett Award in 1984; *Dreams, Like Heretics: New and Selected Poems* appeared in 1997. Her new collection, *Light Year*, was published in 2005.

Gillian Ferguson (b. 1965)

Edinburgh-born Ferguson studied philosophy at Edinburgh University, then tutored for the Open University, and worked as a wildlife and botanical illustrator before moving into journalism. Her first collection, *Air for Sleeping Fish* (1997), was short-listed for the Scottish First Book of the Year. She has been awarded three writer's bursaries by the Scottish Arts Council, including the top award for *Baby: Poems on Pregnancy, Birth and Babies* (2001). Her work appears in various anthologies.

Ian Hamilton Finlay (b. 1925)

Born in Nassau, the Bahamas, Finlay is also a visual artist. Associated in the public mind with concrete poetry, he has published more than a hundred collections or pamphlets, some through his own Wild Hawthorn Press. He lives at Little Sparta, Biggar, where his garden illustrates his themes most effectively. His *Glasgow Beasts, an a Burd Haw, an Inseks, an, Aw, a Fush*, a pioneering poem in the Glasgow dialect (1961), was republished in a single volume with *The Dancers Inherit the Party* in 1996.

Lillias Scott Forbes (b. 1918)

Born in Glasgow, daughter of the composer Francis George Scott, she now lives in St Andrews. Her *Poems of Love* (1966) was followed in 1998 by *Turning A Fresh Eye*. Hugh MacDiarmid considered that the virtues of her verse amounted to 'simply integrity'.

Veronica Forrest-Thomson (1947–75)

Forrest-Thomson grew up in Glasgow and studied at the Universities of Liverpool and Cambridge, and subsequently taught at the Universities of Leicester and Birmingham. Four books and pamphlets of poems were published during her lifetime, and one posthumously, brought together with variant readings in *Collected Poems and Translations*, edited by Anthony Barnett (1990). Also published posthumously was her critical study *Poetic Artifice: A Theory of Twentieth-Century Poetry* (1978). *Selected Poems* (1999) includes corrections to the collected edition and some newly discovered early material.

G. S. Fraser (1915–80)

Glasgow-born Fraser was a graduate of St Andrews University and served in South Africa during the Second World War. His academic career included a readership in poetry at Leicester University, whose press published his *Poems* (1981). A literary critic and reviewer, and a member of the New Apocalypse group, he also wrote books on Lawrence Durrell and Alexander Pope as well as *Metre, Rhyme and Free Verse*, *Essays in Twentieth Century Poetry*, and an autobiography, *A Stranger and Afraid*.

Hugh Frater (see collaboration with Duncan Macrae)

Robin Fulton (b. 1937)

Robin Fulton graduated from Edinburgh University (MA, PhD) and held the writers' fellowship there (1969–71). He edited Lines Review and the associated books (1967–76). Publications include two books of essays (1974, 1989), *Selected Poems* (1980) followed by other collections in 1982, 1990 and 2003, and a goodly number of translations from Scandinavian poets.

Robert Garioch (1909–81)

Robert Garioch was the pen-name of Robert Garioch Sutherland, a reluctant schoolteacher, but a virtual reincarnation of Robert Fergusson in his poetry in vigorous Scots of the street life of Edinburgh. His translations, again in powerful Scots, from the Latin of George Buchanan's plays and from the Romanesque of Giuseppe Belli's sonnets, were masterly. Robin Fulton edited Garioch's *Complete Poetical Works* (1983).

Flora Garry (1900–2000)

A North-East poet with a distinctive lyric voice, not widely known outside her own area until late in life, she died three months short of her hundredth birthday. Brought up in an Aberdeenshire 'fairmtoun', she celebrated, through her writing, the threatened doric dialect of her childhood. Her husband, Robert Campbell Garry was Regius Professor of Physiology at Glasgow University. Explaining her lateness in turning to poetry Flora Garry said that just as happiness has no history, neither does it write poetry. (See obituary in *The Herald*, 24.6.2000.)

Magi Gibson (b. 1953)

Magi Gibson lives in Glasgow. Four collections of her poetry have been published and *Wild Women of a Certain Age* (2000) is now in its third print run. Her most recent collection is *Graffiti in Red Lipstick*. She was co-winner of the *Scotland on Sunday* / Women 2000 Poetry Prize and has held writing fellowships with the Scottish Arts Council and the Royal Literary Fund.

Valerie Gillies (b. 1948)

Born in Alberta, Canada, Gillies was educated at Edinburgh University and at the University of Mysore, India. She is one of the best-known contemporary Scots poets writing mainly in English. Her collections include *Bed of Stone* (1984), *The Chanter's Tune* (1990), *The Ringing Rock* (1995), *Men and Beasts* (2000) and *The Lightning Tree* (2002).

Duncan Glen (b. 1933)
Born in Cambuslang, Glasgow, Glen attended Edinburgh College of Art. His book *Hugh MacDiarmid and the Scottish Renaissance* appeared in 1964 and *The Poetry of the Scots* in 1991. His *Selected Poems* and *Selected New Poems* have also been published. He inaugurated, in Lancashire, the first degree course in publishing and subsequently became Professor of Visual Communication at Nottingham Trent University. He founded the magazine *Akros*, which provided invaluable service to Scottish literature, and now edits Zed_2O.

W. S. Graham (1918–86)
Born and brought up in Greenock, Graham trained as an engineer and attended Newbattle Abbey. Early books published in Glasgow and London were followed by *The White Threshold* (1949), *The Nightfishing* (1955), *Malcolm Mooney's Land* (1970), *Implements In Their Places* (1977), and *Collected Poems* (1979). Early literary influences included Dylan Thomas, James Joyce and T. S. Eliot. The influence of Scottish language, literature, landscape and upbringing is clearly evident throughout his poetry. His *New Collected Poems* appeared in 2004.

Sir Alexander Gray (1882–1968)
Dundee-born Gray was educated at Dundee High School and the universities of Edinburgh, Göttingen and Paris. His distinguished academic record as an economist culminated in the Professorship of Political Economy at Edinburgh University. He was associated with the Scottish Renaissance and his poems 'Scotland' and 'On a Cat Ageing' have been widely anthologised. He also translated numerous Scandinavian ballads into Scots as well as the poems of Heinrich Heine.

Andrew Greig (b. 1951)
Born in Bannockburn, Stirling, and now living in Orkney and the Lothians, Greig has published six collections of poetry, including *Men on Ice* (1977), *The Order of the Day* (1990), and *Western Swing* (1994), on themes ranging from mountaineering to love, as well as two books about his Himalayan expeditions. His latest poetry collection, *Into You* (2001), is a life-affirming volume after his recovery from near fatal illness.

George Campbell Hay / Deòrsa Mac Iain Dheòrsa (1915–84)

Born in Elderslie, Renfrewshire, the son of the parish minister John MacDougall Hay, author of the novel *Gillespie*, Hay was educated at Fettes College and Oxford University. A poet in Gaelic, English and Scots, as well as French and Norwegian, Hay, dogged by mental ill-health after war service, was a recognised figure of the Scottish Renaissance, and an associate of MacDiarmid, Douglas Young, Sorley MacLean and Francis George Scott. His *Collected Poems and Songs* were published in 2000 for the Lorimer Trust by Edinburgh University Press in two volumes which also contain biographical and critical material.

Hamish Henderson (1919–2002)

Blairgowrie-born Henderson was educated locally and at Dulwich College, London, and Cambridge University. After wartime soldiering, which inspired his early poetry, he became a lecturer at the School of Scottish Studies, Edinburgh, then a fellow. He was an enthusiastic collector of folk material. He won the Somerset Maugham Award in 1949 and was the recipient of several honorary degrees. His masterpiece is generally held to be the *Elegies for the Dead in Cyrenaica*, based on his wartime experiences in North Africa. His *Collected Poems and Songs* appeared in 2000. See also special Henderson issue, *Chapman* No. 42, and his obituaries in the leading English and Scottish broadsheets (2002).

J. F. Hendry (1912–86)

Glasgow-born Hendry was educated at Whitehill School and Glasgow University. During the Second World War he served in the Intelligence Corps and was subsequently a translator with various agencies in the United Nations. With Henry Treece he was one of the founders of the New Apocalypse Movement, later joined by G. S. Fraser and Norman MacCaig. He was editor of the movement's three anthologies, *The New Apocalypse* (1940), *The White Horseman* (1941) and *The Crown and the Sickle* (1945). Poetry collections include *The Bombed Happiness* (1942) and the *Orchestral Mountain* (1943). He wrote *Fernie Brae* (1947) and *The Sacred Threshold: A Life of Rilke* (1982).

W. N. Herbert (b. 1961)

W. N. Herbert was born in Dundee in 1961, and educated there and at Brasenose College, Oxford, where he published his doctoral thesis on Hugh MacDiarmid (*To Circumjack MacDiarmid*, OUP, 1992). He has produced six volumes of poetry and four pamphlets, and is widely anthologised. His last four collections – *Forked Tongue* (1994), *Cabaret McGonagall* (1996), *The Laurelude* (1998) and *The Big Bumper Book of Troy* (2002) – have won many accolades, the last being shortlisted for the Saltire Prize. He currently teaches creative writing and modern Scottish poetry at Newcastle University.

Alan Jackson (b. 1938)

Edinburgh-born Jackson has lived most of his life in his native city. His poetry collections include *The Grim Wayfarer*, *The Worstest Beast* and *Heart of the Sun*, all brought together in *Salutations: Collected Poems 1960–1989* (1990).

Violet Jacob (1863–1946)

Poet and novelist, Violet Kennedy-Erskine was born in Montrose, the daughter of the 18th Laird of Dun whose family had held the lands of Dun since the fifteenth century. She married Arthur Otway Jacob and spent much of her married life in India before returning to her native place. She contributed poems both to Hugh MacDiarmid's *Northern Numbers* (1920–22) and to John Buchan's more traditionalist *The Northern Muse* (1924). Her splendidly colloquial Scots poems are collected in *The Scottish Poems of Violet Jacob* (1944). Better than her several books of short stories is her novel *Flemington* (1911). She also wrote her family history in *The Lairds of Dun* (1931).

Kathleen Jamie (b. 1962)

Kathleen Jamie was born in the West of Scotland and studied philosophy at Edinburgh University. She has received various high prestige awards for her poetry including the Forward Prize and a Creative Scotland Award. She lives in Fife and teaches Creative Writing at St Andrews University. Her collections include *Jizzen* (1999); a composite volume of poems from 1980 to 1994, *Mr and Mrs Scotland are Dead* (2002); and *The Tree House* (2004).

Jackie Kay (b. 1961)

Kay was born in Scotland and grew up in Glasgow. Her first collection, *The Adoption Papers* (1991), tells her story of a black girl's adoption by a white Scottish couple. It received a Scottish Arts Council book award and a Saltire First Book of the Year Award and a Forward Prize. She won a Signal Poetry Award for *Two's Company*, her book of poetry for children, and a Somerset Maugham Award for *Other Lovers* (1993).

I. W. King (b. 1955)
Dunfermline-born publisher and poet King runs the Diehard Press with fellow poet Sally Evans. His *The Deid Sheep on Lumphinans Bing* was published in 1977 and his work has appeared in other poetry pamphlets.

Norman Kreitman (b. 1927)
Kreitman lives in Edinburgh and was formerly engaged in social and psychiatric research. His poetry collections include *Touching Rock* (1987), *Against Leviathan* (1989), and *Casanova's 72nd Birthday* (2003). His *Roots of Metaphor*, on poetics, appeared in 1999.

Frank Kuppner (b. 1951)
The prolific Kuppner is a Glaswegian with, to date, seven poetry collections. These include *A Bad Day for the Sung Dynasty* (1984), *The Intelligent Observation of Naked Women* (1987) and *Ridiculous! Absurd! Disgusting!* (1989) which combined poetry and prose. *What? Again?: Selected Poems*, which appeared in 2000, is the best introduction to his work. It was followed by *A God's Breakfast* in 2004. He has been described as 'a kind of Glaswegian Kierkegaard' and has been writer in residence at Edinburgh University, and subsequently at Glasgow and Strathclyde Universities.

R. D. Laing (1927–89)
Glasgow-born Laing studied medicine at Glasgow University and gained an international reputation as one of the most controversial and innovative psychiatrists of modern times. In *Wisdom, Madness, and Folly: The Making of a Psychiatrist* (1985), he tells his own life story, while his son Adrian's posthumous biography tells how his father's relationship with a distant and undemonstrative mother 'laid the foundations for a lifetime of pioneering work on madness and the family'. Laing's collection of 38 *Sonnets* (1979) reflects his considerable abilities as a poet, a side of his creative talent foreshadowed by his 1970 volume *Knots* (a series of witty trains of thought and exchanges that could be read as poems or brief plays).

Helen Lamb (b. 1956)

Stirling-born Lamb won the *Scotland on Sunday* / Women 2000 writing competition with a short story. Her poems and stories have appeared in many magazines and her work has been widely broadcast. Her poetry collection *Strange Fish* was published in 1997 with co-author Magi Gibson.

Tom Leonard (b. 1944)

Glasgow-born Tom Leonard graduated from Glasgow University aged 32 and has worked in a variety of jobs, including several stints as a writer-in-residence. His poetry collection of 20 years, *Intimate Voices*, appeared in 1984 and its sequel, *access to the silence*, in 2004. Edwin Morgan has said of him: 'He is an instantly communicative poet whose work, including its "bad language" about which there will always be diverse views, nevertheless repays close attention on the printed page.' He teaches part-time as Professor of Creative Writing at Glasgow University.

Maurice Lindsay (joint editor)

A Glaswegian, Lindsay, born in 1918, trained as a musician, served in The Cameronians (Scottish Rifles) and the War Office, 1939–46, and was music critic of *The Bulletin*, *The Herald*'s now defunct sister-paper, and a broadcaster till 1961 when he became programme controller of Border Television. In 1967 he was appointed first director of the Scottish Civic Trust and from 1983 to 1990 was honorary secretary-general of Europa Nostra. His *Collected Poems 1940–1990* (1991) was followed by *News of the World* (1995) and *Speaking Likenesses* (1997), among other collections. The fourth edition of his *Burns Encyclopaedia* appeared in 1995 in paperback, the third edition of *The Castles of Scotland* in 1994, and the fourth edition of *A Book of Scottish Verse*, which he edited, in 2001. See Donald Campbell, 'A Different Way of Being Right' in *Akros* No. 74, Lorn Macintyre 'The Poetry of Maurice Lindsay in *Akros* No. 42, and Christopher Rush in the *Scottish Library Journal* No. 12 (1980).

Liz Lochhead (b. 1947)

Born in Motherwell, Lochhead studied at Glasgow School of Art (1965–70) and worked for several years as an art teacher. Her plays, more than a dozen to date, have achieved popular success, especially *Mary Queen of Scots Got Her Head Chopped Off*, which takes an irreverent look at Scottish history. Her first poetry collection was *Memo for Spring* (1972). *Dreaming Frankenstein & Collected Poems 1967–1984* encompassed her work to that date and was reissued in a new edition in 2003. Her most recent collection is *The Colour of Black and White: Poems 1984–2003*. She was appointed Glasgow's Poet Laureate in 2005 in succession to Edwin Morgan.

Roddy Lumsden (b. 1966)
Born in St Andrews, Roddy Lumsden now lives in Bristol, where he is a freelance writer and puzzle compiler. A first book, *Yeah Yeah Yeah* (1997), was short-listed for Forward and Saltire prizes. As 'poet-in-residence' to the music industry in 1999, he co-wrote *The Message*, a book on poetry and pop music. He has been vice-chairman of the Poetry Society. A second collection, *The Book of Love* (2000), was a Poetry Book Society choice and short-listed for the 2000 T. S. Eliot Prize and the John Llewellyn Rhys Prize. *Roddy Lumsden is Dead* appeared in 2001, *The Bubble Bride* in 2003 and *Mischief Night: New and Selected Poems* in 2004.

George MacBeth (1932–92)
Though born in Scotland, MacBeth preferred 'to live and work within sight of the Thames'. He wrote ten novels, edited seven anthologies, and published eighteen collections of poems, including *Collected Poems 1958–70* (1971) and *Collected Poems 1958–1982* (1989). He worked for some time as a BBC producer. Gavin Ewart drew attention to the 'submerged cruelty and menace and the expressive beauty that MacBeth has made his own'.

Brian McCabe (b. 1951)
Born in a small mining community near Edinburgh, McCabe now lives in the capital and has worked extensively in schools and been a Scottish/Canadian exchange fellow, writing fellow for Stirling Libraries (1984–6), novelist-in-residence at St Andrews University, and William Soutar fellow in Perth. His collections include *Spring's Witch* (1984), *One Atom to Another* (1987) and *Body Parts* (1999).

Norman MacCaig (1910–96)
Edinburgh-born and educated, MacCaig was a schoolteacher and headmaster before becoming a lecturer and reader in poetry at Stirling University (1970–77). He was awarded the Queen's Medal for Poetry in 1986 and held many awards, including honorary

D.Litts. from Stirling, Edinburgh and Dundee Universities. He was also a fellow of the Royal Society of Edinburgh, and had an OBE. His *Collected Poems* appeared in 1985. A comprehensive volume, *The Poems of Norman MacCaig*, appeared in 2005. See also *Norman MacCaig: Critical Essays* (1990).

Hugh MacDiarmid / C. M. Grieve (1892–1978)

Born in Langholm, Dumfriesshire, where his English teacher was the composer Francis George Scott, MacDiarmid had a varied career as a journalist, notably in Montrose and London, with a stint of engineering work in Glasgow during the Second World War, having previously spent several years in Whalsey, Shetland. His final home at Brownsbank, Biggar, is now preserved as a memorial and as a home for a Scottish writing fellowship. His works include *Sangschaw* (1925), *Penny Wheep* (1926) and *A Drunk Man Looks at the Thistle* (1926). MacDiarmid has established himself alongside Dunbar and Burns as one of Scotland's greatest poets. His devotion to Communism and his later political free verse, though still showing flashes of genius, generally marked a decline. His *Collected Poems* appeared in 1962 and his *Complete Poems* (two volumes) in 1978. There are innumerable studies of his life and work. His complete works, including his autobiography *Lucky Poet*, are currently being published by Carcanet.

Ellie McDonald (b. 1937)

Dundee-born McDonald's collection *The Gangan Fuit* published in 1991; her pamphlet *Pathfinder* appeared in 2000. She believes in the living validity of the Scots language and thinks it is not the poet but the message that matters.

Pittendrigh Macgillivray (1856–1938)

Sculptor and poet, Macgillivray was born in Inverurie, Aberdeenshire, the son of a sculptor. He studied under William Brodie and John Mossman. His major sculptures include the statue of Robert Burns in Irvine, the memorial to Gladstone in St Andrew Square, Edinburgh, that of the Marquis of Bute in Cardiff, the Byron statue in Aberdeen, and the John Knox statue in St Giles', Edinburgh. His poetry collections were *Pro Patria* (1915) and *Bog Myrtle and Peat Reek* (1922). He was appointed King's Sculptor in Ordinary for Scotland in 1921.

Matt McGinn (1928–77)

A Glaswegian with an international profile, Matt McGinn was a singer, song-writer, raconteur and humorist, and played a major part in the British folk-music and protest movements of his times. His songs were not only performed by himself – in a voice once characterised as 'a mixture of lumpy porridge and broken glass' – but by stars such as Pete Seeger and Tom Paxton. A posthumous volume of his best-known pieces, *McGinn of the Calton*, was published by Glasgow District Libraries in 1987.

Alastair Mackie (1925–95)

Born in Aberdeen, Alastair Mackie was schooled at Robert Gordon's College, and after war service in the Navy studied English at Aberdeen University. He became an inspirational teacher in Stromness, Orkney, and Anstruther, Fife. Greatly influenced by MacDiarmid's early collection, *Sangschaw*, he wrote his poetry in the Scots of the North-East. As well as his original work, he translated into Scots from Latin, French, German, Italian and Russian. His works include *Soundings* (1966), *Clytach* (1972), *At the Heich Kirk-Yaird* (1974), *Back Green Odyssey* (1980) and *Ingaitherins: Selected Poems* (1987).

Albert D. Mackie (1904–85)

A journalist, poet and playwright, Mackie was born in Edinburgh and after graduating from Edinburgh University in 1927 taught briefly before embarking on a distinguished career in journalism, culminating in the editorship of the *Edinburgh Evening Dispatch* (1946–54). His *Poems in Two Tongues* appeared in 1928 and he also wrote several plays for Edinburgh's Gateway Theatre. He was known by the pen-name Macnib.

Rayne Mackinnon (1937–2002)

In spite of debilitating mental illness, Mackinnon 'maintained an intellectual life of great integrity', as one critic put it. He was received into the Roman Catholic Church while a patient in a high security hospital and also became an associate of the Community of the Transfiguration, whose rule is based on simplicity and prayer. He said that Edwin Morgan's poetry had been his 'fifth gospel'. His collections include *The Spark of Joy and Other Poems* (1970), *The Hitch-hiker and other Poems* (1976) and *Northern Elegies* (1986).

Hamish MacLaren (dates and life unknown)

Alasdair Maclean (1926–94)
Born in Glasgow, Maclean was a mature student at Edinburgh
University and had strong family links with Ardnamurchan.
Influenced to some extent by MacCaig, his work is contained in
From the Wilderness (1973) and *Waking the Dead* (1976). He also
wrote *Night Falls on Ardnamurchan: The Twilight of a Crofting
Family* (1984).

Sorley MacLean / Somhairle MacGill-Eain (1911–96)
Born on the island of Raasay in 1911 into a family with strong
Gaelic traditions, he took a first class honours degree in English
at Edinburgh University, agonised over the Spanish Civil War and
served in North Africa in the Second World War, thence returning
to school teaching. His *Dàin do Eimhir agus Dàin Eile* (*Poems to
Eimhir and Other Poems*) was published in 1943 and established
him as a major figure of the Gaelic renaissance. His volume of
*Selected Poems, 1932–72, Reothairt is Contraigh / Spring Tide and
Neap Tide*, was published in 1977. *O Choille gu Bearradh / From
Wood to Ridge*, his *Collected Poems in Gaelic and English*, appeared
in 1989.

Robert McLellan (1907–85)
McLellan was born in Kirkfieldbank, Lanarkshire, and brought up
on his grandparents' farm, which exerted a strong influence on much
of his work, especially his *Linmill Stories* (collected 1977). From
1938 until his death he lived on the Isle of Arran, which was the
setting for *Sweet Largie Bay* (1956) and *Arran Burn* (1965), a long
poem for television. He was, however, best known for his plays,
The Flouers o' Edinburgh (1947) and *The Hypocrite* (1967), but
especially *Jamie the Saxt* (1937), a corner-stone of the Scottish
theatrical repertoire.

Anne MacLeod (b. 1951)
Anne MacLeod was born of Anglo-Irish parents and lives in
Fortrose. She studied medicine at Aberdeen University and is a
dermatologist. Her poetry volumes are *Standing by Thistles* (1997)
and *Just the Caravaggio* (1999).

Hugh McMillan (b. 1955)
A history teacher in Dumfries, McMillan won the Scottish National

Poetry Competition in 1984; in 1988, 1991, and 1993 he was awarded Scottish Arts Council writer's bursaries. His poetry collections include *Tramontana* (1990), *Horridge* (1994) and *Aphrodite's Anorak* (1996). He also writes short stories.

Adam McNaughtan (b. 1939)
Adam McNaughtan was born in Dennistoun, Glasgow. He stopped being a teacher more than 20 years ago and, as he puts it, moved into education, as a second-hand bookseller. His involvement with the Scottish folk song revival, as singer and researcher, dates from the late 1950s. His rhyming activities go back to his childhood, though he has never been prolific. The language of his songs is a Glasgow amalgam fashioned from literature, everyday speech, music hall, musicals, the Kailyard, Scottish Community Drama Association one-acters, traditional folk song and Hollywood movies. He thinks of it as English, but is not offended when people call it Scots.

Aonghas MacNeacail (b. 1942)
A poet in Gaelic and English as well as a broadcaster, journalist and librettist, MacNeacail has had several writing fellowships including that at MacDiarmid's former home, Brownsbank, Biggar. He has written *An Seachnadh / The Avoiding* (1986), *Rock and Water* (1990) and *Oideachadh Ceart / A Proper Schooling* (1996).

Hugh Macpherson (d. 2001)
Edinburgh-born Macpherson worked as a diplomat in Turkey, Sweden, Croatia and Brazil, and received, in 1998, the fourth Robert Louis Stevenson Memorial Award. His poems appeared, among other places, in *Stand*, *Poetry Review*, and *The London Magazine*. He was shortlisted for the Poetry Society's Geoffrey Dearmer Prize in 1999.

Duncan Macrae (1905–67)
Duncan Macrae, the greatest Scots comic actor of his generation, for whom plays were written by Robert McLellan, Alexander Scott and others, collaborated with Hugh Frater on the comic gem published in this anthology. When Macrae declaimed it, it could reduce audiences to helpless laughter.

Gerald Mangan (b. 1951)
Born in Glasgow in 1951 Mangan worked as a medical artist there

after leaving university. He was resident playwright at Edinburgh's Theatre Workshop in the mid 1970s and later poet-in-residence at Dundee College of Art. He has lived mainly as an artist and journalist in various parts of Scotland, Ireland and France, and is now based in Paris. His book of poems *Waiting for the Storm* was published in 1990.

Angus Martin (b. 1952)
Born in Campbeltown, Argyll, into a fishing and seafaring family, Martin has collected for the *Historical Dictionary of Scottish Gaelic* and records Scots and Gaelic words in Kintyre for the *Scottish National Dictionary*. His poetry collections are *The Larch Plantation* (1990), *The Song of the Quern* (1998), and *The Silent Hollow* (2005).

Gordon Meade (b. 1957)
Perth-born Meade is a former writing fellow of Duncan of Jordanstone College / Dundee District Libraries and the recipient of four Scottish Arts Council bursaries. His collections are *Singing Seals* (1991), *The Scrimshaw Sailor* (1996), and *A Man at Sea* (2003). He lives in the East Neuk of Fife and since 2001, has been leading creative writing workshops for vulnerable young people in East Lothian and Fife.

Elma Mitchell (1919–2000)
Airdrie-born Mitchell gained attention with her prize-winning poem 'Thoughts after Ruskin', which has been much anthologised. Her collections include *The Poor Man in the Flesh* (1976), *The Human Cage* (1979), *Furnished Rooms* (1983) and *People Etcetera: Poems New and Selected* (1987). After studying at Somerville College, Oxford, and taking a diploma in librarianship at University College, London, she worked for the BBC and for the British Employers' Federation. Fluent in several languages, including Russian, she finally lived in Somerset.

Naomi Mitchison (1897–1999)
Scion of the distinguished Haldane family, Mitchison was born in Edinburgh and educated at the Dragon School, Oxford. She had strong family links with Edinburgh and Perthshire and lived in Carradale, Kintyre, from 1937 till her death. An extraordinarily prolific writer, she had more than 70 volumes – comprising novels,

travel and history books, and biographies – to her name. She also had a passionate interest in Scottish issues, was a pioneer of sexual freedom, and an honorary African tribal mother. Her indefatigable creativity also took the form of poetry. Her collection *The Cleansing of the Knife* was published in 1978.

William Montgomerie (1904–94)
The Glasgow-born son of a Plymouth Brethren evangelist, Montgomerie rebelled against his family religion. Poet, writer and teacher, he spent most of his spare time collecting and recording Scottish folk songs, ballads, tales and traditional rhymes. With his wife, Norah, he edited several volumes of folklore. Early publications of his poetry were *Via* (1933) and *Squared Circle* (1934). His poems were published in journals and anthologies and his later range is reflected in *From Time to Time: Selected Poems* (1985). He was Editor of *Lines Review* for several years.

Edwin Morgan (b. 1920)
Glasgow-born Morgan, possibly the most versatile Scottish poet of the twentieth century, was educated in Rutherglen, Glasgow, and at Glasgow University. His subsequent academic career culminated in a titular professorship of English at Glasgow University (1975–80). He has received numerous honours including D.Litt. degrees from Loughborough, Glasgow and Edinburgh Universities. He is the recipient of a medal from the Hungarian PEN and was made an OBE in 1982. His *Collected Poems* was first published in 1990 and his *New Selected Poems* in 2000. His latest volumes, *Cathures* and *Love and a Life*, appeared in 2002 and 2003 respectively. He is also an accomplished translator and opera librettist and was the first Glasgow Poet Laureate. He was awarded the Queen's Gold Medal for Poetry in 2000 and was appointed National Poet of Scotland in 2004.

Ken Morrice (1924–2002)
A native of Aberdeen and a medical graduate of its university, Ken Morrice later specialised in psychiatry and lived and worked in Britain and abroad. His various volumes of poetry include *The Scampering Marmoset* (1990), *Selected Poems* (1991) and *Talking of Michelangelo* (1996).

Edwin Muir (1887–1959)

Born in Deerness, Orkney, the son of a crofter, Muir came to Glasgow at the age of 14, an experience he did not relish and which he described in *The Story and the Fable* (1940) and *An Autobiography* (1954). He travelled to London and on the Continent, having married the novelist Willa Anderson (1890–1970). After some years in Sussex and St Andrews, he served with the British Council in Prague and Rome, spending a year as Professor of Poetry at Harvard University before settling near Cambridge. His eight volumes of verse began with *First Poems* (1925), being finally collected in *Collected Poems* (1952). He also wrote the controversial *Scott and Scotland* (1936), which queried the validity of Scots as a living language for contemporary poetry, thus incurring the life-long wrath of C. M. Grieve (Hugh MacDiarmid), which Muir bore with dignified calmness.

Stephen Mulrine (b. 1937)

Poet, playwright and translator, Mulrine has also written extensively for radio and television. His translations, mostly of Russian drama range from Gogol, Turgenev and Chekhov, to contemporary works by Gelman and Petrushevskaya. See also *Poems by Alan Hayton, Stephen Mulrine, Colin Kirkwood, Robert Tait: Four Glasgow University Poets* (1967) and *Poems by Stephen Mulrine* (1971).

Neil Munro (1864–1930)

Inveraray-born Neil Munro was bilingual in English and Gaelic. At 18 he went to Glasgow, eventually finding a job and swift promotion on the *Evening News*, which for a time he edited. His book of short stories, *The Lost Pibroch* (1896), was a breakthrough in the authentic presentation of the Highlander. His first novel, *John Splendid*, appeared in 1898 to be followed by others, notably *The New Road* (1914), reviewing which, John Buchan described Munro as 'the foremost of living Scottish novelists'. Since his first Para Handy tale appeared in the *Evening News* in 1905 the Master Mariner has never been out of print, as well as translating successfully to television. *The Poetry of Neil Munro*, collecting material written over many years, was published posthumously in 1931. A biography by Lesley Lendrum appeared in 2004.

Charles Murray (1864–1941)

Born in Alford, Aberdeenshire, Murray trained as a civil engineer, and had a successful career in South Africa, where from 1910 till his retirement in 1924 he was Secretary for Public Works for the recently created Union of South Africa. His poems were written in the Aberdeenshire dialect and the best of them are to be found in *Hamewith* (first published in 1900, definitive edition 1909), which was one of the most popular books of vernacular verse up to the Second World War. Murray retired to Scotland in 1924 and died in Banchory, Kincardineshire. *Hamewith: The Complete Poems of Charles Murray* was edited by Nan Shepherd in 1979.

Donald S. Murray (b. 1956)
Murray is from Ness on the Isle of Lewis and is principal teacher of English at Sgoil Lionacleit, Benbecula. His short story collection *Special Deliverance* was short-listed for the Saltire First Book Award in 1998 and his poetry has been widely published in anthologies and literary magazines.

William Neill (b. 1922)
Ayrshire-born Neill was educated at Ayr Academy and later took an honours degree in Celtic Studies and English at Edinburgh University. He writes in all three Scottish languages, English, Scots and Gaelic. His awards for poetry include the Grierson Verse Prize (1970), the Sloan Prize (1970) and a Scottish Arts Council book award (1985). His *Selected Poems, 1969–1992*, appeared in 1994 and *Caledonian Cramboclink* in 2001.

Siùsaidh NicNèill (b. 1955)
NicNeill moved for economic reasons from Lewis to Skye in 1988 and now works for an independent Gaelic broadcasting company as a producer/director. She has been published in various anthologies, Scottish and international. *All My Braided Colours* (1996) is her first collection.

Dennis O'Donnell (b. 1951)
Born in West Lothian, where he still lives, O'Donnell is very much steeped in the post-industrial heritage of his native county. His collection *Two Clocks Ticking* was published in 1997, to be followed by *Smoke and Mirrors* in 2003.

Donny O'Rourke (b. 1959)
Port-Glasgow-born O'Rourke is a journalist, songwriter, translator,

broadcaster, television producer, and has been Edinburgh Book Festival writer-in-residence. He teaches the Scottish Cultural Studies programme at Glasgow School of Art and creative writing at Pembroke College, Cambridge; he is also a former creative writing fellow at Glasgow and Strathclyde Universities. His collections include *Second Cities* (1991), *The Waistband and Other Poems* (1997) and *On a Roll: A Jena Notebook* (2001). His latest book is *The Lovely Word Republic* (2005).

Janet Paisley (b. 1948)

Paisley is a poet, playwright and scriptwriter for radio, television and film. Her awards include a Scottish Arts Council Creative Scotland Award, a Canongate Prize and Peggy Ramsay Memorial Award, and she has held various fellowships. She co-edits *New Writing Scotland*. Her collections include *Wild Fire* (1993), *Alien Crop* (1996), *Reading the Bones* (1999), *Ye Cannae Win* (2000) and *Not for Glory* (2001).

Don Paterson (b. 1963)

Paterson was born in Dundee but on leaving school at 16 moved South to pursue a career in music. He returned to Dundee in 1993 as writer-in-residence at the university and subsequently became poetry editor at Picador. He now lives in Kirriemuir, where he continues his work as musician, editor and writer. His first collection *Nil Nil* (1993) won the Forward Prize for best first collection that year. *God's Gift to Women* (1997) won both the Geoffrey Faber Memorial Prize and the T. S. Eliot Prize for Poetry. Further collections include *The Eyes* (1999) and *Landing* Light (2003). The last won both the Whitbread Prize for Poetry and the T. S. Eliot prize, making Paterson the only poet to have won the T. S. Eliot prize twice.

Walter Perrie (b. 1949)

Born in Lanarkshire and now living in Perthshire, Perrie was educated at Edinburgh and Stirling Universities. He is the author of eight collections of poems as well as travel writing and criticism. *Decagon: Selected Poems 1995–2005* appeared in 2005.

Tom Pow (b. 1950)

Edinburgh-born Pow lectures in creative and cultural studies at Glasgow University's Crichton Campus, Dumfries. He has written several radio plays, received four Scottish Arts Council book awards, been a Scottish/Canadian exchange fellow, and is the author of the poetry collections *Rough Seas* (1987), *The Moth Trap* (1990), *Red Letter Day* (1996) and *Landscapes and Legacies* (2003). *In the Palace of Serpents: An Experience of Peru* was published in 1992. He was writer-in-residence at the 2002 Edinburgh International Book Festival.

Richard Price (b. 1966)
Price grew up in Renfrewshire, and studied at Napier College and Strathclyde University. Since 1988 he has lived in London where he is Head of Modern British Collections at the British Library. He has written a study of Neil M. Gunn. His poetry books include *Sense and A Minor Fever* (1993), *Tube Shelter Perspective* (1993), *Marks and Sparks* (1995), *Hand Held* (1997), *Perfume and Petrol Fumes* (1999), *Frosted, Melted* (2002) and *Lucky Day* (2005).

John Purser (b. 1942)
Skye-based Purser is a poet, composer, playwright and musicologist. He has won the McVitie's Scottish Writer of the Year Award, a Giles Cooper Award and a Sony Gold Medal. He lectures in Scotland and abroad, and is author of the ground-breaking *Scotland's Music* (1992) and a study of Jack Yeats. His poetry includes *The Counting Stick* (1976), *A Share of the Wind* (1980) and *Amoretti* (1985).

David Purves (b. 1924)
Selkirk-born Purves was educated in the Borders and at Edinburgh University, where he took a Ph.D. in biochemistry, and subsequently worked as an agricultural chemist. His scientific works include *Trace Element Contamination of the Environment* (2nd edition, 1985). His Edinburgh Festival Fringe play, *The Puddock an the Princess* won a Fringe First in 1985 and was published in 1992. He was editor of the magazine *Lallans* (1987–95). His collection *Hert's Bluid* appeared in 1995.

Kathleen Raine (1908–2003)
Born of a Scots mother and brought up in Northumberland, Raine had from childhood a 'sense of identity within the tradition of Scotland', and Scottish themes and landscapes loom large in her writing. An eminent literary figure of the twentieth century as poet, scholar and editor, she studied science at Cambridge University,

where Jacob Bronowski was among her contemporaries. She published more than a dozen volumes of poetry as well as works of scholarship on William Blake, W. B. Yeats and others, and has been translated into many languages. She received the Queen's Medal for Poetry, a CBE in 2000, and was made a Commandeur de l'Ordre des Arts et des Lettres for her distinguished services to literature. Her first *Collected Poems* (1956) were hailed by Edwin Muir. Her final *Collected Poems* appeared in 2000.

Tessa Ransford (b. 1938)

A former editor of *Lines Review*, Ransford has published a succession of poetry collections including *Light of the Mind* (1980), *Shadows from the Greater Hill* (1987), *The Medusa Dozen* (1994) and *When It Works It Feels Like Play* (1998). Awarded an OBE and an honorary degree, she has been a Royal Literary Fund fellow and is the current president of Scottish PEN. She was founder and first director of the Scottish Poetry Library and the motive force in the creation of the Callum Macdonald Memorial Award for poetry pamphlets.

Alastair Reid (b. 1926)

Born in Whithorn, Wigtonshire, Alastair Reid is a poet, a prose writer, a translator, and a traveller. He grew up in Scotland, and since the fifties has been a foreign correspondent and frequent contributor to *The New Yorker Magazine*. He has published more than forty books – poems, prose chronicles, translations – and has translated the work of many Latin American writers, Borges and Neruda in particular. He lives sometimes in the Americas, North and South, and sometimes in Scotland. *Weathering*, his collection of poems and translations, appeared in 1978.

Robert Rendall (1898–1967)

Rendall ran a draper's shop in Kirkwall, Orkney, and was an expert on molluscs and sea-shells. As a poet, he began by translating from the Greek (a language he taught himself) and by writing poems in Orcadian dialect. His collections, including *Shore Poems* (1957) and *The Hidden Land* (1966), are well represented in *An Island Shore: The Life and Work of Robert Rendall* (1990).

Alan Riach (b. 1957)

Riach was born in Airdrie, Lanarkshire, and educated at Cambridge and Glasgow Universities, gaining a PhD in Scottish Literature from the latter. He was associate professor of English at Waikato University, New Zealand, before his appointment to the Scottish Literature department of Glasgow University, of which he is currently head. His poetry collections include *First and Last Songs* (1995) and, most recently, *Clearances* (2001). His study of *Hugh MacDiarmid's Epic Poetry* was published in 1991. He initiated the publication of the *Complete Works of Hugh MacDiarmid* and is the general editor of Carcanet's multi-volume edition.

James Robertson (b. 1958)
Angus-based Robertson studied history at Edinburgh University and worked as a bookseller for seven years before being appointed first holder of the Brownsbank writing fellowship in 1993. He has published two books of short stories, two novels and other works as well as poetry collections. These include *Fae the Flouers o Evil: Baudelaire in Scots* (2001) and *Stirling Sonnets* (2001), the latter winning the Callum Macdonald Memorial Award for poetry pamphlets in 2002.

Robin Robertson (b. 1955)
Robin Robertson is from the north-east coast of Scotland. He has published two collections of poetry, *A Painted Field* (1997) and *Slow Air* (2002), with a third due in early 2006. He has received a number of awards for his work, including the Forward Prize, the Saltire Scottish First Book of the Year Award and, in 2004, the E. M. Forster Award from the American Academy of Arts and Letters.

David Rorie (1867–1946)
Though born in Edinburgh, Rorie spent most of his childhood and student days in Aberdeen, where he became a general practitioner at nearby Cults. Having previously been a colliery doctor in Fife, he published an essay, 'The Folk Lore of the Mining Folk of Fife'. He served in the 51st Highland Division during the First World War and was awarded the DSO and the Legion d'Honneur. His poetry is contained in *The Auld Doctor* (1920) and *The Lum Hat Wantin' the Croon* (1935).

Dilys Rose (b. 1954)
Dilys Rose grew up in Glasgow and now lives in Edinburgh. She has published poetry, *Madame Doubtfire's Dilemma* (1989), *Lure*

(2003); short fiction, *Our Lady of the Pickpockets* (1989), *Red Tides* (1993), *War Dolls* (1998); and a novel, *Pest Maiden* (1999). Her work has received various awards. Recent work includes libretti for composers Stephen Deazley (*Fatal Attraction*) and Rory Boyle (*The Fires of Bride*), and a collaboration with the painter Moyna Flannigan (*Once Upon our Time*). A new collection of short fiction (*Lord of Illusions*) is due out in 2005.

R. Crombie Saunders (1914–91)

Saunders edited the wartime *Scottish Arts and Letters* and eventually settled in Killin, where he became postmaster. He has two books of verse, *The Year's Green Edge* (1987) and *This One Tree* (1987).

Alexander Scott (1920–89)

Aberdeen-born Scott returned to graduate at Aberdeen University after distinguished war service. He became lecturer then reader in Scottish Literature at Glasgow University, and taught a whole generation of Scottish literature scholars and writers. He wrote several plays for both stage and radio. *Still Life*, the standard biography of William Soutar, appeared in 1958. Scott's own collections include *The Latest in Elegies* (1949), *Mouth Music* (1954), *Selected Poems* (1975), and *Collected Poems* (1994). Like Garioch, he was a natural master of spoken Scots.

Tom Scott (1918–95)

Born in Glasgow, Scott was the son of a shipyard worker. In 1929 his family moved to St Andrews, and on leaving school at fifteen he worked there as a labourer in his grandfather's building firm. After Army service he attended Newbattle Abbey College and then Edinburgh University, gaining a PhD for his work on Dunbar. Written almost exclusively in Scots, his published works include *Seeven Poems o Maister Francis Villon* (1953), *The Ship* (1963), the sequence *Brand the Builder* (1975), *The Tree* (1975) and *The Dirty Business* (1986). He was editor with John MacQueen of the *Oxford Book of Scottish Verse* (1966) and also edited the controversial *Penguin Book of Scottish Verse* (1970). His *Collected Shorter Poems* appeared in 1993.

Charles Senior (1919–75)

Born in Glasgow, Senior worked for many years as a clerk in

Beardmore's Foundry, Parkhead. He was self-educated. His *Selected Poems* appeared in 1966 and *Harbingers* in 1968. He spent his final years in Orkney.

Robert Service (1874–1958)
Born in Preston of a Scots bank clerk father, Service was raised in Scotland but emigrated to Canada at the age of 22 and settled in France before the First World War. His *Songs of a Sourdough* (1907), celebrating the Yukon Gold Rush and including 'The Shooting of Dan McGrew' and 'The Cremation of Sam McGee', proved phenomenally popular and had sold three million copies by 1940. In spite of his success he always considered himself a versifier rather than poet. He produced more than a dozen other books of verse, six novels and two autobiographies, and also worked as a journalist and war correspondent.

Burns Singer (1928–64)
Born in New York, Singer was brought up in Glasgow, abandoning studies in English and zoology on the suicide of his mother. After four years as a marine biologist in Aberdeen, he became a literary journalist in London. His collection *Still and All* and a study of the British fishing industry, *Living Silver*, appeared in 1957. He died of heart failure in 1964. A new edition of his *Collected Poems* was published in 2001.

Iain Crichton Smith / Iain Mac a'Ghobhainn (1928–98)
Poet and novelist from the Isle of Lewis, Smith was educated in Stornoway and at Aberdeen University. He taught in Clydebank, Dumbarton and Oban, retiring in 1977. He was a versatile writer in English and Gaelic (under the name Iain Mac a'Ghobhainn) and a man of great personal charm. His first collection, *The Long River*, appeared in 1955, and his *Collected Poems* in 1992. His novels include *Consider the Lilies* (1968) and *My Last Duchess* (1971), while his most engaging short story character Murdo first appeared in *Murdo and Other Stories* (1981).

Sydney Goodsir Smith (1915–1975)
New Zealand-born Smith was the son of Sir Sydney Alfred Smith, who was appointed Professor of Forensic Medicine at Edinburgh University in 1927. The poet studied at Edinburgh University and Oriel College, Oxford. *Skail Wind* (1941) was followed by several

other volumes in Scots, notably *Under the Eildon Tree* (1948), a sequence of 24 poems dealing with the world's greatest loves and the poet's own experiences, and *Orpheus and Eurydice* (1955). His play *The Wallace* was commissioned for the Edinburgh Festival in 1960. He was a witty man and his sense of fun is preserved in his novel *Carotid Cornucopius* (1947).

Charles Hamilton Sorley (1895–1915)

Born in Old Aberdeen, Sorley moved with his family to Cambridge at the age of five, when his father was appointed Knightsbridge Professor of Moral Sciences at Cambridge University. Sorley himself was educated at Marlborough College and spent a year in Germany before being commissioned on the outbreak of the First World War. He was killed by a sniper's bullet at Loos in October 1915. His *Marlborough and other Poems* were published by Cambridge University Press shortly after his death. His *Poems and Selected Letters*, with a preface by Lord Butler, were published in 1978.

William Soutar (1898–1943)

Born in Perth, the son of a joiner, Soutar was educated at Perth Academy and conscripted into the Royal Navy (1916) where he contracted a form of spondylitis, which confined him to bed for the last 13 years of his life, though not before he had studied English at Edinburgh University. His *Conflict* appeared in 1931, followed by *Seeds in the Wind* (1933) for children. *Poems in Scots* (1935) established his reputation. Later volumes followed in Scots and English, including a poorly edited *Collected Poems* (1948) by Hugh MacDiarmid and the remarkable prose *Diaries of a Dying Man* (1954), edited by Alexander Scott and reissued in 1988. Further volumes of selected poems appeared in 1961 and 2000.

Muriel Spark (b. 1918)

Edinburgh-born and educated, Dame Muriel Spark has an international literary reputation. Though it rests mainly on her novels, of which *The Prime of Miss Jean Brodie* (1961) is perhaps the best known, she has had a lifelong interest in poetry, and ran the Poetry Society and edited the *Poetry Review* from 1947 to 1949 before turning to fiction. A volume of her *Collected Poems* was published in 1967, and a subsequent collection, *Going Up to Sotheby's*, in 1982. The definitively entitled *All the Poems*, incorporating compositions from the 1940s to the present day, was published in 2004.

Lewis Spence (1874–1955)

James Lewis Thomas Chalmers Spence was born in Broughty Ferry, Dundee, and studied dentistry in Edinburgh before turning to writing. His subsequent expertise in mythology is represented by his *Dictionary of Mythology* (1913) and his *Encyclopaedia of Occultism* (1920). He was one of the founders of the Scottish National Party. His poems in Scots are collected in *The Phoenix* (1923) and *Weirds and Vanities* (1927). His *Collected Poems* appeared in 1953. Unlike MacDiarmid's approach, Spence's efforts to resuscitate Scots took the form of attempting a kind of updating of Middle Scots which did not have the energy of MacDiarmid's Lallans.

Kenneth Steven (b. 1968)

Born in Glasgow, Steven has, apart from university years, lived in Perthshire where the landscapes and people have been the major inspiration for his writing. His poetry has been published in periodicals in Britain, and in Canada, Australia and the USA. Poetry collections include *Remembering Peter* (1993), *The Missing Days* (1995), *The Pearl Fisher* (1995), *Iona* (2000) and *Wild Horses* (2002).

William J. (Bill) Tait (1918–92)

Bill Tait was born on the Shetland island of Yell. He studied at Edinburgh University and subsequently taught English in Shetland, England and Dundee. His *Collected Poems: A Day Between Weathers* (1980) was the culmination of 40 years' writing, though he had been widely published previously in England, Scotland and his native Shetland, as well as featuring in translation on the BBC Swedish Service and in the Danish press.

Derick Thomson / Ruaraidh MacThomais (b. 1921)

Born in Lewis, Thomson studied at Aberdeen University, Emmanuel College, Cambridge, and Bangor (Wales). He taught at the Universities of Edinburgh, Aberdeen and Glasgow, being Professor of Celtic at the last from 1963 to 1991. He has published seven collections of Gaelic poetry with many English translations – see *Creachadh na Clarsaich / Plundering the Harp* (1982) and *Meall Garbh / The Rugged Mountain* (1995) – and has also written *An Introduction to Gaelic Poetry* (1989) and the *Companion to Gaelic Scotland* (1994).

Valerie Thornton (b. 1954)
Thornton is a creative writing tutor currently working online for the
Open University. She has recently completed a three-year fellowship
with the Royal Literary Fund. A former English teacher, she writes
poetry and short stories and is currently editing *New Writing
Scotland*. Her creative-writing textbook for schools, *Working Words*
(1995), was awarded joint first prize as Scottish Education Book of
the Year by the *Times Educational Supplement Scotland* and the
Saltire Society. Her first poetry collection, *Catacoustics*, appeared in
2000.

Ruthven Todd (1914–78)
Edinburgh-born Todd was educated at Fettes College and Edinburgh
College of Art. He worked for two years as a farm labourer on Mull
and then as a journalist in Edinburgh, before moving to London
in 1933 and the USA in 1947, where he remained till his death. He
wrote adventure stories under the pseudonym of R. T. Campbell, but
is best remembered for his editions of the *Poems of William Blake*
and, of course, his own poetry, including *Garland for the Winter
Solstice* (1962).

Sydney Tremayne (1912–86)
Born in Ayr, Tremayne spent his working life as a Fleet Street
journalist. His collections include *The Rock and the Bird* (1955),
The Swans of Berwick (1962) and *Selected and New Poems* (1973).
See also 'The Poetry of Sydney Tremayne' by George Bruce in *Akros*
No. 38 (1978).

Gael Turnbull (1928–2004)
Born in Edinburgh, Gael Turnbull returned to the city in 1989 and
lived there until his death in 2004. He grew up in the north of
England and in Winnipeg, Canada, but returned to Britain to study
Natural Sciences at Cambridge University. He subsequently qualified
as a doctor at the University of Pennsylvania, USA, and worked as
a general practitioner and anaesthesiologist in Canada, the USA
and England. He founded Migrant Press in 1957. His publications
include *A Trampoline* (1968), *A Gathering of Poems* (1983), *While
Breath Persist*, published in Canada in 1992, and *For Whose Delight*
(1995).

Anne Turner (b. 1925)
Anne Turner's poetry appeared in *The Glasgow Herald*, *The Saltire Review*, *Akros* and *Outposts*. Her short collection, *Sudden Shards*, was published in 1968.

W. Price Turner (1927–98)
Though born in York, Turner returned with his parents to their native Scotland as an infant. He left school at fourteen and spent his early adult years in Glasgow. His collections include *The Rudiment of an Eye* (1955), *The Flying Corset* (1962), *The Moral Rocking Horse* (1970) and *Fables for Love: New and Selected Poems* (1985).

Raymond Vettese (b. 1950)
Born in Arbroath, and now living in Montrose, Vettese has worked as a journalist, barman, process worker, teacher of Scottish studies to Americans, and supply teacher. He was awarded the Saltire Society's Best First Book Award (1989), the William Soutar writing fellowship, Perth (1990–91) and was president of the Scots Language Society, 1991–94. His publications include *The Richt Noise* (1988) and *A Keen New Air* (1995).

Val Warner (b. 1946)
Warner studied history at Oxford and has worked as a librarian and teacher. She has been writer-in-residence at the University College of Swansea and the University of Dundee. Her first collection, *These Yellow Photos*, appeared in 1971, *Under the Penthouse* in 1973 and *Before Lunch* in 1986.

Roderick Watson (b. 1943)
Poet, critic and academic, Watson was born and raised in Aberdeen, completed a doctorate on Hugh MacDiarmid's poetry, has worked in Cambridge, Canada and Edinburgh, and is currently a professor at Stirling University. His *True History on the Walls* was published in 1976. *Into the Blue Wavelengths*, his latest publication, appeared in 2004.

Kenneth White (b. 1936)
Born in Glasgow and brought up in Ayrshire, White graduated with a double first in French and German from Glasgow University, and has a state doctorate from Paris. After years of travelling he settled in France, where he held the Chair of Twentieth-Century Poetics at

the Sorbonne. He has been awarded some of France's leading literary prizes, including the French Academy's Grand Prix du Rayonnement (1985) for the totality of his work and the Prix Medicis Etranger for *The Blue Road*. His writing has been widely translated and groups following his 'geopoetics' cultural concept exist in various countries, including France, Belgium, Canada, the West Indies, Serbia, Macedonia, Italy and Scotland. His first collection, *The Cold Wind of Dawn*, was published in 1966; *Handbook for the Diamond Country: Collected Shorter Poems 1960–90* appeared in 1990; *The Bird Path: Collected Longer Poems* was published in 1989. *Open World: The Collected Poems 1960–2000* appeared in 2003.

Colin Will (b. 1942)
Will is a former librarian of the Royal Botanic Garden, Edinburgh, and of the British Geological Survey, a background that informs his poetry. His publications include *Thirteen Ways of Looking at the Highlands* (1996) and *Seven Senses* (2000); his work has also appeared in various periodicals.

Jim C. Wilson (b. 1948)
Born in Edinburgh, Wilson studied English at Edinburgh University, taught at Telford College (1972–81), was Writing Fellow for Stirling District (1989–91) and has run Poetry in Practice sessions at Edinburgh University since 1994. He took first prize in the Scottish International Open Poetry Competition (1996). His publications include *The Loutra Hotel* (1988), *The Happy Land* (1991), *Cellos in Hell* (1993) and *Spalebone Days* (2002). He was a Royal Literary Fund fellow from 2001 to 2005.

Andrew Young (1885–1971)
This poet cleric was born in Elgin and educated at Edinburgh University and New College, Edinburgh. Ordained a United Free Church minister in 1912, he became successively an English Presbyterian minister in Hove, Sussex, and the Anglican vicar of Stoneygate, Sussex. Numerous volumes of poetry from 1910 culminated in his first *Collected Poems* in 1936. Further volumes of collected poems followed, and a *Selected Poems* in 1998. He was also a botanist, producing four books on the botany, history and folklore of the British Isles. He was awarded the Queen's Gold Medal for Poetry in 1952 and an honorary LLD by Edinburgh University (1951).

Douglas Young (1913–73)

Poet, polymath, Scottish nationalist and a political conscientious objector, Young was, physically and intellectually, an outstanding figure of the Scottish Renaissance. Born in Fife, he spent his early childhood in India, attended Merchiston Castle School, Edinburgh, and studied Classics at St Andrews University and New College, Oxford. Chairman of the Scottish National Party, he was imprisoned in 1943 for refusing war service, except at the call of an independent Scotland. He lectured at Aberdeen University, University College, Dundee, and St Andrews University before holding professorships in Classics and Greek at McMaster University, Canada, and the University of North Carolina, USA, respectively. He published three collections of poetry – *Auntran Blads: An Outwale o Verses* (1943), *A Braird o Thristles* (1947) and *Selected Poems* (1950), as well as translating work by the Gaelic poets Sorley MacLean and George Campbell Hay into Scots, and producing Scots versions of Aristophanes' comedies, *The Birds* and *The Frogs* (transmogrified into *The Burdies* and *The Puddocks*) in the late 1950s.

Title Index

Index of First Lines